Praise for

A timely study of Britain's first investigative journalist …
with impeccable research, Mr Robinson elegantly pieces
together the back-story.
Tobias Grey, *Wall Street Journal*

A lively and laconic biography.
John Pemble, *London Review of Books*

I grew to quite dislike [Stead] as I read *Muckraker*, but that's
because Robinson knows how to tell a story.
Jonathan Mirsky, *The Spectator*

W. Sydney Robinson's admirably thoughtful and economical
biography could hardly be better timed. Closely researched and
briskly written, it does an excellent job of explaining one of the
most extraordinary individuals in journalistic history.
Dominic Sandbrook, *Sunday Times*

With a lovely eye for detail, a wry sense of irony and a fine
grasp of character, it brings alive an age in which sensationalist
papers went further in search of a story than even Rebekah
Brooks would think appropriate.
Prospect

W. Sydney Robinson's energetic, thorough and
hospitable new biography spares nothing.
Jonathan Barnes, *Times Literary Supplement*

Robinson is a resourceful investigator and a
connoisseur of human paradox.
Irish Times

A timely, well-written biography of the brilliant,
flawed Victorian journalist.
Bel Mooney, *Daily Mail*

Tragically compelling.
Toby Thomas, *Literary Review*

This is, quite simply, a marvellous book, the best I have read this
year so far. Every politician and journalist should slip a copy of
this slim, brilliantly written volume by a new young author
into their holiday luggage this summer.
Lord Lexden, *The House*

W. Sydney Robinson has produced an entertaining and clear-eyed
introduction to an extraordinary life.
Robert Gray, *The Tablet*

An engrossing biography.
Times Higher Education

Gives a singular editor his rightful place
in the history of journalism.
Western Mail

An excellent account.
The Oldie

MUCKRAKER

W. T. Stead at the height of his powers as a journalist (age 40). 'He is a sort of man who in days of active revolution might be a serious danger. I looked at him, thinking if it should ever be my lot to have to hang or shoot him.' Field Marshal Garnet Joseph Wolseley, 1st Viscount Wolseley to his wife, 1890.

MUCKRAKER

The Scandalous Life and Times of

W. T. STEAD

Britain's First Investigative Journalist

W. SYDNEY ROBINSON

The Robson Press

Paperback edition published in Great Britain in 2013 by
The Robson Press (an imprint of Biteback Publishing Ltd)
Westminster Tower
3 Albert Embankment
London SE1 7SP

ISBN 978-184954-585-3

10 9 8 7 6 5 4 3 2 1

A CIP catalogue record for this book is available from the British Library.

Set in Adobe Garamond Pro
Cover design by Namkwan Cho

Printed and bound in Great Britain by
CPI Group (UK) Ltd, Croydon CR0 4YY

Do I contradict myself? Very well then. I contradict myself.
I am large. I contain multitudes.
Walt Whitman (1819–92)

Most mischievous foul sin, in chiding sin,
For thou thyself hast been a libertine.
Shakespeare, *As You Like It*, Act II, vii, 64–5

Northumberland Street, Strand, at the time of the 'Maiden Tribute' sensation. A rival publication denounced Stead's exposure of child prostitution as 'the vilest parcel of obscenity ever issued from the public press', but he was enthusiastically supported by some of the most senior clerics and reformers of the day.

CONTENTS

FOREWORD

I am amazed that, one hundred years after his death aboard the *Titanic*, this is the first major biography of the truly extraordinary W. T. Stead. *Muckraker* is a 'warts-and-all' account of the life of arguably the most important journalist of all time. Many noted biographers have wanted to write about him before, and his contemporary relevance cannot be denied, but for some reason he has never received the sort of attention he so patently deserves.

The father of the modern tabloid newspaper, Stead was certainly no saint but if journalists ever wanted a beatified patron he would have some claim to the title. Daring and reckless; public-spirited and generous – these were the fundamentals of the man. If he went too far on occasion, he at least made sure that others went far enough. He understood that to get at the truth you sometimes have to be 'conscientiously unscrupulous', as George Bernard Shaw once put it. Stead was a master of this art.

Imprisoned for abducting a child in the course of exposing the vicious sex trade that existed in Victorian London, Stead realised, as few before him had, that governments are powerless to resist the co-ordinated voice of the public – when harnessed by a newspaper – to help put an end to such evils. His achievements, ranging from increasing government spending on the military to helping clear London's appalling slums, are impressive by any standard; but, as this well-written biography suggests, he undoubtedly went too far on occasion and had a tendency to exaggerate his influence. Like some in his profession today, he was also liable to forget that newspaper editors are not, generally, supposed to make the news, but to write it.

Allegations of corrupt practices in today's modern media, involving the *News of the World* and others, have brought this once great national institution into disrepute. At the time of writing it is unclear what the repercussions of Lord Justice Leveson's grand inquiry will be, but it seems that nothing will be the same on 'Fleet Street' again. The danger could be that we lose what has traditionally been a valuable part of our national life. Whatever their excesses, the 'red-tops' have often spoken for the powerless, the oppressed and the marginalised. Without them we will all be the poorer.

The story of W. T. Stead is both inspiring and tragic, and I hope that this book contributes to a renewed interest in his truly scandalous life and times.

Tristram Hunt
House of Commons, 2012

PREFACE

When it was revealed in the summer of 2011 that the mobile phone of a murdered schoolgirl had been hacked by a detective employed by the *News of the World*, tabloid journalism hit an historic low. After years of righteously denouncing the shortcomings of others, its oldest and most recognised title lost credibility and collapsed within a week. For once it was the respectable broadsheets which bayed for blood and claimed to speak for the nation. In the *Financial Times* the historian and former newspaper editor Sir Max Hastings decried his 'red-top' brethren as 'wild beasts', while Polly Toynbee, writing in *The Guardian*, cheered: 'Rejoice! Roll on the tumbrils as another News Corp head rolls...'[1] No words were too strong for the scummy underbelly of Fleet Street.

A hundred and thirty years before this crisis, a far more debatable breach of the law was committed by the father of investigative journalism: William Thomas Stead (pronounced 'sted'). Appalled by the prevalence of juvenile prostitution in Victorian London, Stead took it upon himself to 'purchase' a thirteen-year-old child and convey her to a West End brothel to help raise a public outcry. His sensational series of articles, published in a forebear of the *Evening Standard* under the lurid headline 'The Maiden Tribute of Modern Babylon', stirred up a controversy scarcely equalled in the history of journalism. While his supporters, including such respected figures as Cardinal Henry Edward Manning and the pioneers of the National Society for the Prevention of Cruelty to Children, believed Stead to have struck a blow for good, most of his contemporaries denounced him as a monster and a pornographer. To this day, opinion remains divided.

The sensation was characteristic of a man who, ever since

becoming a newspaper editor at the age of twenty-one, saw it as his duty to thrust inconvenient truths in the face of a reluctant public. He was the boldest, most hated 'muckraker' British journalism had ever known. At a time when newspapers contained little besides dry accounts of parliamentary debates and solemn law reports, Stead burst onto the scene with a vigorous, plain-speaking style and a far from sanitised vision of reality. He was imprisoned once and prosecuted frequently for his 'stunts' – and he bore his punishments gladly. It was not dishonourable, in his eyes, to be denounced by the Prime Minister of the day, William Gladstone, as the man who had 'done more harm to journalism than any other individual ever known'. Stead was equally indifferent to personal attack from the era's most acclaimed novelist, George Meredith, who cast him, in an unpublished work, as a filthy newspaper 'Hercules':

> ... [w]hen [Stead] came out from the [Augean] stable, well pleased with the success of his labours, he saw with astonishment that all men turned away from him. At first he could not understand it... Why this cold shoulder? And then poor Hercules discovered that he stank.[2]

Yet, while pioneering the 'dark arts' of investigative journalism and becoming a master of tabloid sensationalism, Stead was also a devout Christian and a strict moralist. This rare combination of attributes served Stead well in his long career as a scandalmonger and reformer. Through his selective deployment of pious horror and righteous indignation, he transformed himself from a poor and uneducated wild 'barbarian of the north' into one of the most powerful people in the country.

Overbearing but also touchingly naive in his egotism, Stead believed newspapers to be the 'only Bible which millions read' and regarded his own position accordingly. His tabloid evangelism won him the grudging respect of many subscribers, including the moralist John Ruskin ('a constant and often grieved reader'), who exempted Stead from his blanket denunciation of the press as so many 'square leagues of dirtily-printed falsehood'.[3]

In the light of his contemporary relevance, it is surprising that Stead is not more widely acknowledged as a maker of modern Britain. This may be partly explained by the fact that journalistic reputations are almost necessarily short-lived. But in his editorship of a great London newspaper, and his later involvement in a bewildering array of international projects, Stead was more than simply a journalist. He viewed himself as a sort of king, who 'filled the whole country with the sound of his voice'.[4] Yet, for reasons this book strives to elucidate, many of his closest friends and admirers wilfully allowed his memory to fade. It was not through laziness or disrespect that it took over a decade for an 'official', family approved account of Stead's life to appear after his death on board the *Titanic*. No fewer than six eminent contemporary writers, and several since, planned to undertake the task, but it seems they were deterred by unwanted discoveries or the objections of the Stead family. A hundred years after his death, these issues are less likely to cause pain and controversy.

The main factual source for Stead's life remains the standard biography by Frederic Whyte (1925). Although too long for modern tastes (two bulky volumes) and excessively laudatory, it contains facts and documents that have not survived elsewhere. I have relied on this source heavily in places. By far the best account of Stead's life, however, can still be found in the relevant chapters of *Life and Death of a Newspaper* (1952) by Stead's gifted sub-editor at the *Pall Mall Gazette*, James Robertson Scott. This veteran of old Fleet Street, who survived well into the 1960s, was the first of Stead's friends openly to admit that the crusading editor had been an improbable guardian of public morality. As well as keeping detailed notes about his sex life, Stead privately considered himself to be the reincarnated spirit of Charles II, the bogeyman of the Puritans. These facts should take little away from Stead's reputation as a journalist. His polemics may have been all the more effective for the fact that he was often, like Shakespeare's Caliban (for whom he felt 'deep sympathy'), 'raging at his reflection'.[5]

A complex subject of this kind presents an obvious temptation to his biographer: to 'unmask' Stead as brutally and unsparingly as he so loved to do in the case of others. This should be resisted. After all, a more self-satisfied Puritan than Stead would surely not have left such a large quantity of 'incriminating' evidence about his private life in the hands of his literary executors. Even after the substantial holocaust of papers which followed the completion of Whyte's authorised account, many of these documents remain extant. It is to Stead's credit that he would not have wished for any of them to be consciously omitted: 'His first instruction to his biographer,' an acquaintance once said, 'would be to be bold and again bold and always bold.'[6] I have attempted to abide by this wise maxim.

Foremost among modern authorities I would like to acknowledge my debt to Professor J. O. Baylen, late of the University of Georgia. Between 1951 and his death in 2009, he published a staggering array of articles and pamphlets about Stead, all of the highest calibre. To his unrivalled scholarship have been added useful studies by Raymond Schults (1972) and Grace Eckley (2007), but the field remains open for the *magnum opus* that a figure of Stead's significance should command.

Although the present volume is hopefully a step in that direction, no single biography of Stead could ever encompass the man in his entirety. As his acquaintance the second Viscount Esher (1852–1930) so rightly observed, Stead simply had 'too many aspects' to be laid to rest in one book alone.[7] Some might feel that my quest for Stead should have included a more detailed examination of his extraordinary circle of friends, which included, at one time or another, two Tsars of Russia, King Edward VII, Cecil Rhodes, Andrew Carnegie and a galaxy of prominent literary figures and society 'beauties'. The decision to keep these connections within reasonable bounds derives largely from my belief that Stead was, at heart, a loner.

I am grateful to the staff and benefactors of several institutions, notably: Churchill College, Cambridge; the British Library; the Bodleian Library; the National Library of Scotland; the National

Archives of Scotland; the Parliamentary Archives; the London School of Economics Archives; the Salvation Army International Heritage Centre; the Women's Library and the Robinson Library, Newcastle, for permission to view and quote from original source material. I would also like to express thanks to the late Lord Rees-Mogg, Sir Harold Evans, Tristram Hunt MP, Prof. Tony Lentin, Dr Robin Darwall-Smith, Ian Hislop, Paul Routledge, Nick Cohen, Daniel Johnson, Robert Low, Chris Lloyd, Neville Bass, Sam Mills, Lorraine Robinson, George Robinson and Paul Charman, all of whom have been particularly generous with their time and support. Special thanks should also be given to my tutors from the universities of Manchester and Cambridge, Prof. S. H. Rigby, Dr R. G. Davies and Prof. Christine Carpenter, who put me in a position to begin this project in the first place. I am also glad to acknowledge the excellent work of my publisher Jeremy Robson, editors Sam Carter and Hollie Teague, and agent James Wills, without whom this book would not have been possible. For what I have written, of course, I alone am accountable.

W. Sydney Robinson
14 March 2012

CHAPTER I

QUEER BILL, 1849–63

*[T]hat uncharitable Philistine bringing-up of yours ... if [only] you had
been taken to the pantomime when you were six...*
George Bernard Shaw to W. T. S. (August 1904)

Shortly before midnight on Sunday 14 April 1912, a stout, prematurely aged gentleman with crystal-blue eyes and a shaggy grey
beard appeared on the foredeck of the *Titanic*. 'What do they say
is the trouble?' he innocently enquired. No one seemed to know.
'Well, I guess it's nothing serious; I'm going back to my cabin to
read'.[8] These were the last recorded words of William Thomas Stead,
the famous investigative journalist who, thirty years previously, had
shocked the world by purchasing a thirteen-year-old girl on the
streets of Victorian London. Two hours later he would be plunged
into the icy waters of the Atlantic Ocean, never to be seen again.

It was a bizarre end for a man who had made his name smiting
'the powers of darkness in high places' on behalf of the 'disinherited
and outcast of the world'. The magnificent ship, legendary in its
vast scale, luxury and exclusivity, represented everything he had
campaigned against during his long career. Yet to contemporaries
there was a grim logic to the tragedy. Not only had a great journalist been lost in one of the most incredible news stories of all time; a
paradoxical man had died in fittingly incongruous circumstances.
Puritan and sex fanatic, Little Englander and Imperialist, 'saint'
and criminal convict, Liberal and Russophile, 'Pope' and clairvoyant: it was somehow apt that W. T. Stead had last been seen turning
the pages of a penny Bible in the first-class reading room of the
world's most expensive passenger liner.

It was this strange combination of grandeur and quaint humility that made – and makes – Stead one of the most intriguing figures of his era. At the height of his fame he thought nothing of breakfasting with a Prime Minister or lecturing an emperor, but he dressed and spoke uncouthly, and even his staunchest admirers often wondered why, despite an undoubtedly striking appearance, he was not 'more beautiful to look at'.[9] For his intermittent contributor and adversary, George Bernard Shaw, the explanation was simple: Stead was an 'outrageously excessive' individual, crippled by the lasting effects of an 'uncharitable' and 'Philistine' Protestant upbringing. If Stead resented these cutting epithets, he certainly did not overlook the significance of his childhood. Even in his most exalted periods of worldly success, when he likened himself to 'an uncrowned king' and the 'father confessor' of mankind, he never entirely escaped the shadow of the Old Manse at Embleton, deep in the heart of rural Northumberland, where he was born on 5 July 1849.

His father, the Reverend William Stead, had arrived here in the winter of 1845 to be installed as the minister of the village's austere Presbyterian church. By background and training he belonged to a slightly less severe Nonconformist sect, the Congregationalists, but his staunch conservatism and fondness for the gloomy prophesies of Hosea, particularly concerning adulterers and idolaters, rendered him entirely suited to his position as eagle-eyed shepherd of his flock. After some years as apprentice to a cutler in his native Sheffield, he had worked by tireless reading and study to amass a store of knowledge that would have graced an Oxbridge-educated Anglican vicar. This was useful. Too poor to send his six children to school, he taught them at home and lived long enough to see the survivors of their pinched childhood succeed in a variety of occupations. 'Oh! My dear, my patient, long-suffering father!' his son eulogised in 1884. 'How utterly inadequate are my poor words to express in merest outline the debt I owe to you... To your fundamental virtues and capacities ... to your education and example, to your encouragement and inspiration, I owe under God and my mother all that I have, all that I can do'.[10] It was no blind filial outburst. In many ways Stead's extraordinary career is best understood as a long attempt to attain the impossible ideals instilled in him by this brilliant, high-minded Nonconformist parson.

The minister's marriage in 1846 to Isabella Jobson would have consequences well beyond the confines of Embleton. She was the sprightly young daughter of a local farmer who had made a small fortune buying up land cheaply during the Napoleonic wars. The value of her inheritance was substantially diminished by the repeal of the Corn Laws in the year of her marriage, but Isabella proved to be a 'sweetening and liberalizing influence' on her husband's less sanguine temperament, and brought with her an enthusiasm for art and literature unusual in their community.[11] These interests she bequeathed to her son, as well as a deeply held conviction that man must always uphold the rights of woman. A favourite memory of Stead's was of his mother leading a local campaign against the government's controversial Contagious Diseases Acts, which required prostitutes living in garrison towns to undergo mandatory medical examination. Stead later wrote:

> It was one of the subjects on which I have always been quite mad. I am ready to allow anybody to discuss anything in any newspaper that I edit: they may deny the existence of God, or of the soul, they may blaspheme the angels and all the saints, they may maintain that I am the latest authentic incarnation of the devil; but the thing I have never allowed them to do was to say a word in favour of the C. D. Acts, or of any extension of the system which makes a woman the chattel and slave of the administration for the purpose of ministering to the passions of men.[12]

This was curious. Not only was Stead known, on occasion, to explode with rage about atheistic submissions, he also had a 'saving vein of Rabelaisianism' to his character.[13] Women who knew him only through his thundering attacks on immorality in articles such as 'Should Scandals in High Life Be Hushed Up?' and 'The Maiden Tribute of Modern Babylon' were invariably shocked by his unreserved flirtatiousness. Yet Stead somehow managed to keep this aspect of his personality unknown to the outside world. Even today, the judgement of his acquaintance, the sexologist Havelock Ellis, that 'his self-control kept him in the narrow path' is largely accepted, notwithstanding the insightful rider that 'in his interests and emotions he was anything but a Puritan'. The first of these claims does not entirely stand up to the evidence. But Ellis was surely correct in supposing that Stead's 'repressed sexuality was ... the motive force of many of his activities'.[14] This is not hard to reconcile with Stead's acceptance that his often fanatical crusaderism on behalf of women stemmed from a deep regard for his mother. 'I have a prejudice in favour of mothers,' he used to tell critics between heavy drags on a cigarette, 'having myself been born of one, a fact which, I am afraid, you think unduly colours the whole of my thinking.'[15]

Such sentiments were underscored by the family's fervent religiosity, which Stead claims to have differed from conventional Christianity in its emphasis on the equality of the sexes. Yet for all its seeming modernity, the family's piety was almost wilfully antiquated. Like the seventeenth-century Puritans described by Lord Macaulay, they were not satisfied to catch 'occasional glimpses of the Deity through an obscuring veil', but preferred to 'commune with him face to face'. Implicit reliance on God would remain Stead's mantra throughout his life. 'That,' he would often say when confronted with some difficulty, 'I leave to the Senior Partner' – as he styled the Almighty. Such unselfconscious faith also stemmed from his beloved mother. On her deathbed in 1875 she told her husband not to hurry in gathering the children to her side, as 'Jesus is preparing a place for me' and would not call her to heaven 'until it is quite ready'.[16] This was the origin of Stead's lifelong faith that he was constantly guided by an unerring hand.

Their home for most of these years was not at Embleton, but Howdon, a small mining town a few miles to the east of Newcastle. The minister was strangely drawn here by the fact that the previous incumbent had been dismissed from office for 'ungodly' conduct, almost certainly involving drunkenness and debauchery. Not even the most exacting member of the congregation would be able to find fault with the new incumbent. For over thirty years his pulpit quaked under the force of such characteristic utterances as:

> [W]hen you and I meet at the throne of God and the Judge says: 'Stead, did you warn that man?' I shall say: 'Yes, September 1874, first Sabbath...'

But his son never warmed to the town. He would later remember it as 'that grimy spot, befouled and bemired, poisoned by chemical fumes and darkened by the smoke of innumerable chimneys ... Howdon-on-Tyne'.[17]

The family home was a squat cottage situated at the foot of the town's great basalt hill, with views of the 'roar and the flame' of Palmers Steel Works across the Tyne. At first the future editor had only one playmate: an older sister called Mary Isabella or 'Isie' (1847–1918), on whom he doted. Other siblings soon followed, but only John Edward (1851–1923), Francis Herbert (1857–1928) and Sarah Annie (1857–96) survived into adulthood. A bubbly, fun-loving younger brother called Joe was carried off by cholera aged fifteen, much to the family's grief. Yet it was the diseases of society that particularly weighed on the minister. For this reason, he kept a watchful eye over his children and had them protected from idle callers by a fierce dog that stalked the garden like an ecclesiastical Cerberus.

This provided the backdrop for the children's intensive schooling, which began each day at six in the morning and lasted almost until nightfall. The curriculum was highly ambitious. It included Latin and Hebrew as well as French and German, although Stead would never become particularly expert in any foreign language. The influence of the outside world was kept to a minimum, and the amusements of their neighbours were roundly castigated. The theatre was 'the devil's chapel', cards were 'the devil's Prayer Book' and novels 'a kind of devil's Bible'. Only the hours of prayer and occasional walking expeditions suspended the constant grind of the Rev. Stead's pedagogy.

The Sabbath was the sole day when these strictures were relaxed. But any notion of Sunday as a holiday would be misleading. As well as attending chapel and ministering to the needs of the Sunday school, the children were required to reproduce independent summaries of their father's lengthy sermons before partaking of a modest Sunday lunch. This exercise, however, proved excellent training for the future editor. When he came to pioneer the newspaper interview at the *Pall Mall Gazette* thirty years later, Stead boasted a memory so well-trained that all note-taking was superfluous. Unlike his brother Herbert, who went up to university and enjoyed a more conventional career in journalism, Stead never entirely succeeded in mastering shorthand.

All this lay in the future. What immediately concerned Stead was his first great discovery – his ardent love of girls. It is impossible to say when exactly this developed, but, as is often the case with highly pressurised boys shut off from female company yet devoted to their mothers, he was precocious. Before he was even a teenager he had developed a 'very intense awareness of my own sinfulness', and required maternal reassurance before putting out the oil lamp in the little room he shared with his sister. The first object of his passion, however, was a picture-book illustration of Queen Elizabeth I. The Virgin Queen was an unlikely first love, yet Stead was besotted. 'I remember distinctly feeling about her,' he later mused, 'exactly what you would feel about a woman with whom you are in love… You are greatly interested to hear everything about her that you can; you believe that she is the peerless of all women; and you regard all her enemies as enemies of the human race, who ought to be exterminated.' Stead was accordingly much gratified by the fate of her cousin. 'To this day,' he wrote as a fully grown newspaper editor, 'I have never been able quite to get over the feeling of exultation that Mary Queen of Scots had her head cut off.'[18]

It was not long before Stead began to notice living specimens as well. 'The love affairs I had between 1861 and 1871 were numerous,' he recalled happily. Yet, as Stead was the first to admit, these 'affairs' were almost entirely one-sided. 'It was thought in the village that I was a little "daft",' he confessed, 'and the girls did not care to receive the attentions of a suitor who was more or less looked down upon and ridiculed by local public opinion.' Known as 'queer Bill', Stead developed several of the eccentricities that would characterise his maturity. He invariably preferred, for example, both as boy and man, to run everywhere rather than walk. When he first arrived in London in 1880, he casually told his unlikely mentor, the cagey, old-maidish man of letters John Morley: 'If I felt cold any day I would not hesitate at running as hard as I could from one end of Pall Mall to the other.' Stead noted 'with some amusement' the bewildered expression that inevitably ensued. Like the little girls of Howdon, Morley would discover that his deputy had a fund of energy that would spasmodically explode much as a 'mainspring uncoils when it has been wound too tight'. So it was to be always.

The first girl to be swept up in his whirls of amorousness was young Lizzie, whom Stead vividly recalls coming to play with his older sister in a 'little dimity apron, which was rather stiff'. Stead remembered the apron 'because the first time I kissed her I had a battle with it'. In the course of a rare break from study, the eight-year-old conspired with Mary Isie to pin the girl down so that he could land a kiss on her lips, a feat he pulled off 'in spite of vigorous scratches'. It is not clear how long this violent embrace lasted, but he never forgot it: her name was prominent in his curious list of 'Girls, Howdon', which he treasured in old age.

A few years later, Stead became aware of Lydia. 'She was the belle of the village, and all the boys were crazy over her,' he wrote. 'Alas! She was two years older than I was, and when you are eleven, two years is a lot.' This did not stop the young Stead from tracing her footprints through the snow; an occupation which left him 'inexpressibly happy'. Nothing and nobody was allowed to taint this sweet, innocent girl – not, at least, if he could not. This led to a much-discussed tussle with another boy, who appears to have been equally captivated by Lydia's charms. Stead's clerical biographer, the Rev. Benjamin Waugh, reconstructs the story to illustrate the editor's irreproachable knight-errantry, but this was certainly not the full story. 'Like most historians,' the hero privately reflected, 'he ignores that very vital consideration, precise truth, in order to make it appear that my battle was on behalf of her modesty or from general devotion to ideal virtue, whereas it was really inspired by a very devoted love for the girl herself.' Luckily for Stead, the matter never reached the ears of his father. Like his son, the Rev. Stead was prone to beating his children for their misdemeanours.[19]

From this environment Stead was sent away at the end of 1861 to a private Congregationalist academy, Silcoates School in Wakefield. The twelve-year-old must have been an odd figure, strutting around the playground of that humble school, asking the more or less conventional boys if they too conversed with the Almighty. By his own reckoning the school was 'not distinctly religious'. That would soon change. Encouraged by one or two other pupils who were equally 'under deep conviction of sin', Stead worked up a 'Revival' in the school. The letters he wrote to his family at the time give a delightful picture of his profound earnestness. 'Now my dear sister,' he wrote in one, 'unless you have already given your heart to God, give it to Him now.' 'My dear Mary Isie,' he continued, 'turn, oh turn, why will ye die, have you any objection to come to Him who is altogether lovely? Oh that I could love him more... Oh how great the danger is and how many walk on with their eyes shut to hell, oh that awful place.' After a dozen more lines of this frenzied plea, Stead closes abruptly: 'Now my dear sister I must bid you good-bye. Give my love to Mrs Bell and all the children. I hope Mama is in perfect health.'[20]

The older boys at Silcoates were not amused by these entreaties. Stead's son Henry recounts that his father used to be 'pulled across the playground on his back by the hair of his head' for his zeal in the cause of evangelical religion. Yet for Stead these attentions were all part of the fun. On other occasions he would complain of being ignored. '[H]ow I walked long with them and talked with them,' lamented Stead to his mother, 'and apparently they took no notice at all [but] when another boy [said] just two or three words to them they would burst out crying and in a few minutes they would find peace.'[21] A religious revival was all very well, but it was best if he was its leader. Even fifty years later, at the time of his death, an Old Silcoatian felt it necessary to write to the *British Weekly* to clarify that the excitement was in fact 'fired by a boy called Waite'.[22]

The same writer agreed that while Stead was 'not especially proficient in any department of work or play ... his pluck was magnificent'. This was consistent with Stead's own self-estimation as a muscular Christian and a sportsman. 'I went [there],' he explained, '...full of romantic idolatry of Scott and Byron, [but left] when I was fourteen, crazy about cricket and cricketers'.[23] Such reminiscences were no doubt intended to reinforce the editor's self-image as a successful autodidact, owing little to his teachers, but his time at school was actually a very significant stage in his intellectual development. It was here, among the Congregationalists – 'the heirs of Cromwell' – that the young man immersed himself in the heavy volumes of the Lord Protector's letters and speeches edited by Thomas Carlyle. This was to have a great bearing on his future career. 'When I read the *Pall Mall Gazette*,' his often alarmed friend, Cardinal Manning, would say, 'it seems to me as if Cromwell had come to life'.[24] This was one of Stead's most cherished anecdotes: a tribute to his restless two years at the obscure Nonconformist academy.

It would be some time before Stead would become familiar with such exalted personages as cardinals and monarchs, not to mention the other alleged *bête noire* of the Puritans – sex. But by the standards of his class and time, he had already reached maturity when he left Silcoates in 1863. Perhaps with more money or greater inclination he might have been able to stay on and even go up to university. His future business partner, Sir George Newnes, who was two years junior to him at the school, would succeed in moving from Silcoates to study alongside a future Prime Minister, H. H. Asquith, at the City of London School. But this was not to be Stead's destiny. Even following his father into the dissenting church, for which he was evidently suited, was discouraged. No

doubt his mother made him aware of the improvidence of attempting to marry and raise a family on a modest clerical salary.

So, with a heavy heart, Stead put aside childish things and found
himself a position in a counting-house in Newcastle. It was to be
the only job outside journalism he would ever have – or desire.

CHAPTER 2

TO BE AN EDITOR!

I was intensely ambitious, with a personal ambition that led me to wish to make a name for myself and to be great and famous.
W. T. S., 'Autobiographical Fragment' (1893)

The world into which Stead emerged, aged fourteen, was hardly a suitable environment for a sheltered youth of his disposition. Each day, with his lunch lovingly tucked into his knapsack by his mother, Stead ventured into some of the most depraved backstreets in England. It could not be helped, for his workplace, Carr & Co., merchants of 27 Broad Chare, was situated in the midst of one of Newcastle's most notorious districts: the Quayside. According to a celebrated local antiquarian, Eneas Mackenzie, the very alleyway through which Stead passed each morning on his way from Manors Railway Station was thronged at all hours by 'very dangerous, though not very tempting females', who solicited trade from idle clerks and wearied sailors. Stead did not expand on Mackenzie's theme of their relative desirability, but would never forget these 'wretched ruins of humanity, women stamped and crushed into devils by society'.[25] One feels that he was both fascinated and disillusioned.

Stead was kept in line by his genial employer, Charles Septimus Smith, who was almost certainly a friend of the family. After his parents, this man was the greatest influence in Stead's early life. He took his work seriously, was intensely devout and aspired to be 'useful' in the community; he went on to become an alderman. In Stead he recognised a man after his own heart, and once made an extravagant gift to him of a considerable sum of money and a silver watch, which Stead wore on a chain all his life. More importantly, as the Russian vice-consul in Newcastle, he bestowed to Stead a lasting sympathy for all things Russian, which inoculated the young man against the Slavophobe prejudice of the times.

Though Stead would sometimes contrast, with apparent bitterness, his adolescence with those of his 'more favoured contemporaries' who were then beginning their public-school careers, he appears to have greatly enjoyed his time as a clerk. His hours were apparently shorter than was customary, leaving him free to devote the long evenings to earnest self-improvement. This was probably an exaggeration, but there is no doubt that Stead was a regular visitor to the Mechanics' Institute library on Blackett Street, which did not usually close its doors until 10pm during the week. The library had been founded by the city's mercantile elite in the 1820s with the commendable intention of placing 'general knowledge within the reach of the humblest individual of the community' – an ideal greatly appreciated by the young Stead. For only six shillings a year he had access to the world's knowledge and was able, so he claims, to make serious inroads into subjects as weighty and diverse as ancient history, science, comparative religion, geography and music. Although it was somewhat ironic in the light of his later career, Stead evidently benefited from the Board's strict prohibition of any 'books of mere amusement or ... modern works in which fiction and fact are so strangely blended'.[26] By nature, Stead's tastes were never uniformly highbrow.

Yet Stead was always careful to nurture the legend that he had been a precocious youth, unusually godly, intelligent and industrious. He claims, for instance, that after continuing his studies a little further, he had seriously contemplated writing 'the whole history of the Puritan Movement' from 'where Froude left off the History of England and Macaulay began it'.[27] Stead's efforts in this direction got no further than a modest essay on Oliver Cromwell, for which he received, aged fifteen, a guinea from the editor of the *Boy's Own Magazine*. In more candid moments, the youth admitted to more mundane interests: poring over 'reports of cricket-matches and novels'. These temptations, as Stead viewed them, were exceeded by an unlikely fascination with horses and horse-racing. Characteristically, although Stead boasted of becoming 'familiarised with all the prize horses' and getting 'tremendously excited about the winners', he never allowed himself to succumb to the 'betting mania'.[28]

This paradox – Stead's obvious liking for the things which he denied himself – was illustrated even more forcibly a few years later when he fell madly in love with an actress. Abiding by his father's solemn warning to eschew the theatre, Stead did not enter a building containing a functioning stage until he was in his fifties – and in that case it was principally to denounce it for promoting levity. Yet when he heard that a beautiful young woman was playing Ophelia in *Hamlet* at the city's theatre (he had fallen in love with this character, as he had Queen Elizabeth, straight off the page), he was almost overcome with excitement. To the obvious amusement of his fellow clerks, Stead wanted to know everything about the woman who was playing the role, and even went so far as to carry her portrait about in his breast-pocket 'for a couple of years'. More disturbingly, Stead took to 'haunt[ing] the square in which she lived', in the hope of seeing his 'idol' at the window. Such behaviour would lead Stead to reflect, with obvious self-knowledge, that youth was, indeed, 'a rare self-torturer'.[29]

But Stead did not always lust after the unobtainable. At the age of eighteen he claims to have had 'one of the most useful love affairs' of his life. It was with a woman ten years his senior, the sister of the village doctor, who passed an otherwise uneventful summer in Howdon. For once his attentions were not unappreciated. 'She was the first woman outside my own family,' recollected Stead, 'who ever said a civil word to me.' He told her that he loved her and gleefully turned the pages of her music book while she sang Scottish airs at the piano. But after 'some months of very delicious experience', during which Stead was 'allowed to make love to her' (i.e. to cuddle her), she returned to her native Edinburgh to be married to a young naval officer to whom she had been engaged. Stead was devastated: 'I felt as if the sun had gone down in mid-heaven.' But he kept up a voluminous correspondence with the woman until, at length, she seems to have ceased to answer his letters.[30]

Such tender experiences hardly foreshadowed Stead's career as, so *The Times* sneered, the 'self-elected guardian of morals'. Yet Stead always had an inkling that this was his true calling. He once told his doubtless proud father that he wanted God to give him a 'big whip' in order to 'go round the world and whip the wicked out of it'. The Rev. Stead, who had some legitimate concerns about his son's desire to become a journalist, reflected that he knew of only one instrument that could wield such a power: a newspaper. Consciously or not, he was echoing the words of Thomas Carlyle, who, forty years previously, had wondered if the journalist of the future would not be an iconoclastic mendicant friar who 'settles himself in every village, and builds a pulpit, which he calls Newspaper'. Stead grew to be a passionate disciple of this ideal but, typically, claims not to have learned it from Carlyle (who famously changed his views), but from James Russell Lowell, the obscure American humorist and poet. This author's 'Pious Editor's Creed' was a great inspiration to Stead, despite the fact that it was almost certainly intended as satire. It depicts the perfect newspaper as

a Bible which needs no translation, and which no priestcraft can shut and clasp from the laity – the open volume of the world, upon which, with a pen of sunshine or destroying fire, the inspired Present is even now writing the annals of God![31]

By the time that Stead read these magnificent lines, he must have already come into contact with a newspaper in the Mechanics' Institute newsroom which at least attempted to conform to its lofty standard: the *Newcastle Daily Chronicle*, owned and edited by the popular local entrepreneur Joseph Cowen. Cowen had purchased the paper in 1859 and instantly brought to Newcastle a flavour of the highly personal journalism that had been pioneered by Horace Greeley in the United States. Like Greeley, whose inspired editorship of the *New York Tribune* between 1841 and 1872 brought him within sight of the White House, Cowen made it his duty not merely to serve up the events of the previous day, but to agitate, educate and enthuse his readers with the force of his character. His journalistic achievements were impressive: as well as mobilising a band of Newcastle volunteers to fight alongside his friend Giuseppe Garibaldi in the Italian War of Independence, he was also party to an attempt on the life of the French Emperor, Louis Napoleon III. Through his editorial columns he became a daily presence in the lives of the population, whom he presumed to instruct for their betterment.

This was exactly the kind of journalism which Stead himself would develop on an even grander scale. Yet, strangely, Stead denied Cowen as an influence – he could not abide the man's 'arrogant domination'. Not even the unsurpassed Greeley received the recognition that he deserved. Implausibly, Stead credited the more stolid *Spectator*, edited at the time by a heterodox theologian called Richard Hutton, as the originator of his lifelong romance with newspapers. He never forgot his first encounter with that publication. Before he had even read three pages, he claims to have discovered 'an entirely new thing': 'a man with strong convictions, speaking with unconventional earnestness and perfect simplicity exactly what he thought of the public questions of the day'.[32] From that moment, Stead traced his desire to become an editor.

But how to realise that ambition? Stead possessed none of the usual prerequisites of editorship. He had not been to university, had few family connections, no capital and was politically insignificant. He had not even reached the age of majority. But Stead persevered and even managed to turn some of his apparent failings to his advantage. Unlike so many aspiring journalists, he did not attempt to write upon topics about which he had only a superficial grasp. Instead, he made it his model always to write directly from experience.

It was, then, perhaps unsurprising that Stead's first noteworthy contribution to appear in the columns of a newspaper concerned what he saw around him in Broad Chare. In an attempt to put his

Christian values into practice, Stead had given an overcoat, a Bible and some money to one of the vagrants who assembled outside his office on payday. But after directing this man to a local doss-house and being 'very friendly and brotherly to him', Stead was mortified when the recipient took flight, leaving behind nothing but his Bible. Appalled and betrayed, Stead immediately penned a powerful attack on indiscriminate alms-giving, which he forwarded to every newspaper editor in the north-east.

Stead's article appeared on the morning of 7 February 1870 in the pages of a journal recently founded in the neighbouring town of Darlington, the *Northern Echo*. It suggested both Stead's huge potential as a publicist as well as his lifelong hypersensitivity. 'Conventional charity,' he thundered, did not produce 'good, but evil – curses instead of blessings; it debases instead of ennobling, and it is the fruitful parent of vice, indolence, ignorance, falsehood, and crime.' Accordingly, those who solicited such aid were said to be

> dirty, vicious, drunken, and deceitful. Their capital is impudence and lying. They are a curse to the country, a terror to society, and the despair of social reformers. They rear children like themselves; they form the recruiting ground for our criminal army; they are increasing daily; and why? Because they find begging pays better than working.

Hardly anything of this kind had appeared in a newspaper before. Although not exactly 'well-written', it was easily digestible, and carried a clear and righteous message. For better or for worse, this would become the keynote of Stead's style – a foretaste of the tabloid journalism of the future.

Stead had good reason to be pleased with his handiwork. But he caused considerable annoyance to some distinguished citizens of Newcastle by sending them cuttings of his article as a means of rousing them to action. Aside from being thought excessively brash and presumptuous, this was a grave breach of the convention that all journalistic contributions were supposed to be anonymous. Such niceties would not survive the advent of 'W. T. S.'

According to Stead, the result of his article was instantaneous: a mendicant society was established to ensure that the unemployed of Newcastle were properly monitored. This was surely an embellishment, coloured by Stead's subsequent achievements as a crusading journalist, but it is true that a society of this kind gradually came into being, and that Charles Septimus Smith was recruited as its general secretary. Stead, who promised to write any speeches that might be required, had his first, delightful taste of importance. It would become an addiction.

The editor of the *Northern Echo*, Jonathan Copleston, was a man of relatively limited ability, but he instantly recognised Stead's usefulness. 'If you do write again,' he wrote, *'and will allow me to use your mind,* I shall be gratified.' It was a backhanded remark, made considerably worse by his refusal to offer Stead any remuneration for his articles, which were nevertheless accepted, week after week, over the course of the following nine months. Although Stead was greatly piqued by this at the time, he later claimed not to have been put off or embittered in the least. In an essay for the benefit of aspiring journalists written at the height of his fame, Stead realistically observed that newcomers to the profession must humbly accept the fact that they will be unpaid throughout their long, hard years of dreary 'apprenticeship'.[33]

Unbeknown to Stead, his entrance into the world of journalism coincided with a serious dispute between Copleston and his acting proprietor, John Hyslop Bell. It may have resulted from the editor's lack of piety, for what precipitated the row appears to have been a contribution entitled 'Christianity and Democracy', which Bell, though apparently not Copleston, had thought worthy of commendation. After a heated debate, Bell wondered if he should offer the editor's chair to the unknown contributor. The contributor, of course, was Stead. If local legend is to be believed, Bell immediately journeyed up to Newcastle to make enquires. On reaching the Stead family home he was informed by the perplexed minister that there had been some mistake – he had never submitted anything for publication in the *Northern Echo* in his life. Then the truth dawned on him. 'Oh,' he stammered, 'it is Willie you are seeking. He is in the field playing cricket.' The would-be editor was a young man of only twenty-one.[34]

Bell was obviously startled by this revelation, but he saw no reason why Stead's youth should be an impediment. He already had several experienced journalists on his staff and proposed to recruit a skilled sub-editor, Mark Fooks of the *Northern Daily Express*, to act as Stead's mentor. In order to prepare him for the challenge which lay ahead, Bell allowed Stead to take some preliminary lessons in newspaper editing from Copleston, who by this time had decided that he would like to emigrate to the United States. Subsequently Bell advised Stead to visit another man who, with a similar background to his own, had also been given command of a newspaper in his early twenties. This was Wemyss Reid of the *Leeds Mercury*.[35]

Reid was neither an elderly nor a stuffy editor, but he immediately felt himself to be 'one of the old fogeys of the Press' when Stead arrived in his office late one evening in the summer of 1871. 'For hour after hour,' he recalls, the 'ugly duckling ... talked with an ardour and a freshness which delighted me.' If Stead had come in the guise of a pupil he 'very quickly reversed our positions, and lectured me for my own good on questions of journalistic usage which I thought I had settled for myself a dozen years before I had met him'. Stead, clearly enjoying one of his first visits to a newspaper office, went on to outline his journalistic ideal: a paper that would expose injustices, reform morals and topple errant regimes. 'I see you think I am crazy,' he beamed at one stage. Reid did not entirely demur: 'If you were ever to get your way,' he said, 'you would make the Press a wonderful thing, no doubt; but you would make the Pressman the best-hated creature in the universe.' And so the conversation went on until dawn, when Stead shot up 'with an air of bewilderment' and declared: 'Why, it is daylight! I never sat up till daylight in my life before.'

Reid's memory may have been adversely affected by his subsequent dislike of Stead and his methods, but there is no doubt that the young man was exceedingly full of his ideas. In a diary fragment, scribbled just before setting out to take up his position at Darlington, Stead spoke his mind no less unblushingly:

> To be an editor! ... to think, write & speak for thousands... It is the position of a viceroy... But ... God calls ... and now points ... *to the only true throne in England, the Editor's chair, and offers me the real sceptre... Am I not God's chosen ... to be his soldier against wrong?*[36]

Stead was obviously desperate to make a start. But, as was forever to be the case, he felt it incumbent on him to make a great profession of humility. In a toe-curling letter to the Congregationalist minister of Darlington, the Rev. Henry Kendall, Stead, Cromwell-like, outpoured his worries. Would it be right to accept a position which involved 'Sunday work'? And although Stead had recently asked (unsuccessfully) if Bell would increase his proposed salary from £150 to £180, he emphasised that he was not in the least motivated by the prospect of material gain. If anything, he proudly alleged, the editorship of the *Northern Echo* would entail a sacrifice. His 'governor', Smith, had offered to double his wages to match Bell's offer 'rather than lose me'.

Stead needed no words of encouragement from Kendall. His mind was firmly made up: he saw before him a 'glorious opportunity of attacking the Devil'.[37]

CHAPTER 3

ATTACKING THE DEVIL, 1871–80

I often advise young people, who ask me what would be the best school in which to learn to write well – to fall in love with a clever woman a dozen years older than themselves, who lives at a distance from them, and can only be communicated with by writing.

W. T. S., 'Autobiographical Fragment' (1893)

Stead's appointment as Britain's youngest newspaper editor coincided with an important phase in the growth of the British press. Only fifteen years earlier, taxes on every conceivable aspect of the trade had made it impossible for a daily journal to be sold for less than about five pence: a price equivalent to a meal at a restaurant or two hours' unskilled wages. This impediment to circulation was exacerbated by the low levels of general education and, more importantly, the limited nature of the political franchise, which gave the vote to scarcely a fifth of adult males. By the time of Stead's arrival in Darlington, however, sweeping political and fiscal reform had begun to change this state of affairs. William Forster's Elementary Education Act of 1870 meant that children would be entitled to a free, comprehensive education for the first time in the nation's history. Britain stood on the brink of a media revolution.

The north of England's contribution to this great social and political change is relatively unsurprising. London papers such as *The Times*, which had long dominated the market, could only nominally claim a national circulation since their editions had to be transported significant distances before reaching the provincial centres. This created a time-lag which businessmen were only too willing to convert into profit. Moreover, local worthies, who were no longer immune from public criticism, had to find a means of speaking directly to the newly enfranchised segment of the population.[38]

The *Northern Echo* was born with just such a consideration in mind. Several years before its inception, the Liberal establishment of Darlington, headed by the Pease family, had come under fire from a radical coal merchant named Henry King Spark, who had used his fortune to take control of the town's only newspaper, the *Darlington and Stockton Times*. Like many 'New Men' of the nineteenth century, Spark desired to convert his wealth into political power. His plan was to use his newspaper to propel himself to Parliament over the heads of the Peases, who had been slow to realise the influence the press would come to wield.

Between the time when Spark took charge of his newspaper in 1864 and the launch of the Peases' *Northern Echo* on 1 January 1870, the town was convulsed by much 'Sparkite' agitation. Workmen put their weight behind his campaign to have Darlington made into a parliamentary borough, rather than an appendage of the South Durham constituency as it had been since the Great Reform Act of 1832. This in itself might not have been a direct threat to the Peases, but his demand for the Board of Health to be replaced by an elected town council, with himself as mayor, was more threatening, as the Board was entirely controlled by the family.

Spark narrowly missed being elected to Parliament in 1868, when the first of his radical demands had been sanctioned by law. If it had not been for his Liberal opponent, Edmund Backhouse (a crony of the Peases), demanding a written ballot rather than the still not unusual show of hands, he would probably have romped to victory. As it was, the Peases used the time between the hustings – where Spark had been on the verge of being declared the winner – and the ballot to intimidate voters. The day after his defeat, Spark railed in his paper: 'Early in the morning, ward after ward was visited, and in ward after ward, the screw [of the Peases] was unmistakably present.'

Less than two years later, the Peases dispensed with such old-style politics by founding a newspaper of their own. To assist them they drew in the experienced proprietor and sometime editor of the *South Durham Mercury*, John Hyslop Bell, whose journalistic sense would be proved by his early recognition of Stead. He created for the Peases a daily publication that could be sold for just a halfpenny, providing 'rich and poor simultaneously' with 'a carefully collected and neatly printed digest of the latest authentic intelligence on all the matters of social, commercial, or political interest'. This was radical in itself, since halfpenny newspapers were rare at the time and typically consisted of little more than evening summaries of the day's news. At such a price, the paper was unlikely to make a profit, although the founders' manifesto boldly anticipated 'a commercial success'. What is more likely is that it was designed to undercut its rivals, giving the Peases undisputed mastery in the region.

Stead does not appear to have had any great objection to this situation, but he was more wary of some less pleasant aspects of the nascent modern press. In a letter to Bell shortly before taking up his position, he had alluded to certain 'inexperienced suggestions' he had made, which actually show him to have been farsighted rather than naive. It seems that he had been eager to flesh out every aspect of the terms of his contract in the belief that 'matters of business arrangement could never be too clearly defined among gentlemen in any profession'.[39] Like those in his position today, Stead realised that he could be greatly compromised by the dictates of his backers upon whose salary he depended. This difficulty was circumvented when Bell informed Stead that he would not have to write anything contrary to his convictions, but it still appears that the young man was expected to write his daily leading article (or 'leader') on a theme chosen by his superiors. Bell also demanded that his new editor wear a top hat and cease his 'undignified running', which appears to have been the cause of some embarrassment.[40]

Despite their initial uncertainties, the two men enjoyed a good working relationship for the best part of a decade. Bell would have been flattered by the description of his newspaper made by Stead's future colleague, James Robertson Scott, as a cross between 'the *Tribune* ... *The Christian World* and *John O'London's Weekly*'.[41]

The remark was intended to convey the winning formula of piety, self-improvement and quality writing which gave distinction to its pages. By the mid-1870s Stead and Bell had established the *Echo* as one of the most widely read journals in County Durham and the North Riding of Yorkshire; some copies even made it as far as Edinburgh and London.

Though it only consisted of four broadsheet pages, the paper was packed full of interesting information; a far cry from rival publications, which were principally vehicles for disseminating leading articles. Stead's innumerable daily notices, ranging from tales of child murderers to discussions of international affairs and summaries of periodical literature, were genuinely novel. There was also a 'housewife's corner' with prices for the day's foodstuffs, which would later become one of the staples of the media revolution sparked by Alfred Harmsworth's *Daily Mail*. The essential difference was that the *Northern Echo* was still printed in the mercilessly small type that had characterised the press prior to the lifting of the 'taxes on knowledge' twenty years earlier. This may have been because of financial considerations, but it is equally likely that Stead's uncontrollable itch to write forced him to cram as much as possible into the limited space provided. By his own testimony, nearly every line was by his own hand, though his staff included at least five full-time reporters, including his brother Herbert and several editorial assistants, some of whom would later follow him to London.

The newspaper was conducted from a nondescript former thread factory in Priestgate, near the centre of Darlington. The main benefit of this location was that it was close to the post office, where telegrams from the capital, and even the Continent, could easily be picked up by the office boy. Stead made no secret of not wanting to live near the site, where he was expected to put in a day's work beginning late in the afternoon and often running into the early hours of the following day. He first lived in a pleasant cottage outside the town but subsequently rented rooms at a more central location, which he loathed. He described the terraced houses that he could see through his study window as 'rows of slated hideousness', and seldom deigned to raise the blind.[42]

Stead's plight was ended in the summer of 1873 when he married Emma Lucy Wilson, who had been a great friend of his sister's throughout his youth. Their courtship began when the three of them, accompanied by Emma's sister, had gone on holiday to Edinburgh while Stead was still working at the counting-house (later, however, Stead claimed to have fallen in love with his wife 'for the first time' – of three occasions – when he was just thirteen). As was often the case with women whom Stead fell for, both before and after, Emma was slightly older than him and prone to bossiness – a reflection of the combination of adoration and pity that he frequently aroused in women. The bridegroom's only stipulation was that they made their home an attractive country house some way from Darlington, Grainey Hill Cottage, where they could keep a pony and be surrounded by riverbanks and orchards.

Within days of the marriage, Emma became pregnant with their first child, 'Willie' (b. 1874). The couple went on to have three more children in Darlington: Henry (b. 1875), Alfred (b. 1877) and Emma Wilson, always known as 'Estelle' (b. 1878). Although Emma must have been pleased to be settled, she did not find their home especially comfortable, and spent much of her time looking after the 'little monkeys', as Stead called the children, in a worker's cottage which they rented in town. Her husband's attitude was that it was her role 'to mould, and to direct them', but he conceded that 'she is welcome to get as many laughs as she can get out of the operation'.[43] Despite not having the same amount of time to devote to his children as his father had, Stead made a point of taking them for a ride on the pony whenever possible.

Emma's remoteness from her husband soon proved to be more than merely geographical. As a young country girl, she can hardly have known anything of the neglect typical of wives of provincial journalists, let alone ones with aspirations well beyond the confines of County Durham. Almost from the first this presented her with a serious grievance against her husband, which in some ways was only exacerbated by the frequency with which she fell pregnant. That Stead was quietly aware of these issues is demonstrated by a diary entry in which he lamented Emma's 'reproaches more often implied than spoken' on account of his 'intense absorption in politics to the exclusion of family, social or any other life'.

The first major breach between the pair occurred during a holiday in Keswick a few years after their marriage, when Stead indulged in a 'fortnight's flirtation' with an unnamed 'Scottish lassie' (probably a 'Miss Johnson' who came to look after the children). 'I liked the girl very much and like her still', Stead privately wrote. Presumably unlike Emma, '[s]he was a good listener, had good spirits, good complexion and told me her troubles'. But he was clearly interested in more than just talking. 'I kissed her a good deal more than was wise or right,' he admitted, 'but I was on my holidays and had better spirits and was more in the mood for any kind of fun than I had been for long.' Only when the young woman returned to Scotland did Stead realise that his wife disapproved of the affair, writing incredulously that she 'deprecates the continuance of the correspondence'. With typical assuredness, Stead mused that 'Emma would have felt less lonely if she had gone about with tracts, taught classes or in other ways gone about doing good,' much as his own dear mother had. Bringing up his four – soon to be five – children was apparently not as wearying as the 'treadmill round' at the office.[44]

Stead's seemingly chauvinistic attitude was not entirely unjustified. He was living through some of the busiest years of his life, desperately trying to keep abreast of the latest news while at the same time plugging substantial gaps in his general knowledge. Undoubtedly he was aided by more experienced colleagues such as Fooks and Bell, but the paper's early leaders bear his unmistakable stamp. The ridiculous pomposity of Copleston, whose lyrical description of the Oxford–Cambridge boat race of 1870 summed up everything that could be pointless and pretentious about a local newspaper, had been replaced by powerful, often vitriolic, prose, principally adhering to the Liberal creed: Home Rule for Ireland, non-intervention in foreign affairs, Free Trade and land reform. 'I am today what I was in 1869,' Stead often boasted. It was only a slight exaggeration, though in later years the editor became a much firmer supporter of the British Empire, which could only cautiously be mentioned in Bell's presence.

Another important feature of Stead's early journalism was his ostentatious rejection of the methods of 'Society' editors, for whom he would always show the utmost disdain. In one characteristic leading article opposing the state financing of the Thames Embankment, he decried 'the pressures of Cockneydom, in the clubs and its journals, brought to bear upon the national representatives'.[45] It was the sort of irreverence that won Stead a few readers in the capital, who might have felt aggrieved by the fact that social and political power was held by so few. Later in his career, however, Stead would become the most unashamed of all newspaper editors in bringing his publications 'to bear upon the national representatives', boasting excessively of his influence on Parliament. It was an important feature of a man who broke all the rules – sometimes hypocritically – partly because, as George Bernard Shaw quipped, he never learned 'that there was any game to play'.[46]

During this time Stead also published a variety of articles on the subject forever associated with his name: prostitution. As a man who worked unusual hours, often returning to the cottage by pony well after midnight, he would have known more about Darlington's sex trade than most other professional men in the town. But, as with his experiences in Broad Chare, it is impossible to know whether he ever visited these women 'on business'. The only evidence that exists suggests that he was naive – perhaps wilfully so – in 'helping' them. He told a close female friend in the autumn of 1879 that he had heard a woman sobbing in the street 'saying a scoundrel had attempted to outrage her'. Apparently unaware that he was being led on, Stead gave her his arm and walked her home. 'Before she got there,' wrote Stead, 'she calmly proposed that I should complete the offence and [I] discovered that my desolate damsel was a common prostitute!' Stead, who once expressed profound

'respect and admiration' for prostitutes, dutifully reported the incident to the police.[47]

Whatever his personal experiences, Stead displayed expert
knowledge of the subject in his newspaper and was never guilty of
mincing his words. In one robust leader he spoke provocatively of
'wealthy men, churchwardens and deacons, husbands and fathers,
not only in the habit of frequenting houses of ill-fame but even
acting as "dealers in the very evil traffic"'. His approach to other
issues typically ignored by his rivals was equally uninhibited.
Speaking of a proposed Health Bill, he noted: 'We know that
scarcely one in the public in ten care anything about sanitary legislation. It is dry, and it bores them; it does not matter though it kills
them as well.'[48] Such powerful – and surely intentionally amusing
– language earned the editor something of a reputation.

But the campaign that really made Stead famous, putting
Darlington and himself on the journalistic map, was the war
he waged against the government at the time of the Bulgarian
Atrocities in 1876. These were a series of bloody reprisals carried
out by Turkish irregulars in response to a nationalist uprising on
the western fringe of the Ottoman Empire. To this day no one
is sure of the exact number of innocent men, women and children who were slaughtered in the mayhem, though 8,000 can be
taken as a conservative estimate. At the time, the news came out by
instalments, mostly through the Constantinople correspondent of
a fervently Liberal newspaper, the *Daily News*. For the first time in
British history, barring perhaps William Howard Russell's pioneering reportage during the Crimean War (1853–6), the government
lost its inherent monopoly on international news and its foreign
policy was dictated by 'the Fourth Estate'.[49]

The difficulty for Prime Minister Benjamin Disraeli and his
colleagues was that Turkey was an important ally of Britain, protecting her interests in the Mediterranean and Middle East from her
historic enemy, Russia. They had no intention of reversing the carefully worked system of alliances that underpinned this policy just
because the Pasha had put down a worrying nationalist rebellion

with too much vigour. Moreover, as the Foreign Secretary, Lord Derby, warned: 'Too many newspaper sensations have proved to be exaggerated to be alarmed about this one.' Despite the existence of influential editors such as John Delane, who was then coming to the end of a celebrated thirty-year editorship of *The Times*, complacency of this kind still abounded in the upper reaches of government.

With the benefit of hindsight, Stead's early denunciation of the atrocities is something his admirers are right to emphasise. But he went too far in his blanket indictment of the Conservative government, which he rather hastily dismissed as a collection of 'moral eunuchs'.[50] The worst criticism that can actually be made of Disraeli, whom Stead came to loathe with a passion, is that he had less information available to him than the press; and it was by no means perfect. Queen Victoria's ambassador in Constantinople, Sir Henry Elliot, was repeatedly asked by the Foreign Office to comment on the situation – often with articles from the *Daily News* enclosed within official documents – but he proved lethargic, uncritically accepting the denials offered by the Turkish authorities.

Nevertheless, if Disraeli sensed the magnitude of the brutalities while refusing to overturn twenty years of careful diplomacy, his caution was not unjustified. The crimes perpetrated against the Bulgarians were not carried out by the regular army, but a hodge-podge militia of 'bashi-bazouks', who had clearly embarrassed their overlords. Furthermore, the revolt which had triggered the brutal suppression was fairly horrific in its own right, with many innocent Muslims killed by Christian separatists. If any other inconvenient truths needed to be squared up to, it was the fact that Russia's record on tolerance, liberalism and democracy was little better than Turkey's. That these facts were played down or even flatly denied by agitators such as Stead suggests that their interest in the 'horrors' was not as saintly as they alleged.

Stead's overriding ambition was twofold. Firstly, he wanted to help return the Liberal opposition to power; a consideration he once claimed to be every newspaper editor's moral obligation. Secondly, he wanted to elevate himself to the circles of power and influence to which he naturally aspired. Though he hotly denied both of these 'allegations', the facts paint a different picture. Both objectives were spectacularly realised on the bandwagon of the Bulgarian agitation. This was largely thanks to the involvement of the supposedly retired former premier, William Gladstone, to whom Stead sent marked-up copies of his leading articles – which he also posted to some 'two hundred' other public men. In his zeal to be heard, Stead enclosed a long and overexcited letter to the veteran statesman suggesting that recent events might help return him to power.

Gladstone's reaction to these entreaties was lukewarm. But as he started to realise the full scale of the atrocities (and their potential for political leverage) he began to make extravagant claims about the small County Durham newspaper. His gratified correspondent even believed that the 'Grand Old Man's' famous pamphlet, 'The Bulgarian Horrors', was a direct response to his prodding.[51]

This was only partly true. Stead would not have been able to whip up anything like the level of public interest in the subject had it not been for the famous reportage of J. A. MacGahan, who was sent out to the Balkans by the *Daily News* towards the end of July. His articles gave graphic descriptions of rape and destruction; villages 'festering with dead bodies partly covered – hands, legs, arms, and heads projecting in ghastly confusion'. No one can be sure of how accurate these Bunyanesque descriptions actually were: one critical newspaper fairly observed that MacGahan had disguised the fact that his reports were not actually first-hand. But Stead not only drew on MacGahan, he made his accounts yet more vivid:

> At night the sky glares red with the flames of burning villages, by day the horizon is dark with the smoke from their smouldering ruins. The ground is strewn with the remains of the mutilated dead. Herds of swine are feasting upon the limbs of their former owners, while the house dogs are fattening upon human flesh... A cry is

heard from the midst of the bloody mass – it is a little child at the breast of his slaughtered mother endeavouring in vain to draw the milk from the death-cold corpse.[52]

With the help of such imagery, Stead launched a national protest movement against the government, beginning with an 'indignation meeting' at Darlington on 25 August. But while Stead was aiming for the moral high ground, the cause was almost from the first a political one. His farfetched claim that '[t]he honour of Bulgarian virgins is in the custody of the English voter' effectively portrayed Conservative supporters as co-conspirators in rape and torture, a contention more opportunistic than accurate. Any woman who had been assaulted by the Sultan's army of 'savage dogs' was unlikely to receive any redress from a new government, especially a Liberal one whose commitment to non-intervention went back at least as far as the great Liberal pamphleteer and statesman, Richard Cobden, whom Stead and his confreres revered.

The underpinnings of Stead's sensationalist approach can be guessed at by his unintentionally cynical journal entry that a 'keen sense of female honour is a more potent force to arouse men to generous action than any mere massacre'. It is no wonder that many of his enemies had such a low opinion of the campaign that he was running, even though some of the crimes that he referred to were later confirmed by a relatively impartial report from the American official, Eugene Schuyler. By September, not even Disraeli's quick wit could redress the situation: his plea for his compatriots to ignore the newspapermen's 'coffee-house babble' failed to win the day.

In the coming months, Gladstone's praise for the *Northern Echo* increased significantly. Towards the end of 1877 he declared that to read the paper was 'to dispense with the necessity of reading other papers'. The element of self-interest in these statements was undeniable. At the same time as making them, Gladstone was dropping 'general clue[s]' to the still relatively unknown 28-year-old provincial editor on how to handle the crisis and the ensuing war between Russia and Turkey. This would be unsurprising: political manipulation of the press was in its heyday, with Liberals no less domineering than the media-savvy Tories. However, Stead did not need much prompting from Gladstone, whose opinions and values at the time were almost indistinguishable from his own. In later years, Stead, too, would become the sort of 'people's champion' who might – as A. J. P. Taylor wrote of Gladstone – 'step into a carriage and drive off to the mansion of the Duke of Sutherland or the Duke of Westminster ... immediately after a great oration to tradesman and farmers'.[53]

The first sign that Stead was leaning in this direction was his unlikely correspondence with the Oxford historian Edward Augustus Freeman. This maverick Liberal don was a quintessential English scholar of pre-professional days, churning out innumerable volumes on his chosen subject, the Norman Conquest, without so much as deigning to visit an archive or examine a manuscript. His inspiration came not from facts, but from deep and burning prejudices, which owed more to the current political climate than the hard grind of historical research.

In many ways, the two men were brought together by their preference for instinctive writing, a trait far more forgivable in a journalist trying to predict tomorrow than a scholar who was meant to be describing events of the distant past. Nevertheless, the young editor was something of an amateur historian himself, enjoying playful quotations to illustrate the myth of England's 'ancient nobility' and writing a competent entry on the history of Darlington for the *Encyclopaedia Britannica*. In one important leading article, in which Stead introduced an idea that would dominate his later career, he even likened the notion of an international system of arbitration to the centralising policies of the monarchs of the Middle Ages.[54] Such allusions, especially when combined with his passionate attacks on Turkey and Disraeli, were well designed to prepare the way for a swift courtship of the influential historian. The main difference between their political standpoints was that Stead's dislike of Disraeli was not aggravated, as Freeman's was, by violent anti-Semitism.

The pair's connection began when Freeman received a copy of the *Northern Echo* in the great mail-shot let loose by Stead in the summer of 1876. It is unlikely that Freeman had heard of the paper at this time, but by the following March he was describing it as 'the best paper in Europe'. As with Gladstone's eulogies, Freeman's words were just as much intended to highlight the perceived inadequacy of the Metropolitan press: in later years neither man could remember the paper's title. Freeman's interest in furthering the cause of the Liberal party was equally pressing, making him doubly sympathetic to the reports that so damaged the moral credibility of the government. Together the three men constituted a formidable alliance that combined contacts and political power with energy and a growing readership.

Freeman's most important contribution to Stead's career was to forward the paper to his friend, the curious Russian émigré, propagandist and self-styled 'Her Excellency' Madame Olga Novikov, née Kireev, who wrote in the press simply as 'O.K.'. This 37-year-old god-daughter (and likely biological daughter) of Tsar Alexander II was the wife of an elderly Russian officer and the sister of a volunteer killed fighting against the Turks. Though her temperament proved to be remarkably like that of the young editor, she lived in a far more exalted sphere. Her year was divided between St Petersburg and Claridge's Hotel, where she kept a salon attended by such Liberals and luminaries as Gladstone, Thomas Carlyle, James Anthony Froude, Alexander Kinglake and Freeman himself. Her aim was to win these influential figures over to the unlikely cause of Russian autocracy, an objective in which she apparently had some success. Though most journalists viewed her with suspicion mitigated by ridicule, Stead was quickly bowled over by her warm entreaties.

Before meeting the flirtatious north-countryman, Olga had already been connected romantically in the press with Gladstone. This may have been unlikely, but it is true that the premier offended against Victorian etiquette by taking her arm after a public address. Another member of her circle, the historian Alexander Kinglake, claimed her smile meant more to him than 'the raptures of ninety-nine marriages', while the British diplomat to Russia, Sir Robert Morier, bluntly described her as 'an extremely accomplished whore'.[55] Though such epigrams were undoubtedly cruel and overstated, it is likely that she used her sexual allure to control the minds of influential men. To describe her as beautiful or influential, however, might be an exaggeration: Gladstone's private secretary, Sir Edward Hamilton, dismissed her as 'a rather masculine looking and pushing woman' who 'bored' and 'pestered' his master with 'notes and invitations'.[56]

Olga's courtship of Stead – or, possibly, his of her – began during the white heat of the Bulgarian controversy, a period in which Emma had grown especially distant from her husband on account of her relatives being unsympathetic to the newspaper's stance. Alone in his cottage, Stead probably felt more inclined than ever to contemplate an adulterous relationship, not least because his chances of succeeding with 'Her Excellency' seemed so remote – and exciting. For her part, it seems that the Russian temptress initially wanted to seduce her correspondent purely in the political sense, not least because she had assumed from the authoritative tone of his leading articles that he was a much older man. Be that as it may, she soon roused the young man's passion.

'My correspondent is as fair as she is noble' gushed Stead in a letter acknowledging her photograph, which portrayed a slightly rotund older woman with soft skin, emerald earrings and elegant clothes. Evidently alarmed, Olga suggested that he should write to her as if she were an 85-year-old babushka. 'It is impossible,' retorted Stead. 'I cannot conceive the possibility of a grandmother retaining unimpaired ... all the freshness, the enthusiasm and the glow of youth which are the characteristics of she who writes the letters signed "Olga Novikov née Kireeff".' So enamoured was Stead that he boldly suggested that she come and stay alone with him at his 'little hermitage' for a few nights. To this, Olga predictably gave him a fierce rebuke, which almost scuppered their friendship before it had even begun.[57]

In desperation, Stead disingenuously claimed that both he *and* his wife had invited her, insinuating with slightly too much vehemence that her rejection was based on class prejudice as opposed to moral propriety. 'Madame,' he wrote back, 'it was wrong of me to invite you here. It is not for a poor and humble individual as my wife and myself to entertain Excellencies. We do not associate with the aristocracy. We don't even associate with the local grandees of our town ... they do not mix with such humble people as newspaper editors... Social superiors I suppose are much the same all over the world.' But Olga did not react badly. Indeed, she appears to have been moved to pity by her grovelling correspondent, whom she reassured in comforting tones that he was already becoming 'quite a personage'.

Over the next two years it seems that Olga felt strongly enough about Stead to allow him to become her lover. He went down to visit her in London whenever he could, though this cannot have been often since the combined burden of his work and family lives in Darlington was still great. He was also intensely guilty about the situation and asked Olga to cease all communication with him for one year beginning in October 1878, since, he explained, 'you know how you would feel if you were in her [i.e. his wife's] place'.[58]

Just six months later, however, on another visit to the capital, Stead could not resist calling at Olga's suite, perhaps reassured by the foreknowledge that she would not be there: 'Your salon seemed empty. Bedroom ditto. It was very sad.' Later in the same year he again broke his silence to observe: 'Ever since I first saw you not a day, not a night, has passed without my thinking many, many times of my dearest O.K. ... It is not easy to forget, even when we try.' Such sincere affection inevitably rekindled their romance; indeed, Olga came to stay with Stead during November 1879, a period in which his wife was conveniently in town tending to a 'fine fat baby of the female sex'. Stead claimed to have only invited Olga to help him work on a book about Russia they were supposed to be writing together, but the fact that he did not dare forward her 'sarcastic' thank-you note to his wife suggests that they had other things on their minds.[59]

The most important aspect of Stead's relationship with Madame Novikov in terms of his career was the many doors she opened for him in the capital. 'You seem to know everyone,' he gawped in one of his starry-eyed dispatches. But not everyone in Olga's cosmopolitan circle warmed to her new friend. Only Freeman saw the absolute necessity of courting journalists in order to give them a public platform; most of the others viewed them with the utmost contempt. The historian J. A. Froude summed up the group's collective opinion in a letter to their hostess in which he contrasted the rise of the political press with the fall of individual liberty: 'The people are losing all capacity for self-government,' he lamented. 'They no longer think for themselves. They repeat only what they read in the newspapers and the worst results may be expected for the Constitution.' Carlyle, however, by then an old man in his eighties, apparently enjoyed the two or three occasions on which he met the editor, describing him as 'that good man Stead' and laying off his usual criticism of anything associated with news reporting.[60]

Stead was comforted and flattered by these acquaintances, who gave him a glimpse of an entirely new world. His self-confidence, never needful of encouragement, soon grew to such an extent that he dispensed with any residual pretence that he needed to placate the likes of Bell, who had conveniently been on holiday in Switzerland at the time of the outbreak of the Bulgarian agitation. Even so, Stead's later claim that he experienced his first mystical 'premonition' at this time, which anticipated his call to London to edit a newspaper, was a piece of retrospective make-believe. Certainly he was aware that his new connections could be put to good effect in the capital, but he actually renewed his contract with Bell shortly before receiving the news that Olga had used her influence, almost certainly with Gladstone, to secure him the deputy editorship of the *Pall Mall Gazette* in the summer of 1880.

Stead claims to have been unsure about whether to accept this offer, partly because he had such a strong hatred of the capital and did not want his children to grow up 'Cockneys ... reared in Babylon'. But this was just another aspect of his confused personality, which made him outwardly embarrassed at his burning ambition. In reality, there was never a moment of doubt that he would leap at the chance of entering so forcefully into the London scene – via the *Pall Mall Gazette* or anywhere else that would have him. His claim that it would take whips to force him down to the capital – 'the grave of earnestness' – was merely hyperbole designed to assuage the likes of his father, who asked him at this time, plaintively, whether it would not be better to 'leave God to manage His universe in His own way'. Thankfully for Stead, Bell and the others at the *Northern Echo* let him out of the contract he had signed, freeing him to make the move that would secure him a place in history. Like other newspaper proprietors to come, they were also partly relieved: Stead had become a loose cannon.[61]

Stead journeyed down to London at the end of 1880 with the intention of practically never returning to the north again. Behind him he left his wife and four young children, who would have to wait anxiously for several months until he had found them a new home. The change was to herald one of the most important developments in his life – and would revolutionise journalism forever.

CHAPTER 4

MORLEY'S APPRENTICE

It is a great venture. If I succeed, in a year or two I may be one of the most powerful men in London.
W. T. S. to Madame Olga Novikov (August 1880)

The London newspaper scene at the time of Stead's appointment as deputy editor of the *Pall Mall Gazette* was a strange amalgam of two very different, yet in some respects related, worlds: Clubland and Grub Street. The former was the sphere of the wealthy 'man of letters', who could pass the day reading in his favourite armchair at White's or the Athenaeum with little worry about the source of his evening meal. The latter was the metaphorical home of countless impoverished hacks, many of whom had enjoyed the benefits of an expensive education, but were now compelled by economic necessity to live upon their pens. As ever, their ranks were swelled by a considerable body of young men from decidedly less genteel origins, such as Stead, who had to find their feet in the cut-and-thrust world of daily journalism.

Rather curiously, it was these characters that the snobs of Grub Street – who might easily have outnumbered those of Clubland – detested most of all. No source bears greater testimony to this than the lives and novels of two of the most eminent writers to make the transition from the garret to the Garrick: Anthony Trollope and William Makepeace Thackeray. For both men, literary wealth and the acceptance of high society went hand-in-hand with an acerbic contempt for the mass of jobbing writers they left behind in the depths of the literary marketplace. It was a class personified by Trollope's creation, Quintus Slide, editor of 'The People's Banner' in the Palliser novels. Like the new arrival at Northumberland Street,

Strand, Slide was principally hated for the fact that he combined uncouthness with influence. He was

> ...a young man under thirty, not remarkable for clean linen ... [a] well-known and not undistinguished member of a powerful class of men... And though he talked of ''ouses' and 'horgans' he wrote good English with great rapidity, and was possessed of that special sort of political fervour which shows itself in a man's work rather than in his conduct.

Stead cannot have been the man that Trollope had in mind when Slide first appeared on the pages of his series in 1868, but the editor's enemies must have been quick to make use of the cruel, if serviceable, caricature. It reflected the stock prejudices of the entire class of 'arriviste' men of letters, to which both Trollope and Thackeray belonged. For this reason it is no small irony that the name of the newspaper where Stead presently found himself as assistant editor came from the pages of Thackeray's classic satire of mid-nineteenth-century journalism, *The History of Pendennis*. In that novel, a young man trapped in the mire of Grub Street – the debtor's prison – proposes to found a newspaper that will be of much higher quality than the sort lampooned by Trollope. 'The *Pall Mall Gazette* is,' the protagonist proudly declares, 'written by gentlemen for gentlemen.' In effect, it was the prototype of everything that Stead thought a newspaper should not be.

When the *PMG* (as the paper came to be popularly known) issued its first number in February 1865, the reference to Thackeray, who had been dead for only two years, was far from incidental. It was his deputy and protégé, Frederick Greenwood (originally a humble 'printer's devil'), who was the paper's first editor, while the finances came from Thackeray's former publisher, George Smith. Smith had formerly employed both men on the staff of his influential literary journal, *The Cornhill Magazine*.

Greenwood had been reluctant to accept Smith's proposed title, preferring 'The Evening Review'. But Thackeray's fictional creation was an inspired choice, befitting a proprietor known to be as shrewd as he was ruthless. Not only did it provide an excellent daily advertisement for one of his most celebrated authors (among whom he listed the Brontë sisters, John Ruskin and George Eliot), it also tapped into the demand of Clubland for an evening paper that could be trusted as much as *The Times*, yet also incorporated some of the lighter touches that were beginning to make other newspapers attractive to a wider audience. As the historian of that long-lived publication observes, Smith's brainchild was intended to appeal to 'those who disliked the vulgarity, as they considered it, of the *Daily Telegraph* and the stiffness of the *Standard*'.[62]

On this model, the *PMG* strove to woo the rich and powerful rather than secure a popular readership – a strategy curiously antithetical to the modern methods soon to be pioneered by Stead. For its first fifteen years of existence, it scarcely exceeded the *Northern Echo*'s provincial circulation of between five and ten thousand, yet it rapidly became the paper of choice for statesmen, aristocrats and, fittingly, 'gentlemen' of the Thackerean mould.

Politically, the paper was hostile to Liberalism and almost as pragmatic in its approach to foreign affairs as Disraeli. During the great Bulgarian Atrocities campaign, for example, Greenwood had denounced the likes of Stead and Madame Novikov as 'irresponsible journalists' and 'hired agencies', who had exaggerated the scale of the atrocities with a 'sham sympathy ... for false purposes'. As a clearer picture of the facts started to emerge, Greenwood rather callously observed that a massacre of 10,000 Christians was only a small proportion of the region's population, and was certainly not substantial enough to warrant a change in Britain's carefully worked foreign policy.[63]

These views were naturally received with indignation by Stead in Darlington, who took a strong dislike to what Virginia Woolf's father, Leslie Stephen, described as 'the most relentlessly anti-Gladstonian, thoroughly jingoistic newspaper' in the land.[64] Stead even went so far as to describe Greenwood's great coup of persuading the government to purchase the Suez Canal from Egypt as 'the most dismal of modern fiascos'. In later years, however, when its shares were yielding an annual dividend of almost £1.5 million for the national exchequer, Stead conveniently 'forgot' this youthful blunder, disingenuously claiming to have 'always been a firm supporter of the purchase'. Greenwood, for his part, had not even attempted to publicise his triumph: an indication of the very different schools of journalism that the two men would come to represent.[65]

Greenwood's control of the *PMG* did not outlive the ministry of the Conservative government that he had done so much to support. In 1880, when Gladstone replaced Disraeli as Prime Minister for the second time, it was presented as a wedding gift to Smith's son-in-law, Henry Yates Thompson, an Old Harrovian manuscript collector with little genuine interest in newspapers. Described by one of his staff as 'absolutely submissive', 'Thompy' (as he was known, though not to his face) was never particularly loved or loathed by anybody. Nevertheless, Stead anticipated that he would be unlikely to get along with his new employer, who had thoughtlessly asked him to negotiate the terms of his contract on the Sabbath. Writing to excuse himself, Stead had tactfully observed that it would 'be awkward to be away from the wife on a Sunday'. But the seed of doubt had been firmly planted in his mind. In the same letter Stead warned Yates Thompson that he might be unsuited for the position on offer since he was a wild 'barbarian of the north', 'more of a farmer ... than a West-ender'. The proprietor's views on the matter are not known, but he would come to regret hiring Stead in such haste.[66]

For all his mixed emotions, Stead had many reasons to be grateful to Yates Thompson. It was only because of his opportunistic decision to change the political stance of the paper from Conservatism to Liberalism that the opening of the assistant editorship had even arisen. Unwilling to countenance such a shift in policy, Greenwood and his team dispelled the popular assumption that journalists have forever been purely mercenary by resigning en masse to form a rival newspaper, the *St. James's Gazette*, in order to provide support for the Tory party in opposition. It was always a source of pride for those associated with the *PMG* that the same remarkable action was repeated a mere decade later when the newspaper reverted back to its former colours under the ownership of the first Viscount Astor (1848–1919). In that case the new publication formed was a Liberal one, the esteemed *Westminster Gazette,* underwritten by Stead's school friend, the future Sir George Newnes, though by that time the famous editor had spun off in another direction.

In the midst of these dramas, Yates Thompson had briefly found himself as the sole hand at the editorial wheel, an experience which may have instilled in him an uncommon respect for the often thankless task of newspaper editing. Somehow he managed to keep the paper alive for several fraught weeks during which he searched for a replacement. The candidate to emerge was John Morley, the celebrated editor of the *Fortnightly Review* and author of several historical and philosophical studies including *Edmund Burke* and the highly influential essay *On Compromise.*

Morley, despite his attainments, was a surprising choice of replacement for his predecessor. Not only was he an unashamed 'little Englander', thoroughly opposed to meddling in international affairs, he was also an intellectual aristocrat, not naturally predisposed to the rough and tumble of the penny press. When friends valiantly attempted to contradict this, as well as the popular image of him as an austere schoolmaster, they tended to do so with reference to his secret 'femininity' – which can hardly have been intended as flattery. In a satirical essay published ten years after their first meeting, Stead compared his former 'chief' to 'a lovesick schoolgirl', lamenting how he 'looked down with infinite contempt upon most of the trifles that interest the British tomfool, as the general reader used sometimes to be playfully designated'.[67] Not even the theatre and the arts were allowed to pollute his pristine pages of indigestible politics, as George Bernard Shaw humorously recounts:

> When, as a beginner, I got an introduction to Morley (not then Lord Morley), and he asked me what I thought I could do, I threw

away the opportunity by saying that I thought I could write about art. In utter disgust he turned away, flinging over his shoulder a muttered 'Pooh! ANYBODY can write about art.' 'O, CAN they???' I retorted, with great self-restraint in not adding 'you wretched Philistine second-hand Macaulay.' That concluded the interview; and Morley missed his chance of becoming my editor.[68]

Although this *enfant terrible* went on to describe Stead as 'an abyss of ignorance' in relation to cultural matters, it cannot be denied that the latter played an important role in launching his career, as well as those of William Archer and Oscar Wilde. All three contributed regular articles and reviews to the *PMG* after Morley 'abandoned journalism for politics' in mid-1883. But Stead does not appear to have valued their submissions especially highly, nor did he attempt to befriend them personally or give them the privilege of signing their articles. This may explain why each of them, as Shaw later explained, 'moved over to the real editors' and virtually never acknowledged Stead as an important figure in their careers.[69]

For the time being it was only Stead's relationship with Morley that counted. Initially they appear to have been blissfully unaware of the utter irreconcilability of their personalities. 'I feel a terrible responsibility when I consider how much you forgo,' the older man had written when trying to persuade Stead to accept Yates Thompson's offer in August 1880. With even greater warmth, Morley admitted that 'it will make all the difference to have some-one with whom I can discuss every day the line of the paper. My official [i.e. political] friends can be busy, and besides my notion is that we should inspire them rather than they us.' All seemed to bode well for their budding relationship – Morley even went up to meet Stead at Darlington, while Stead was a guest at Morley's Putney home for several weeks when he first came to London.[70]

The illusion that the two men were kindred spirits may have been reinforced by the fact that the only practical difference of opinion that Stead could detect from a thorough perusal of the back issues of the *Fortnightly Review* was in relation to the Contagious Disease

Acts, which Morley later agreed should be repealed. The two men were also superficially linked by the fact that they came from relatively similar backgrounds: Morley was the son of a Dissenting (though later Anglican) physician from Blackburn, and had endured many years of hardship before finally establishing himself as an author and journalist in London.

Yet these similarities only served to accentuate how different the two men really were. Morley had played the game of social advancement with far more skill than his new assistant editor by winning scholarships to private schools from an early age, and rounding off an impressive education with a prestigious exhibition to Oxford. Though financial difficulties and a major breach with his father (resulting from his loss of religious faith) eventually led Morley to leave the university without a degree, there is little doubt that he would have found a high-paying job in the civil service, or a seat in Parliament, had it not been for his lack of connections and resources. In later years he would become a senior politician, Gladstone's official biographer and a viscount.

The truth about Stead's appointment was that Morley was tiring of his work at the *PMG* and wanted someone to deputise for him while he went off to complete a popular biography of Richard Cobden for Macmillan. Soon after Stead had settled into this role, Morley informed his sister Grace that his burden had been 'much lightened' by this 'queer child of nature', whom he described, perhaps a little prematurely, as 'a nice and good fellow'.[71]

Stead's appointment also owed much to the proprietor's belief that Stead would be content to receive a considerably lower salary than would have been necessary to attract a more established figure. This was betrayed by Yates Thompson's suggestion that his prospective employee should receive less than a quarter of Morley's salary: £400 as opposed to £1,700, though topped up by so many pence a line for his 'copy'. In effect he was treating his experienced new assistant editor as though he were merely a regular contributor, albeit one with a handsome retainer. It may have made sound business sense, but it irritated Stead beyond measure and almost led him to refuse the offer outright. In the end, no doubt under Morley's influence, a workable compromise was agreed upon, but Stead's improved salary of £800 was only slightly better than what he had commanded shortly before leaving Darlington.

Stead stretched his resources by taking out a mortgage on a large detached villa overlooking Wimbledon Common, grandly called Cambridge House. Morley said with honesty that it needed 'a good deal of repairing', but Stead was happy to do without the 'mighty works' that his chief was carrying out to his own house and garden in the neighbouring borough.[72] Rather than a launch-pad into 'society', Stead wanted a secure and comfortable environment for his growing brood; a retreat from his hectic daily routine, which began with early morning dumbbell training after which he attempted to read every British and European newspaper 'down to the police reports' before arriving at the office a little before 8am.[73]

This ambitious routine did not prevent Stead from finding time to take his children for an occasional pony-ride on the Common, much as he had at Darlington. Aaron Watson, who wrote 'turnovers' (short articles following the front-page leader) for the newspaper at the time, claims that the new assistant editor once arrived for work on this unlikely animal (which he incorrectly recollected as a donkey) – in his dressing gown! The story may have stemmed from Stead's later reputation as one of the worst-dressed men in London, but it is equally plausible that Stead really had been too impatient to await the first train, which took him each morning to Waterloo Station.

Other staff members recalled seeing their new colleague trudging across Waterloo Bridge swinging a battered leather bag from his elbow. Besides bundles of proofs and foreign newspapers, it contained the sandwiches which Stead consumed at great speed for his lunch, often washed down with a glass of stout preheated on top of a grotty water tank by his secretary. This improvised meal would typically take place as soon as the first edition was out, a little after noon, though a political crisis or announcement might require a fresh leader to be written, legend had it, 'between 11.57

and 12.01'. In such instances, there were angry shouts from the mysterious business managers upstairs, who seldom mixed with the editorial team, and had surprisingly little influence over the contents of the newspaper. James Robertson Scott, who joined the staff as a sub-editor in the late 1880s, could not even remember the name of the advertising manager – now one of the most important positions on a newspaper's staff.[74]

❧

It is hard for a modern visitor to Northumberland Street to imagine such a vanished world. Though still a 'mean-looking thoroughfare, more like a passage than a street', the lane has inherited some of the order and security that characterises the Strand, into which it runs at the south end of Trafalgar Square.[75] This part of London was not so fashionable in Stead's day. His fellow newspaper editor Robert Blatchford depicts it vividly:

> There are thieves in the Strand, and prowling vagrants, and gaunt hawkers, and touts, and gamblers, and loitering failures, with tragic eyes and wilted garments; and prostitutes plying for hire.[76]

Stead was working in the same land of brothels and coffee-houses in which the eighteenth-century poet Richard Savage had run a man through with his sabre and Ben Johnson had set to work on his first Latin primer.

More coincidentally, Northumberland Street was also the location of a famous fracas involving Alexandre Dumas and a crazed, gun-wielding loan-shark, described in Thackeray's *Roundabout Papers*. In his retelling of the story, the newspaper's spiritual grandfather spoke of an office behind 'those blank windows in Northumberland Street ... a cavern of terror ... with its splendid furniture covered with dust, its empty bottles, in the midst of which sits a grim "agent", amusing himself by firing pistols, aiming at the unconscious mantel-piece, or at the heads of his customers!'

Whether it was by design or coincidence that the same chair was now occupied by the moth-eaten John Morley cannot be known. But it was certainly the ideal location for a newspaper of the *PMG*'s pretensions, which came so close to grandeur, yet somehow fell short of the desired ideal. Its location opposite the tradesmen's entrance of Northumberland House, which had been a centre of political intrigue in the seventeenth century but had since been converted into an expensive hotel, was a fitting allegory for its position in the world. Though close to power and opulence, it enjoyed little reflected glory.

The building was a strange rabbit warren of poky rooms, connected by a series of sliding panels and approached by a 'dark narrow stair'. As Robertson Scott recalls, 'there may have been less convenient, darker and grubbier daily newspaper offices in London but I never heard of them'.[77] In the rat-infested basement, steam printers shipped in from America spewed out thousands of editions of the paper each afternoon, the text having been fumbled into square blocks by an army of skilled young compositors. Surviving photographs of the editor's 'big room' – cramped and paper-strewn – confirms this desolate image. One can almost smell the varnish and lamp oil rising from the dusty, ink-stained chaos.

These discomforts excepted, 2 Northumberland Street remained a place of considerable influence – it was no exaggeration to say that nearly all the most influential people of the day traipsed up its staircase at one time or another. They did so principally to see the editor, whose custom was to receive visitors into his office, withdrawn from the swarm of drones who scribbled furiously in the adjoining compartments. It is easy to imagine his annoyance when his new assistant editor took to interrupting these private colloquies with long lists of premeditated questions 'on any subject in which [the guest] could possibly be interested'. Watson believes that many distinguished callers who came expecting a ponderous conversation with Morley about Diderot or the latest developments in Comtean philosophy went away 'feeling that they had been interviewed by a hurricane'. With the exception of an abortive dinner party at the Yates Thompsons and the occasional reappearance at Madame Novikov's salon (allegedly in a 'deplorable check suit'), this was how the presence of Stead was first felt on the London newspaper scene.

The contents of the paper at the time were almost exclusively confined to Ireland, whose inhabitants had flared up to an unprecedented extent on account of Anglo-Irish landlords driving up rents, or evicting tenants entirely, as they shifted from arable to more lucrative (and less labour-intensive) pastoral farming. Stead later claimed to have converted Morley to Home Rule (Irish quasi-independence) as a means of redressing these grievances, but his influence in schooling the future Irish Secretary was probably less than he supposed. For most of their time together it is likely that the younger man was on the receiving end of most of the office pedagogy. As Stead admitted, Morley used to 'bore me to death on Ireland'.[78]

But Stead succeeded in teaching Morley a fair amount about the more practical aspects of newspaper editing, about which the younger man knew a great deal. One of his innovations was to incorporate some modest maps and diagrams into the paper, which were at the time very rare features in daily journalism. The first to appear was a crude representation of troop movements at the battle of Tel el-Kebir in September 1882, which Mr Hunt, the assistant to the foreman in the composing room, 'solely constructed out of brass rules and type'. Stead's other innovations were to expand the paper's summary of the morning's news, to enliven the gossipy 'Occasional Notes', and to break up longer articles with 'crossheads' (subheadings), which had never before been seen in an English newspaper.

These reforms were the seeds of the radical changes that would follow once Stead was in absolute control, but they were scarcely a full indication of what was to come. Unsurprisingly, they did not entirely meet with the approval of the editor, who Stead remembered as 'a chilly frost on the exuberance' of his 'more youthful enthusiasm'. Morley's reticence must have been aggravating for his young assistant, who, after a decade in command of the *Northern Echo*, was now reduced to the same level as the young striplings, 'learning the job as they went along'.[79]

Stead's frustration was compounded by the fact that the most prominent of this small body of men was a pair of swaggering Oxford graduates who carried themselves, as Watson recalls, 'with a lofty air that was plainly anticipatory of future greatness, and was, indeed, only excusable on that ground'. These were the future Viscount Milner and Sir Edward Tyas Cook – the former a distinguished graduate of Balliol College who would follow Morley into politics; the latter an eminent biographer and government censor of newspapers during the First World War. Though they often saw past their social differences, Milner later reflected that Stead 'had a very just contempt for my powers as a journalist'. In all likelihood the younger men thought themselves rather too good to work beneath Stead, as is suggested by Cook's boast to a friend that 'you never know whether you will hear the voice of culture (that's me, you know, and Milner) or the blatantest vulgarity [i.e. Stead]'.[80]

Somewhat incongruously, Morley wanted Stead as nothing more than a technician to oversee the churning-out of polished 'Morleyese', freeing himself to continue with his other projects, including the editorship of the *Fortnightly Review*, a position he somehow managed to retain. Stead claims to have had no objection to this, but those who could remember their stormy morning conferences were less prone to downplay the scale of their disagreements. 'We differed on absolutely everything,' Stead later confessed, 'from the Providential government of the world to the best way of displaying the news in the "Extra Special".' Entire lines were struck out of his leaders, while Morley 'was always down on' his deputy's 'besetting temptation to bawl when a word in the ordinary tone would be sufficient'.[81]

As Morley was increasingly absent from the office, he was provoked to send angry missives to his deputy. 'I have read your two [Occasional] Notes with the same satisfaction with which a man received two black eyes,' he observed upon reading a pair of stinging salvos that Stead had unleashed against *The Times*. A few weeks later an article suggesting that Britain and America be linked by Stead's hobby-horse, the 'supreme tribunal', provoked him to write: 'your article this evening has turned my hair grey', while another on Russia compelled him to hurry back to 'rub off the Slavophil label'. When these disagreements were played out in person they could be considerably more ferocious, but there was always an underlying good humour in their mutual antipathy. Watson recalls that Stead used to emerge from their 'morning battles ... beaming as if with the enjoyment of victory, though it may be doubted if he ever really won, John Morley not being at all distinguished for a giving-way temper'.[82]

One area in which Stead and Morley were most obviously at loggerheads was religion. Morley ranked among the most militant atheists of the day (he was the first author to drop the capital letter in 'god'), whereas Stead styled himself as a latter-day prophet of the Puritan faith. But Stead always maintained that the practical manifestations of their world views were easily reconcilable, and – with one notable exception – there were no submissions that he objected to purely on religious grounds. This was largely because Stead's Christianity was generally accommodating of opinions that offered to promote his most cherished values, which were initially pragmatic rather than devotional in nature. When Stead later replaced Morley as editor, this allowed him to continue to accept occasional contributions from the likes of Frederic Harrison and T. H. Huxley ('Darwin's Bull-Dog'), who were widely considered to be the greatest heretics of the hour.

Where their differences were more insoluble concerned what might be called the 'philosophy of journalism'. Morley's attitude was that every article needed to be written by a 'qualified expert', since this provided the most authoritative, rather than entertaining, 'copy'. Stead violently dissented from this view. He did not think that a newspaper should be a forum for dons and civil servants to pontificate on the great matters of the day. Rather, he believed it to be the job of the journalist to stand 'between those who know everything and those who know nothing, and it is his duty to interpret the knowledge of the few for the understanding of the many'. This was anathema to Morley, who mocked his deputy one morning by declaring that he was 'going to write upon the Egyptian question, chiefly because I know nothing about it'. He could not countenance the younger man's views, which Stead enthused about in his diary shortly after his arrival in London:

> [The *PMG* should] lead the leaders of public opinion and combine literary distinction with good journalism; it should interpret the aspirations of the lower, inarticulate classes to those in power; it should combine the function of Hebrew prophet and Roman tribune with that of [a] Greek teacher; and while keeping the public informed about everything that needs improvement it should be at once lively, amusing and newsy.[83]

With views so radical and objectionable to Morley, it was a relief to them both when the editor resigned in order to become MP for Newcastle in the middle of 1883. Although Stead later claimed to have predicted the very month of Morley's departure, Watson was confident that his resignation had not been anticipated by Stead when the death of the incumbent MP was unexpectedly announced in the press. As was so often the case, Stead might not have been unwilling to invent a story which offered to confirm his self-perception as a journalist-cum-clairvoyant, a quirk that could be very trying for those alongside whom he worked. A few years later, when Gladstone offered Morley the highly challenging post of Irish Secretary, it was noted that the task before him was at least easier than keeping control of Stead at the *PMG*. As the outgoing editor's biographer observes:

> It is just possible that Morley found the turbulence of Parnell's House of Commons comparatively easeful after more than two years in a newspaper office which bubbled over with the indiscretions of his brilliant, restless, irrepressible lieutenant.[84]

CHAPTER 5

RUNNING THE EMPIRE

There was ... in the old admiral's eye a certain incredulous wonder at the supreme audacity of the young journalist, who cheerily declared that if only he could secure his facts he could compel any government, even Mr Gladstone's, to grant as many millions as were necessary to restore the sea power of England.
W. T. S., 'The Rebuilding of the British Navy' (July 1897)

It would be an exaggeration to say that Morley's departure unleashed the full force of Stead's radical journalism, but it certainly loosened the chains. Yates Thompson was cautious enough to insist that he, and not Stead, be made the official editor, although this meant little in practice since the owner had no interest in busying himself in the office on a daily basis. It was a purely precautionary act but it says much about the uneasy atmosphere that followed Morley's sudden departure. It was also a tacit acknowledgment of the power that the *PMG* had come to wield.

Stead's first act at the helm was to draw up a thirty-page document seriously entitled 'The Gospel According to the *Pall Mall Gazette*' for the edification of his staff. Under a series of bold subheadings, including 'The Development of the Individual', 'The Independence of Woman' and 'The Establishment of the United States of Europe', Stead outlined the programme he intended the newspaper to follow under his direction. Much of the contents had been anticipated in the pages of the *Northern Echo*, but there was an unmistakable sharpening of Stead's ideas. 'Woman,' began one paragraph, 'no longer the mere ancillary of man, to be petted or enslaved at his will, is to have as independent a voice in the disposal of her life as he.' This was radically different to his predecessor's line. So too was Stead's imperial vision, which accepted editorial responsibility for 'our rowdies, our filibusters, our slave traders, and our rum-sellers' who 'go forth armed with the resources of our civilization to exploit and plunder the native populations of the uncivilized world'. Though Stead believed the British Empire to be 'an evil in itself', he conceded that it must be 'tolerated' on account of 'the time it staves off still greater evils'. Its success was to be measured by the efficiency with which it 'digs [its] own grave'.[85]

As the title of Stead's pamphlet would suggest, it also had a strong religious element. He instructed his team to remember that newspapers are 'the only Bible which millions read', and should accordingly provide moral uplift, not merely light entertainment or titillation. Such entreaties undoubtedly have a quaint ring to modern ears, but there was nothing quaint or platitudinous about Stead's faith. He had the measure of himself when he wrote: 'I ... am so impatient, so vehement, so anxious ever to jog the elbow of the Almighty ... I cannot be moderate, the throbbing of my heart will never cool, the fever burns within my brain.'[86] What he wanted to produce was a recognisably modern newspaper that would nevertheless have appealed to the sympathies of the prophets of the Old Testament. 'Christian is as Christian does,' implored Stead. It did not matter to him whether men or women were actuated by 'heretical dogmas' or even 'blind agnosticism', so long as they ministered to 'the wants and ... aspirations of man'. Everything else was secondary.

It was in this spirit of enlightened evangelism that Stead launched his first great London newspaper campaign: an exposé of the unacceptable living conditions of the poor. The subject recalled Stead's first steps in journalism when he had denounced the evils of 'indiscriminate charity' in the pages of the *Northern Echo*. Since that time, urban deprivation had worsened significantly, particularly in the capital, where migrants both from abroad and the countryside had caused rents to soar and living standards to plummet. Many felt that nothing could be done, besides, perhaps, improving ventilation and sewerage facilities. Yet there was a considerable tinderbox of public opinion that was waiting for ignition. Stead proved, as he would time and again, that he was just the man to 'spark the mine'.

The scene had already been set by novelists of the realist school such as Walter Besant, George Gissing and G. R. Sims, who had created a ripple of sensation in the early 1880s with grim depictions of slum life. But none of these authors had offered any meaningful solutions to the problems they had so eloquently described, let alone mounted an effective campaign to redress them. Gissing's pessimistic early novels, though read intently by Stead, came into few hands, while Sims's classic *How the Poor Live* was little more than a voyeuristic 'tour of the "one-roomed helots" of darkest London'.[87] Something more substantial, dynamic and disturbing was needed to make the nation aware of the seriousness of overcrowding. Having an eye for such things, it was Stead who saw it in a timely booklet entitled *The Bitter Cry of Outcast London* by one of his Congregationalist brethren, the Rev. Andrew Mearns.

To call this work 'sensationalist', as one historian of the Victorian slums has chosen to, does not do the *Bitter Cry* full justice. Unlike Sims, Mearns's primary intention was not to provide his reader with a banquet of horrors but to focus on real people and situations, whose assistance he earnestly believed to be a matter of great public importance. His pamphlet forms part of a literary tradition that reached maturity with George Orwell's *Down and Out in Paris and London* and *The Road to Wigan Pier*, which were themselves greatly indebted to one of the most pioneering 'scoops' ever printed in the *PMG*, 'The Amateur Casual'.

This series of articles had been contributed by James Greenwood, whose older brother Frederick then edited the paper. They offered a powerful description of a night he had spent in the foul-smelling 'casual ward' of Lambeth workhouse, having obtained entry in the disguise of an out-of-work engraver. As though this was not enough to give the Conservative newspaper some right to a radical heritage, Frederick Greenwood had also accepted articles on the Franco-Prussian war from Friedrich Engels (brought to the office in a hansom cab by Karl Marx) and had H. M. Hyndman, who went on to become head of the Social Democratic Federation, on his staff.[88]

It was actually the Liberal tradition that was most unwilling to square up to the awful reality of poverty in the slums. Its proponents – not least Morley himself – had long believed that attempts to reduce the hardships of the very poor tended to worsen misery, not abate it. By the early 1880s, however, there was a considerable body of Liberals who had begun to question this most fundamental principle of their creed. One had written apologetically in the pages of the *Fortnightly Review* late in 1882 that 'the ordinary laws of demand and supply have ... sufficed until now' but were now causing unprecedented suffering to the great underclass soon to be exposed with considerable force by Stead and Mearns.

The agitation began on Tuesday 16 October 1883, with a leading article entitled 'Is It Not Time?' In this seminal piece of journalism Stead chastised Londoners for being 'too busy or too idle, too indifferent or too selfish' to do anything to redress urban deprivation – 'the great scandal of our age ... [a] huge cancer eating into the very heart of the realm'. Stead went on to hint strongly at the necessity of the kind of state intervention that was taking place in Germany, where the 'Iron Chancellor', Otto von Bismarck, was unconsciously laying the foundations of Europe's first welfare state. Aware that this would have been galling for the readership that he had inherited from his predecessor, Stead ingeniously deployed the kind of irresistible logic that would define his mature style:

> If, after full and exhaustive consideration, we come to the deliberate conclusion that nothing can be done, and that it is the inevitable and inexorable destiny of thousands of Englishmen to be brutalized into worse than beasts by the conditions of their environment: so be it.

This set the tone for Stead's ferocious three-week campaign, during which he utilised facts and figures pertaining to rents, birth rates, mortality and poverty in London's poorest boroughs. This was highly original, but what made the campaign especially notable was Stead's focus on issues of class and 'money power', which set him apart from most well-to-do people to venture into the slums. In this connection, Stead inadvertently attacked many of his own readers by speaking candidly of the outrageous profits that these 'fever dens' returned to wealthy landlords, who 'if justice were done would be on the treadmill'. Even more challengingly, Stead compared some of them to brothel-keepers. He was, however, more cautious in alluding to Mearns's grim observation that 'incest is common' in the slums. Rather than tackling this issue head-on, Stead simply reminded his readers that this 'seething mass of misery and vice' where children were 'suckled on gin and cradled in the gutter ... exists at our doors'. 'Many,' he wrote in a phrase that anticipated Lord Beveridge's famous report on deprivation by sixty years, 'are lucky enough to die, others live on, in turn to propagate their kind, and to hand down to another generation the curse which never leaves them from the cradle to the grave.'

Nothing of this kind would have spoiled the pages of the newspaper during the editorship of Morley, for whom the backstreets of London were hardly thought deserving of editorial concern. But readers were clearly interested, since the issue was kept alive on the letters page well into November and December. This was the first time that Stead truly experienced the thrill of being at the centre of a journalistic sensation, revelling in his power to move an unwilling government into action. When a Royal Commission was set up to establish the facts shortly afterwards, he was quick to claim responsibility. Although he had not written the influential pamphlet, Stead was emphatic that it was he alone who had 'called [it to] the attention of the world'.[89]

Stead was justly delighted by the success of his campaign, but by the New Year he was thirsting for a fresh story. The scoop to emerge revealed two sides of the rising editor: both his power and his fallibility.

The background to the sensation was a crisis in the Sudan, where a popular movement against British control in the region had been started by the 'Mahdi', an embittered former slave-trader who claimed to be the new Messiah. Motivated by a wave of religious fervour, the Sudanese rose in rebellion, massacred hundreds of colonialists and left the British garrison under siege at the capital, Khartoum. In a matter of months the region had become unsafe for any foreigner and Gladstone was preparing for a complete withdrawal, a course of action that had been clamoured for in the pages of the *PMG*, first by Morley (who had supported the British invasion of 1882) and now by Stead. The paper's stance was one of 'anti-Imperialist repentance'.[90]

To more unwavering supporters of the Empire, Gladstone's provisional plan to withdraw at all costs was seen as calamitous, not only because the safe retreat of such a large body of men across a hostile desert would have been virtually impossible – it harmed Britain's strategic and commercial interests as well. Nevertheless, the Prime Minister's plan to cut his losses was not irrational, even if it was necessarily hard on the Khartoum garrison which would be left in great danger. Why Stead suddenly dissented from this view towards the end of 1883, when he dramatically opted for a quick-fix solution that would appease his Imperialistic instincts, is unclear. But it was boldly set out at the start of the New Year in a leader in which Stead suggested the deployment of a popular hero to 'smash the Mahdi' and keep Sudan under British control – miraculously without the help of an army. Stead's idea of sending the veteran commander General Charles Gordon, who had been affectionately known to the British public as 'Chinese Gordon' since crushing the Taiping Rebellion some twenty years previously, was inspired, but fatally flawed.[91]

Stead claims that he had not planned to 'send Gordon to the Sudan' until he heard that the soldier had returned to England to resign his commission. This was a serious development, as Gordon, a truly legendary figure in his prime, was controversially planning to transfer his services to a rival kingdom, Belgium – a tragedy for all who shared Stead's admiration for the hero of Taiping. With characteristic self-assurance, the editor telegraphed Gordon at his sister's house in Southampton, informing him that he desired an interview. When he received a reply later that afternoon stating that Gordon had nothing that he wished to say, at least publically, Stead shot back that he would arrive by the last train, as though the veiled rejection were not in earnest.

Upon arrival, Stead found his way to the gloomy townhouse where he hoped to conduct his epoch-making interview – practically the first to appear in a British newspaper. Although the two men were physically and temperamentally alike (Gordon was also a strange contradiction of man of action and religious mystic) the interview cannot have begun as either would have hoped. When a short man with a squeaky voice opened the door and offered to take Stead's overcoat, the editor tentatively enquired, 'If I could see General Gordon?' To this the indignant man responded: 'I *am* General Gordon!' The exchange is the only part of their conversation that has survived verbatim, since what was published the following day was essentially a monologue, suspiciously Steadean in tone.

This was the first of hundreds of interviews that Stead conducted as editor of the *PMG*. His technique was inimitable. According to one contemporary, he would begin by overwhelming his subjects with a dose of 'nerve force': a combination of Stead's live personality and powerful, 'un-English' blue eyes. Stead would then lead his 'victim' through a wide-ranging conversation in a friendly manner, unencumbered by scraps of paper, notebooks or any other journalistic paraphernalia, which Stead believed to be detrimental to candour. Upon the conclusion of the discussion, Stead would return to his office, sprawl himself across a large oak desk, and dictate a supposedly word-perfect transcript of the dialogue to an admiring stenographer. This was obviously impossible, but it was only rarely claimed that Stead had deliberately attempted to belittle or undermine his subject. That was not generally the problem. 'I was interviewed once by Mr Stead', complained T. P. O'Connor, the Irish journalist and MP. '[T]he next day I hid myself: I found myself addressing the world after so infallible, cocksure, and lofty a fashion that I blushed at my own image. I was Steadesque, not statuesque; and though I admire Mr Stead, I prefer to speak in my own character.'[92]

There is little doubt that Stead intended to 'boom' Gordon in the same manner. Though he prefaced Gordon's remarks with the telling observation that the general 'showed considerable disinclination to express his opinions upon the subject' of the Sudan, it would appear from what was published the following afternoon that Gordon was eager to speak of nothing else.

Gordon allegedly told Stead that the garrison at Khartoum could neither be abandoned nor rescued, but needed to be defended in its current position by a strong governor 'at all hazards'. This ambitious policy was supported in Stead's leading article, printed alongside the interview, in which he boldly asked the political elite: 'Why not send [Gordon] out with *carte blanche* to do the best that can be done?' After tirelessly singing the praises of this 'born genius for command', Stead could not quite bring himself to acknowledge how foolish it was to expect a lone veteran, no matter how talented, to stem such a violent tide of messianic fervour. Gordon, he admitted, 'may not be able single-handed to reduce that raging chaos to order', but 'the attempt is worth making' and needed 'to be made at once'. As elsewhere in the course of his rapid campaign, Stead showed surprisingly little regard for the fact that it was apparent from the outset Gordon was likely to be nothing more than a sacrificial lamb on the altar of the preferred Liberal policy of 'non-interventionary intervention'.

Although it went against his instincts, the plan was taken up a mere ten days later by Stead's former patron William Gladstone, who read the *PMG* even more intently than he had read the *Northern Echo*. But the Prime Minister was never truly comfortable with the scheme and appears to have made the appointment against his better judgement, lending at least some weight to Stead's exaggerated boast that he had forced the hand of government. Striding into the newsroom the following day, Stead was almost overcome with self-satisfaction when his assistant editor, Alfred Milner, told him with a metaphorical slap on the back that it was 'the biggest thing you have done yet'. In his leader, written the same morning, Stead grandly commended the government for 'tardily' obeying his instructions.[93]

Gordon's subsequent year at Khartoum is beyond the scope of Stead's life, but it is worth briefly noting how justified Gladstone's reservations had been. As was clear from the outset, sending Gordon to the Sudan was never likely to succeed because it lacked the essential ingredients of a genuine policy. When the town eventually fell to the Mahdi in February 1885, after which all Westerners, including Gordon, were brutally murdered, the government riskily decided that the best way to exonerate itself was to publish Gordon's diary so as to 'reveal Gordon's madness to the public'. The image of the pious fool, who wondered why he had even been appointed, was precious ammunition against him. But the truth is that no mere strongman would have been capable of holding off the rebels with so little material support from Westminster.

Upon hearing the news of the city's fall, Stead deployed the first twenty-four-point headline ever to appear in a British newspaper: 'TOO LATE!' – a reference to the failure of General Wolseley's reserve army to reach Khartoum before the catastrophe. In the editorial features that followed, as ever after, Stead was reluctant to concede that the enterprise had been doomed from the start. Rather than accepting a degree of responsibility for this, Stead attempted to shift blame onto others, before finally dropping the story altogether. Perhaps owing to criticism he received at this time – Morley wondered how he slept at night – the 'Gordon for the Sudan' campaign was one of the few journalistic coups that Stead was not especially eager to publicise. It was only when two retired government officials published their memoirs decades later that Stead sprang back into life to restate his importance in the matter.

This postscript began in 1908 when the most senior British statesman in Egypt at the time, Sir Evelyn Baring, by then Lord Cromer, published *Modern Egypt*, his classic memoir. This berated the press, and Stead in particular, for forcing on him a policy that went entirely against his professional judgement. By contrast to Stead, who saw the affair as the genesis of the democratic 'government by journalism' that he championed, Cromer was angered by what was in effect the usurpation of ministerial responsibility. 'I thought that as everyone differed from me, that I must be wrong,' he lamented. What particularly angered him was that Stead had apparently not even given a fair reflection of Gordon's opinions, since they were 'certainly opposed both to what he wrote about the same time officially, and to what he said when he was on the point of starting for Khartoum'. In the manner of a modern tabloid journalist, it seems that Stead had used his interview with Gordon to blend Gordon's opinions with his own agenda – or someone else's.[94]

Stead was naturally indignant at these charges but he took a certain pleasure in having it confirmed so conclusively that he really had been 'running the Empire from Northumberland Street', as he had claimed all along. In a long rebuttal of Cromer's book in the *Contemporary Review*, he endeavoured to prove that the ex-Consul-General's mistake had not been to accept the policy of the *PMG*, but to have done so with insufficient vigour. As he put it: 'It was the Press which possessed prescience, initiative, resolution and energy, and it was he [Cromer] who was oscillating, procrastinating and always too late.'[95] Although there is an element of truth in this charge, the rapidity with which Gordon was appointed after the publication of Stead's famous interview undermines its substance. There is undoubtedly more to be said for Cromer's observation that Stead's claim to speak with the authority of 'the man in the street', masked by a thin layer of editorial anonymity, was the most deplorable feature of the tragedy, with woeful implications for the future. Like the French revolutionary reproached for obeying the cries of the Jacobin mob, Cromer could only lament the onerous responsibilities of a conscientious modern democrat: 'I am their leader, so must do their bidding.'[96]

Marvellous though this backhanded recognition of Stead's influence must have been, the editor was painfully brought back down to earth three years later when another ex-official, the poet Sir Wilfrid Blunt, published his *Gordon at Khartoum*. In this version, which Stead dismissed as 'a scandalous production ... [drawn from] the idle and malicious gossip of thirty years ago', Cromer was accused of exaggerating Stead's influence as a means of diverting attention from a plot devised by Imperialist rebels in Gladstone's Cabinet. This was substantiated by contrasting the leader from the *PMG* of 20 November, which argued *against* sending a single man to Khartoum 'even if the Mahdi were to rout the whole force', with a private letter written by the chief instigator of the plan, Lord Hartington, to Gladstone just one week later. In this missive the Secretary of War asked:

> Do you see any objection to using Gordon in some way? He has an immense name in Egypt, he is popular at home, he is a strong but very sensible opponent of slavery, he has a small bee in his bonnet. If you do not object I could consult Baring by telegraph.[97]

Over the next few weeks, it was revealed, Hartington and his secretary, Reginald Brett, did everything they could to prove just how 'popular at home' their chosen saviour was so as to overcome the perceived obstinacy of Gladstone and Baring. 'As is usual in such cases,' Blunt knowingly hypothesised, 'the London press was being called in to add weight to opinion on either side.' Whether this was done directly by 'a Ministerial hint of the very directest [sic] kind' to Stead, or through more subtle avenues, remains controversial. There is, for instance, a possibility that the dissident ministers laid the bait for Stead by getting their ally, Sir Samuel Baker, to write letters to the press at the time on the subject of Gordon's suitability. One of these was published in *The Times* on New Year's Day 1884 – ten days before Stead's famous interview with Gordon. This might allow Stead to escape the charge of mendacity, since his confident rebuttal to Blunt that 'the statesman may be in the editorial sanctum and the puppet in Downing Street' would otherwise be all but impossible to explain.[98]

But Stead certainly had a motive to exaggerate his influence and was rarely entirely honest about the sources of his journalistic inspiration. The fact that he made little serious attempt to refute Blunt's convincing argument suggests that this was also the case on this occasion. The proposal of sending Gordon to the Sudan undoubtedly stemmed from Hartington, who used Brett as his agent to leak intelligence to Stead. This is supported, firstly, by the fact that Brett, although not an old employee (as Blunt supposed), had formerly been a contributor to the newspaper and would soon join forces with Stead in a lifelong journalistic and political alliance. Secondly, the language of Stead's leaders bore a striking resemblance to the private dispatches that Hartington had sent to Gladstone and Baring, with 'carte blanche' being a favourite expression. The third, and deciding, consideration is that the Liberal Imperialists in the government were about to collaborate with Stead in launching an even greater crusade: 'The Truth about the Navy'. As the legendary First Sea Lord Sir 'Jacky' Fisher later confided to Brett (who succeeded his father as Lord Esher in 1899): 'What a story the whole thing would make, from those far away times when you and I – unknown to each other – were pulling at dear old Stead.'[99]

The agitation was planned in August 1884, when one of the most cantankerous of the young Liberals, Oakley Arnold-Forster, came to the office at Northumberland Street with details of a Cabinet split regarding the funding of the Navy. He brought with him a summary of Lord Carnarvon's unpublished report on the condition of the Fleet, highlighting the extent to which Britain had declined as a naval superpower since 1878. Britain had extended her sphere of interest considerably since that year, but without making commensurate increases in the funding of her Navy. This was serious, since rivals such as France and Germany had recently begun ambitious shipbuilding programmes, leaving it open to debate whether the nation would be able to stand alone against a coalition of two or more naval powers as she had during the fateful struggle against Napoleon.

Almost from the first, the new scoop took on a domestic air, with Sunday garden parties at Wimbledon being the preferred venue for intrigue. This may have been because the Steads had now furnished a comfortable home, complete with a tennis court and strawberry patch; it is equally likely, however, that there was a strong animosity between Arnold-Forster and *PMG* staff. Only two years previously the newspaper had loudly boasted of securing the dismissal of his adopted father, W. E. Forster, from the position of Irish Secretary. This view is well reflected in a letter written by Alfred Milner to Stead, in which the assistant editor declined to pay a visit to Cambridge House on the grounds that he 'couldn't quite see myself enjoying a very easy time in [Arnold-Forster's] company'.[100] Stead no doubt harboured similar reservations himself, but he was too much of a modern journalist to allow personal or past differences to ruin an excellent story. For his part, Arnold-Forster knew that Stead could be trusted with the leak: not only had he proved his usefulness in the past, Stead's undeniable vanity made him unwilling to admit that he had been used as a tool of others. Perhaps more importantly from Forster's viewpoint, 'responsible' newspaper editors were unlikely to reveal Britain's military weaknesses so frankly to the rest of the world.

Over the course of the next few weeks, Stead acquainted himself with the facts of the situation, which, as a self-confessed 'non-naval journalist', he needed to master before he could hope to challenge the government's proposed cuts in spending. He was helped in this capacity by Fisher (at the time the gunnery commander of *HMS Excellent*) who met him 'like Nicodemus surreptitiously in byways and highways' to discuss exactly what needed to be printed in order to inflict the maximum damage to the advocates of a small navy. 'You have got enough in your wallet to break half the officers in Her Majesty's Service if you split,' the future Sea Lord gleefully told his young confidant. As with Fisher's later attempts to ally himself with radical journalists such as Stead's 'apostolic successor', J. L. Garvin (editor of *The Observer*, 1908–42), he probably asked Stead to incinerate any documents that could compromise his position by marking them 'burn and destroy'. Since none of these letters appear to have survived, it seems likely that Stead lacked the insight of his famous Fleet Street successors, who knew the command to be nothing more than Fisher's shorthand for 'publish as widely as possible, but don't give me away'.

A few days before unleashing the first 'Truth about the Navy' instalment, Brett arranged for Stead to interview the First Naval Lord, Sir Astley Cooper Key, at the Admiralty. This veteran of the Crimean War was well aware of the facts and showed a 'certain sympathetic compassion' to his visitor's entreaties; but he had not yet come to realise the power that the press could wield on his behalf. Stead probably failed to impress this point, since his worn clothes and ragged brown leather bag, which he took everywhere with him, were hard to reconcile with the extravagant claims he made about himself as a rouser of public opinion. As Stead later reminisced:

> There was ... in the old admiral's eye a certain incredulous wonder at the supreme audacity of the young journalist, who cheerily declared that if only he could secure his facts he could compel any government, even Mr Gladstone's, to grant as many millions as were necessary to restore the sea power of England.[101]

Stead left feeling slightly despondent, but this only emphasised in his mind that he had a personal point to prove as much as a patriotic one. A few days later, he published a sobering leader, written with Arnold-Forster at his elbow, in which he stated that 'the scramble for the world has begun in earnest', before asking: 'how far are we able to prevent our own possessions being scrambled for by our neighbours?' Stead listed twelve points of inquiry to determine how ready the Navy was in case of a sudden outbreak of war.

To appease his Liberal readers, who generally favoured a small, inexpensive navy, Stead mischievously quoted a letter from Morley's recently published biography of Richard Cobden, which gave solid backing to the contention that 'Free Trade without command of the seas is death', namely by starvation. This was followed three days later by the first instalment of Stead's official-sounding audit of ships and personnel written by 'One who Knows the Facts', a character few readers would have realised to be Stead himself. These articles combined to good effect with the more high-pitched screaming of Stead's leaders, in which the Empire was likened to an old Spanish galleon, whose precious cargo of bullion would not reach port due to the government's abysmal failure to protect it from the 'hungry buccaneers' that swarmed up its flank.

These articles did much to excite the public, but it is a sign of the times that other newspapers were slow to take up the story. The First Lord of the Admiralty, Lord Northbrook, had not even heard that there was an outcry until arriving back from Egypt at the end of the month, when the storm practically blew up in his face. As a firm supporter of Gladstone's military economies, Northbrook had resisted the demands of the Navy for more supplies, but now, combined as they were with the clamour of Northumberland Street, he was struggling to fend them off. On 2 October his parliamentary secretary regretfully informed him that there was 'sufficient excitement and anxiety felt in the country to prevent the question being shelved or pooh poohed'. Two months later, Stead had 'the supreme satisfaction' of going down to the House of Lords where he heard Northbrook 'beg' for an extra £3.5 million 'from the very bench where, in the month of May, he had declared that the Navy was so perfect he would not know what to do with £2,000,000 if he got it as a gift'.[102] Once again, the editor was exultant in triumph.

છ

These campaigns did much to bring Stead to public notice, but he was generally seen as a nuisance by the elite class to whom he was expected to pander. The towering arbiter of culture Matthew Arnold complained angrily to Stead's predecessor John Morley that the newspaper was 'fast ceasing to be *literature*' (ironically, Arnold-Forster was his nephew).[103] More grave for the editor was the opprobrium with which he was held in the eyes of Gladstone, who felt genuinely threatened by the increasingly hostile position of the paper. Through the medium of his son, Herbert, and private secretary, Horace Seymour, he let it be known that the 'errant' editor had greatly displeased him. Typically sanguine, Stead, merely responded with the admonition: 'If information is not forthcoming from the Prime Minister's office, then it must and will be obtained elsewhere.'[104]

Stead's relationship with Gladstone approached its nadir during the Anglo-Russian Panjdeh crisis in spring 1885, when Stead accused the premier of jingoistic sabre-rattling. This was infuriating for Gladstone, since the Russians were accused of perpetrating atrocities in Afghanistan similar to the ones which Stead had so recently brought to his attention in Bulgaria. Reminding everyone to 'keep cool and be sure of your facts', Stead's loyalty to Russia – or rather to Madame Novikov, who supplied him with confidential material for his articles – dulled his usual desire to unsheathe the sword of righteousness. When discussing the alleged brutality of Russian troops in seizing the frontier city of Merv, the editor adopted a tone that was strangely redolent of Morley's predecessor at Northumberland Street, Frederick Greenwood, in asking statesmen to show 'some sense of proportion to the relative importance of events'. Combining his editorial voice with a suspicious letter from 'Tyneside', Stead implored the government to avoid 'plunging two world-encircling empires into bloodshed and strife' for the sake of a 'miserable little State in Central Asia', namely Afghanistan.

The Prime Minister flew into a rage on reading this article: he must now 'throw Stead over', for he could not tolerate 'one standard of morality for Russia and another [higher one] for the rest of the world'. The sense of love lost was emphasised a few weeks later when Stead proudly boasted of forcing the government to accept arbitration in the dispute – albeit from Denmark rather than his preferred choice of Germany.

Stead was playing a dangerous game with Gladstone. It would be as easy for the Prime Minister to remove him from the *PMG* as it had been to bring him there in the first place. This may explain why Stead now turned his pen to a subject with which both men shared a deep and often troubling fascination: the plight of the 'fallen woman'. But Stead conducted his sensational 'Maiden Tribute' agitation in such a manner that it was impossible for the two men ever to become properly reconciled. Each would forever suspect the other of harbouring secret 'perversions', which both denied, but were nevertheless attributed to them by the rest of society, particularly in the case of Stead. Gladstone may have had a special reason for fearing his old associate hereafter, since Stead claims to have made some regrettable discoveries in the course of his exploration of the seedy underworld. Confiding to his ally Reginald Brett, Stead piously explained that he had been 'horrified' by some of the accounts he had heard of the premier's dealings with prostitutes, but was willing to 'keep it all to myself'. The suggestion of blackmail was undeniable. With the help of Gladstone's most candid biographers, Roy Jenkins and Colin Matthew, it seems likely that Stead had discovered the Grand Old Man's darkest secret: that his 'rescue work' had a 'carnal' aspect.[105]

CHAPTER 6

BABYLON – REVEALED!

I have just interviewed a brothel keeper who has undertaken to procure for my abuse two English girls of 13 or 14 warranted virgins. Price £5 per head.
W. T. S. to Madame Olga Novikov (May 1885)

The campaign that Stead now launched remains central to his contribution to investigative journalism. Some recent commentators have shared the view of Stead's contemporaries: his actions were shamelessly self-aggrandising and scarcely legitimate, let alone justified by the ends.[106] Others, more sympathetic to the editor's professed principles, have viewed the episode with an almost reverential piety, echoing the panegyric of the *Methodist Times*, which claimed the crusade to have been exactly 'what Christ Himself would have done' were he a newspaper editor in late-Victorian Britain.[107] If the truth can ever be established, it will only be detected by examining what was happening in Stead's life and mind at the time, factors which have been strangely omitted from the standard accounts of the campaign, despite the existence of a substantial corpus of unexplored evidence.

Few have contended that the campaign originated entirely from Stead, but it has never been possible to determine who exactly provided him with the encouragement he claims to have required. Depending on whose version is believed, Stead apparently had no intention of delving into the backstreets until he was approached by any one of a multitude of Victorian worthies. These included the early women's rights activist Josephine Butler; the Chamberlain of the City of London, Benjamin Scott; the ex-Commissioner of Scotland Yard Howard Vincent; the secretary of the Society for the

Protection of Children, Benjamin Waugh; and the Salvation Army's 'Chief of Staff', Bramwell Booth. Although all these individuals had an important role to play in the eventual campaign, the fact that each firmly believed that they had initiated the project lends weight to the unorthodox contention that the idea was, in reality, Stead's from the outset. His claim to owe others for 'inspiration' may have been a convenient means of avoiding awkward questions about his true impetus.

Stead's interest in prostitution went back to his earliest days in journalism, when he had decried the hypocrisy of respectable gentlemen who frequented brothels. At that time, the editor had been a reasonably happily married young man and so was unlikely to have had many dealings with prostitutes. But there is reason to believe that for a short period during the mid-1880s his relationship with Emma cooled significantly. This is alluded to in a purposely damaged letter to Madame Novikov, dating from April 1885, in which Stead complained that his wife had become 'cold and distant' towards him on account of not being able to 'respect me anymore'.[108] No doubt exasperated by her husband's continued enjoyment of the occasional 'fortnight's flirtation', and fearful of yet more unplanned pregnancies, Emma might have been keeping her husband at an icy distance within the marital bed. Stead appears to have been resigned to this fate, writing in his diary with unusual frankness that he and his wife had been practising *coitus interruptus* for some time before the likely break.[109]

The obvious person to whom Stead could turn for sympathy was Madame Novikov, but the flame that had ignited their mutual passion had recently been extinguished. This was largely because Stead felt intensely guilty about committing adultery with a woman whom his wife knew of and had reason to distrust. In his diary Stead confided, 'I sin no more in relation to her', but this left him at a loss to know how he could relieve what he regretfully called his 'crazy appetite' for sex.[110]

Someone who might have been willing to help keep Stead's unwanted desires at bay was his new secretary, Hulda Friederichs.

Considered by Robertson Scott to have been 'the first woman journalist treated (more or less) like a man', she was a tough, hard-looking young woman who became known to the *PMG* staff as 'the Prussian Governess' or simply 'The Friederichs'. Stead was evidently highly fond of her and appears to have opened up to her about his personal life. She did not, however, go on to become 'one of his out and out admirers'. At a formal retirement dinner for a later editor of the *PMG*, at which Stead was not present, she upset the 'solemnity of the assemblage' by giving out 'a loud cackle' when a speaker seriously suggested that, whatever his faults, Stead was undoubtedly a 'regenerator of the human race'.[III]

Hulda's apparent dislike of Stead may have stemmed from the 'particular regard' that he privately confessed to have for her. As Stead wrote in his diary at the time, 'it is a ticklish thing to be a private secretary when you are of the same sex as your employer's wife'. Even so, Stead would have been extremely foolish to have considered an affair with someone so easily traceable, which would have allowed his actions to become instantly known to a wide circle of his friends and acquaintances. Instead, he sublimated his apparent love for her so that 'efficiency will supply the place of affection'. Like many Victorian husbands, sexual kicks would have to be found in the underworld or not at all.

Stead had another reason for being interested in prostitution: it fed into his perennial anxieties about class and status. These had been deployed to good effect in Stead's early exchanges with Madame Novikov, when he had accused his correspondent of refusing to stay at his 'little hermitage' on the grounds that 'social superiors are much the same all over the world'. Stead's evident inferiority complex only became more acute when he moved to London, where he often felt himself to be looked down upon. When Stead attempted to make light of this by good-naturedly designating himself a proud 'barbarian of the north', he was only reinforcing a stereotype that he could not avoid. Whether he agreed to attend 'society' dinners or not, he was invariably the instigator of some embarrassment or the butt of an elegant witticism.

This nettled him and goes some way towards explaining why his campaign against child prostitution took on such an aggressive tone against the 'ruling classes'.

Although it seems likely that Stead had been planning his crusade for some time, it was precipitated by a parliamentary debate which took place just before the Whitsun recess, late in May 1885. Its subject was the Criminal Law Amendment Bill, which had been designed to raise the age of consent to sexual intercourse for girls from thirteen to fifteen, giving new powers to police to clamp down on prostitution and the 'white slave trade', whereby young women were duped into lives of prostitution in continental brothels. The Bill had vacillated between the House of Lords (where it originated) and the Commons (where it had failed to be passed into law) for three years, leading many campaigners to conclude that it was unlikely to succeed before the coming election, which was certain to follow the recent collapse of the second Gladstone administration.

Stead's version of the debate was characteristically simplistic: in an Occasional Note he declared that 'the protection of our young girls has been sacrificed to the loquacity of our legislators'. The truth was that the principle of child welfare outlined in the Bill had the backing of both Houses, from the new Prime Minister Lord Salisbury down to the rank and file of the backbenches. Only a small minority of members, notably 'that unrepentant sinner' George Cavendish-Bentinck (an obscure Tory MP much detested by Stead), had serious objections, ostensibly because they feared that the Act would 'outrun public opinion'. For this reason, it was more than a little unfair of Stead to portray Parliament as a seething viper's nest of rakes and debauched old men, wickedly scheming to defend their 'feudal privilege' to corrupt the daughters of the poor.[112] One MP, Sir Baldwyn Leighton, actually forestalled the very point that the editor would soon use against his parliamentary colleagues by observing that the issue was one 'in which the working classes were deeply interested; it was their children and their daughters who were chiefly affected'.[113] Nearly every MP concurred with this sentiment and felt that something needed to be done, but rightly feared that some clauses of the Bill — particularly those which proposed to raise police powers (a concern for Stead also) — could be even more dangerous than the *laissez-faire* arrangement of old. One modern feminist has declared the final Act to have been 'a particularly nasty and pernicious piece of omnibus legislation', which made the lives of prostitutes and vulnerable young women even more dangerous than before.[114]

On the day of the recess, Stead claims to have been visited by an elderly municipal official, the Chamberlain of the City of London Benjamin Scott, to discuss the matter in more detail. Among various other positions, the caller was the chairman of the London Committee for the Prevention of Traffic in English Girls, which had been involved in advising a Select Committee of the House of Lords three years previously. He implored the editor to use his influence to ensure that the motion would be rushed through Parliament, stressing that the cause seemed all but lost. Although Stead always had an eye for this kind of story, the swiftness with which he responded, and the manner in which he ran his campaign, suggests that his motivation was more than simply doing a good turn to this kindly old Quaker banker. His passion came from the fact that he, like Gladstone, probably had intimate knowledge of the sexual underworld and had been appalled by the youthfulness of the girls he had seen on offer.

Immediately after Scott's departure, Stead went to see the Salvation Army's 'Chief of Staff' Bramwell Booth at the organisation's office on Victoria Street. Stead wanted to learn more facts about the 'Shoreham case' to which Scott had alluded. This was an unusual incident in which a young prostitute had escaped from a Pimlico brothel to the sanctuary of the Salvation Army's headquarters, where she had been found early one morning clad only in a nightdress. Having confirmed the story, Booth allowed Stead to interview 'three or four' ex-prostitutes and a retired brothel-keeper whom he summoned into the adjoining room. The transcripts of these conversations have not survived, but it can be assumed that the extract entitled 'Confessions of a Brothel-Keeper', published on the first evening of the campaign, were derived from them. To this day they remain some of the most disturbing revelations of the exposé, but it is likely that the dominant voice was that of Stead himself. As with every other line in his long series of articles, it is impossible to distil fact from fiction: there is simply too much of the reformer's zeal mixed in with the impartial observer's commentary to get a firm hold on reality. Nowhere is this clearer than when the interviewee leaps effortlessly from the world of the believable into the sphere of the scarcely imaginable, as when, after explaining that 'fresh girls' may be acquired by adopting the chilling disguise of an elderly country parson, the brothel-keeper continues:

> Another very simple mode of supplying maids is by breeding them. Many women who are on the streets have female children. They are worth keeping. When they get to be twelve or thirteen they become merchantable... Sometimes the supply is in excess of the demand, and you have to seduce your maid yourself [so as to entrap her into a life of prostitution forever], or to employ someone else to do it, which is bad business in a double sense... I once sold a girl twelve years old for £20 to a clergyman, who used to come to my house professedly to distribute tracts.[115]

Whatever the authenticity of these remarks, Stead emerged from the interview in an uncontrollable rage. Walking over to the desk where the ardent Salvationist was composing a pamphlet on the evils of alcohol consumption, Stead crashed his fist down on the oak 'so that the very inkpots shivered', letting out a great 'Damn!' that echoed throughout the building.

What Stead had learned was confirmed in an interview that he immediately conducted with the veteran policeman, Howard Vincent, at Scotland Yard. In their published dialogue, Stead assumed his favourite role: the curious child, innocently discovering the commonplace wickedness of the worldly wise:

'But,' I said in amazement, 'then do you mean to tell me that in very truth actual rapes, in the legal sense of the word, are constantly being perpetrated in London on unwilling virgins, purveyed and procured to rich men at so much a head by keepers of brothels?' 'Certainly,' said he, 'there is not a doubt of it.' 'Why,' I exclaimed, 'the very thought is enough to raise hell.' 'It is true,' he said; 'and although it ought to raise hell, it does not even raise the neighbours'.[116]

This brilliant piece of theatre perfectly set up the crux of the investigation: the abduction of an 'unwilling maid' by his 'Secret Commission' of which Stead characteristically styled himself 'the Chief Director'.

Stead was well aware of the outrage that this would cause, so wisely took the precaution of informing three prominent churchmen of what he intended to do: the Archbishop of Canterbury, Edward Benson; the Bishop of London, Frederick Temple; and the Archbishop of Westminster, Cardinal Henry Edward Manning. Of these, only the leading Anglican advised against the project, since he saw it as too severe a remedy for the crimes that were allegedly being perpetrated. Foremost in his mind was probably the recent trial of another brothel-keeper, Mary Jeffries, at which it had been suggested that the Prince of Wales (the future King Edward VII) was one of her clients. In order to nip the sensation in the bud, the Establishment had closed ranks, pressuring the madam to change her plea to 'guilty', thereby bringing proceedings to a hurried conclusion. Rumour had it that payment of her £200 fine came from aristocratic sources, perhaps even the Palace itself, but this had never been verified and the story soon died. The thought of a muckraking journalist like Stead reigniting this dangerous fuse was alarming to a cleric whose principal function was to preserve good relations between the classes and to promote the sanctity of the monarchy.

Yet having secured at least a modicum of support, Stead was adamant that he would have no trouble personally carrying out the transaction that would define his campaign – and his career.

He began by leading the life of a depraved streetwalker, returning in the early hours to a small room that he rented on the Strand for the purposes of eating his lunch and other business that could not easily be conducted at home or the office. His method was to ingratiate himself with 'society' brothel-keepers so that they would provide him with a little girl whom he could take away for whatever purposes he desired. 'I go to brothels every day & drink & swear & talk like a fiend from the bottomless pit', he confided to Madame Novikov in a letter marked 'to destroy'.[117] But he seems to have had no luck, only getting so far as to prove that it was possible to sleep with an extremely young woman in return for a sum of about £10 or £20 (between £500 and £1,000 in today's currency). Since these children had no idea about what was potentially going to happen to them, and had only been supplied by relatives greedy for the inflated fee, it is unsurprising that 'Stead's blunt talk thoroughly frightened them'.[118]

Nevertheless, the information that Stead had gathered in this way would easily have been enough to secure his objective. But he wanted something more, apparently taking his failure to convince these madams of his alleged predilections as a personal slight. He therefore demanded that 'certain investigations' be made with the help of an old hand; someone who would be believed by the people on the inside. This formed the crucial, and disastrous, step of turning one of his 'expert witnesses' into an unwilling accomplice.

The woman recruited for this purpose was a reformed prostitute and former brothel-keeper called Rebecca Jarrett, who had recently been brought into the fold of the Salvation Army by Bramwell Booth's mother, Catherine. Excessively penitent and eager to demonstrate her newfound godliness, she personified the values of an institution that saw a virtue in exaggerating the past sins of its members so as to highlight the miracle of their redemption. Although Stead had complete faith in the organisation, many shared the suspicions of his young contributor, George Bernard Shaw, who dismissed the 'confessions' of the likes of Jarrett as no more believable than the tales of a 'millionaire who says he came up to London or Chicago as a boy with only three half pence in his pocket.' Nevertheless, Rebecca greatly impressed Catherine Booth's friend, Josephine Butler, who appointed her as the governess of her refuge for reformed prostitutes in Winchester. Here she excelled, becoming an accepted, if not respected, member of the local community.

Butler heard of Stead's nascent campaign either from the editor himself or through the Booths, and was naturally attracted by its objective.[119] Some years earlier she had contributed to a similar inquiry – in many ways a more conclusive one than the 'Maiden Tribute' proved to be – which Stead had been eager to publish, but had been persuaded by her not to. Possibly Butler distrusted Stead, as is suggested by a letter to a friend dating from February 1885 in which she wrote: 'I don't know whether you ever read the *Pall Mall* (*I hate it*)'. Rather than arousing excessive publicity, she preferred to conduct her campaigns by lobbying the government directly or by writing letters to specialist newspapers such as the *Shield*, which was too obscure even for Stead to read on a regular basis. Yet she had evidently come round to the necessity of using journalists more forcefully to promote her various good causes, as was demonstrated when she assisted a Belgian editor in staving off an assault of the '*police des moeurs*' in 1881. 'For the moment this editor is a great man,' she loftily declared after providing some crucial information for his defence.

Josephine clearly had no idea about what she was getting herself into. Arriving in London with Rebecca towards the end of May, her understanding appears to have been that Stead and some of his male colleagues would continue with the sort of work that they had been conducting for the past week or so. Of this she approved; the idea of kidnapping a child, subjecting her to all kinds of unpleasant experiences before removing her to another country went far beyond what she believed to be the call of duty. Stead, however, could be remarkably persuasive. His life is riddled with instances in which he won the confidence of a reluctant accomplice only to disappoint him by doing what he believed to be right rather than what had been expected. The decisive moment in this instance occurred late one evening when Josephine came to see the 'hagged face[d]' editor after a 'day of hand-to-hand wrestling with the powers of Hell'. Throwing himself at her feet, he let out a great cry 'more like a bereaved or outraged mother ... [than] an indignant man'. He then recounted how, only hours previously, he had sat petting little girls, 'father-like', on his knee in the darkest depths of 'London brotheldom'.

Whatever its motivations, the scene had the desired effect. Within days Butler returned to Winchester, leaving Stead in sole command of her vulnerable protégée. Promises of merely wishing to 'observe' were now utterly dispensed with in favour of more direct action. Stead may have been encouraged in this line by Bramwell Booth, who provided him with a 'rescued' women 'who actually went and placed herself in a brothel as though she were a woman of doubtful character, and lived there for ten days, reporting what happened'.[120] Such instances suggest that both men shared the view of Bramwell's father, the Salvation Army's founder 'General' William Booth, who once said of Stead: '*He* would never make a [Salvation Army] General if he was afraid to sacrifice his men in order to win a battle'.[121] This time, it appears, Stead's concern for the physical and psychological wellbeing of his troops was practically nil. In his eyes Rebecca was little more than a body to be used as he saw fit in carrying out the work of the 'Senior Partner'.

His chosen instrument was a poorly educated woman who, despite being under forty, walked with a heavy limp and had a crooked back; mementos of a miserable former existence. Since meeting the Booths and Josephine Butler about six months previously, her brain had been crammed with visions of hell and damnation, tempered only by vistas of a glorious heaven which could be hers if only she would 'obey'. In Stead's hands such a creature was especially vulnerable. He began to break her down by asking her to recount the story of her life, probably needlessly on account of the fact that he must have already heard it from

Butler, who was soon to pen a short biography of her disciple. With feigned horror, he heard how she had sold innocent children 'to dissolute customers, who for £10 or £20 could purchase liberty to rape with impunity.' This set the scene for his thoroughly indecent proposal: to 'purchase' the little girl he so desperately needed to complete his story. In return, Stead sanctimoniously offered God's forgiveness for her wicked former life. When Rebecca asked if she could consult Josephine beforehand, Stead was forthright: 'Jarrett pleaded to be spared ... I was inexorable.'

Thrust out onto the streets that she had wanted to leave behind, Rebecca hobbled over to Charles Street, Marylebone, to see her old friend Nancy Broughton, with whom she had, coincidentally, worked as a laundress at one of Stead and Madame Novikov's favourite haunts, Claridge's Hotel. Nancy lived here in a damp room with her violent husband Charles, who was known to his friends simply as 'Bash'. Rebecca had stayed on the couple's floor for a short period between losing her job at the hotel and becoming involved with the Salvation Army. There is no evidence that this was a large 'bad house', as Stead alleged in his articles, though it is equally improbable that the room was adorned with 'crucifixes and portraits of popes and cardinals', as a rival publication would later claim. Like all of the poverty-stricken abodes in the area, there was probably a fair amount of what respectable people would have called 'immorality' in the Broughton household, possibly involving Rebecca herself in a former incarnation (less than a year earlier she had written a letter to Nancy in which she euphemistically lamented to no longer having any 'toast and Bash' in the mornings). But their circumstances were by no means as desperate as many of their neighbours, who commonly lived twelve to a room. They were relatively well off since all their children had perished and they were both employed: Nancy as a laundress; 'Bash' as a chimney-sweep.

Perhaps with the intention of impressing her old friend, Rebecca invented a story that she was now married to a wealthy commercial traveller, a 'Mr Sullivan' (actually a brick-layer she had met while

working at a laundry in Chiswick), and required a servant-girl
to do the washing and scrubbing in their six-room house in the
suburbs. Although this must have sounded quite a tall story, it was
not impossible, and evidently created a lot of excitement in the
dingy backstreet. One nineteen-year-old girl, who was sitting with
Nancy at the time, offered herself immediately, but was rejected on
account of being 'too big and too old'. Over the course of the next
hour or so various other applicants were summoned and similarly
passed over. Only when a thirteen-year-old called Eliza Armstrong
appeared clutching her baby brother in the doorway did Rebecca
signal her approval. But the girl's mother could not be found
and the matter was left to be decided the following day – which
happened to be that of the Epsom Derby, easily the biggest and
most memorable event in the Victorian sporting calendar.

In the interval, Nancy sought out Mrs Armstrong, who seems to
have been less than pleased about her daughter's 'teasing' proposal.
She wanted to know why 'Mrs Sullivan' could not find a servant
closer to where she was living. Nancy's soothing response – that
she wanted to do a poor girl a favour by taking her to a 'good
place where she would be well cared for' – must have sounded
appealing to a woman who was routinely abused by her husband
in the tiny room they occupied with their six needy children. With
reluctance she agreed to the proposition, but chose not to tell her
spouse about it, probably because she felt that she alone knew what
was best for her child.

When Rebecca returned the following day, she came with a far
more respectable Salvationist, a Mrs Combe, who must have added
authority to her elaborate tale. The two women took Eliza to buy
some 'neat but not gaudy' new clothes, which probably signified
nothing more than the fact that the child was poorly attired, but
may have been intended to give the subtle impression that she
was to be sold into prostitution as well (one garment was a feather
hat). It is also possible that the mother was asked if Eliza was 'a
good girl', 'a pure girl' or even 'a forward girl', but it seems highly
unlikely that anything more explicit was intimated. So certain

was Mrs Armstrong that everything was above board that she did not even come to see her daughter off, evidently satisfied that she would receive a letter from Eliza every week and that they would meet again in a month's time, as agreed. No wages were advanced nor any down payment, but Mrs Armstrong did take a shilling from Nancy (who received a £2 'gift' from Rebecca) when she called round later that evening in desperation for money to buy a drink. She had good reason to need one, for her husband had beaten her for the second time in as many days upon discovering that his daughter had gone into service without his consent. That night she was found in a drunken stupor while in possession of her baby and was duly fined for disorder.

When Stead was informed of what had apparently been achieved, he was ecstatic. Unaware of the particulars of the transaction, he never would have learned the truth had his scheme not been so ill-fated. It was not in his nature to ask questions about matters that excited his emotions so intensely. And Rebecca had no intention of letting on either: not only was she lauded by Stead as the saviour of womankind, she may have also embezzled about £3 from him, since the quoted price for Eliza (who appeared in his articles as 'Lily') was £5 (£3 down payment, £2 after being certified as a virgin) – a large sum of money for a servant girl, but apparently well below the market rate for a bona fide virgin bought for the purpose of 'seduction'.

After taking the girl by bus from Charles Street, the two women led their captive to a French midwife and likely abortionist, Madame Louise Mourez, who agreed to examine the child and sell them a bottle of chloroform (routinely used to ease the pain of childbirth) for an inflated fee. This unpleasant and unnecessary ordeal – so similar to the horrors that Stead had associated with the much-abused Contagious Diseases Acts – clearly terrified the bewildered child, who vainly tried to escape. Although Stead was not present at the time, and so was unaware that Madame Mourez hardly spoke English, he used the scene to air some of his most sensationalist prose:

'The poor little thing,' ... the hard-hearted old abortionist exclaimed... 'She is so small, her pain will be extreme. I hope you will not be too cruel with her' – as if to lust when fully roused the very acme of agony on the part of the victim has not a fierce delight.

The two women then took Eliza to 32 Poland Street, a West End brothel frequented by an elite clientele. Preparations had been made for them to have the use of two upper bedrooms by another of Stead's accomplices, a Greek private detective called Mussabini who was known (even to the police) under the false name of 'Sampson Jacques'. Since this arrangement threatened to exonerate the brothel-keeper somewhat, who could easily have pleaded ignorance to what was going on, Stead ordered up some whisky, which he – a strict Puritan – had no intention of consuming. This did not prevent Stead from engaging his hostess in a long conversation about what he planned to do to the young girl next door. Her responses were apparently encouraging:

> You can lock the door and then do as you please. The girl may scream blue murder, but not a sound will be heard. The servants will be far away in the other end of the house. I only will be about seeing that all is snug.

Although such vile sentiments may have been common enough in Victorian London, the jarring word 'snug' savours of a journalistic masterstroke.

Inside the adjoining room, with its heavy curtains and double carpet, Rebecca attempted to administer the chloroform to the increasingly distressed child. This was yet another example of Stead taking his experiment beyond the limits of legitimate investigation. Rebecca appears to have relented, however, when Eliza refused to sniff the handkerchief on the second or third attempt. This somewhat spoiled the scene that Stead had envisaged. When he crept into the room clutching a cigar a few minutes later, the child was not unconscious on the bed but sitting up in a terrified state of agitation. As Stead closed the door and proceeded to lock it behind him, she let out 'a wild and piteous cry – not a loud shriek, but a helpless, startled scream like the bleat of a frightened lamb... "There's a man in the room! Take me home; oh, take me home".' In the printed text this scene was followed by a row of asterisks, which was intended to imply a violent rape scene which never took place. 'And then all once more was still.'

After Stead had departed, Rebecca ordered Eliza to dress on account of there being 'too many men in this house'. She was then taken to a far more respectable medical practitioner, Dr Heywood Smith, where she was again chloroformed (this time successfully) and re-examined to ensure that Stead had not sexually assaulted her. This ghastly undertaking showed that, even at this early stage, the editor foresaw the likelihood of legal proceedings following his audacious enterprise, which would make him an object of public hatred as well as what Morley somewhat derisively called 'for a season the most powerful journalist in the island'.[122] All that remained was for the girl to be deposited at Charing Cross Station, where she was taken to France in order to prove how easy it might have been to carry off a real abduction. Rather than being ensnared in a continental brothel, however, Eliza was taken to work as a laundress in the household of Mrs Combe's brother in the South of France. Stead and Booth wished for the child never to see her parents again.

From this time until Stead broke his story in the second week of July, the 'Special Commission' continued with its investigation, though nothing so spectacular was again attempted. It seems that his colleagues at the *PMG* were concerned that their chief had become fanatical about the cause, which few of them actively supported. In later years Alfred Milner would express his view frankly: 'There was another side to it,' he confided in a private letter to Frederic Whyte, 'which revolted me.'[123] Evidently it was believed by some of Stead's friends that he had indulged at one time in the very crimes that he was denouncing. H. M. Hyndman, who was an occasional contributor to the paper, even went so far as to claim that Stead had asked one of his reporters to root around in the Garrick Club library for the banned works of the Marquis de Sade to add 'local colour' to his graphic depictions of sexual abnormality. That may have been an exaggeration, but there is no question that Stead took perverse pleasure in denouncing many of the practices, including extreme sado-masochism, which he explored in unnecessary detail. One of his stories involved a young woman who consented to be 'tied up naked to a nail in the wall … [to be] flogged by a man … [until] the flesh flew and the blood flowed, while her shrieks for mercy were heard all over the house'. Apparently without humour, Stead added that the woman in question had 'got more [punishment] than she bargained for'.[124]

Edward Cook was no less concerned about the campaign than Milner. '[I]t was bad while one agreed more or less with Stead,' he told a friend, 'but … it is rather too much to suffer for one's supposed approval of what one hates.'[125] For weeks on end the editor was driven to distraction, until at last, practically the night before going to press, he frantically dictated the best part of his 50,000-word narrative to relays of shorthand writers – memorably with a wet towel wrapped around his head. He said that he wanted to produce a British equivalent of the American anti-slavery novel, *Uncle Tom's Cabin*, but ended up authoring 'something in theme, language, and self-presentation closer to "Walter's" *My Secret Life*' – a contemporary piece of salacious fiction.[126]

The story was intimated to the public with an unprecedented 'Notice to our Readers' on Saturday 4 July – perhaps not coincidentally the eve of Stead's thirty-sixth birthday. This explained that the editor had in his possession 'the report of a Special and Secret Commission of Inquiry which we appointed to examine' the whole subject of 'sexual criminality which the Criminal Law Amendment Bill was framed to repress'. Explaining that he had 'no desire to inflict upon unwilling eyes the ghastly story of the criminal developments of modern vice', Stead rather clumsily suggested that 'all those who are squeamish, and all those who are prudish, and all those who prefer to live in a fool's paradise of imaginary innocence and purity, selfishly oblivious of the horrible realities which torment those whose lives are passed in the London Inferno, will do well not to read the *Pall Mall Gazette* of Monday and the three following days'. Both *Punch* magazine and the *St. James's Gazette* were fast to observe that a similar gimmick was used by peddlers of backstreet pornography: 'Don't let any good young man buy my little book,' the latter croaked, 'it wouldn't agree with him ... *awful* revelations!'[127]

Perhaps to give his campaign a tentative claim to respectability, Stead entitled his series 'The Maiden Tribute of Modern Babylon' – a strange mélange of Greek legend and Old Testament history that provided the perfect backdrop for his Puritanical melodrama. Stead also had the foresight to call in representatives from the provincial press, whose support he knew would be necessary if he was to maintain the kind of national momentum that had characterised 'his' Bulgarian agitation, to which he fondly compared the present crusade. One reporter, Henry Norman of the *North Eastern News* (who later became a noted foreign correspondent for the *PMG*), recalled the editor lolling back in his armchair with a 'truly American disregard of the angles of Society postures', chatting 'calmly about the Criminal Law Amendment Bill ... as if there were not the slightest possibility that the sturdy Inspector of Police from Bow Street, whom I met at the door, had an uncomfortable missive in his pocket'. Evidently the thunderbolt that Stead was about to unleash had been anticipated by the local constabulary.[128]

The first instalment, which hit the press just a few hours later, was prefaced by a rambling account of the story of Theseus (to whom the editor clearly compared himself), comprising a substantial verse of Latin taken from Ovid. This was followed by a high-minded admonition to his readers, which reminds posterity that whatever his credentials as a journalist, Stead could probably have enjoyed a successful career as a novelist:

>...most of those ensnared tonight will perish, some of them in horrible torture. Yet, so far from this great city being convulsed

with woe, London cares for none of these things, and the cultured man of the world, the heir of all the ages, the ultimate product of a long series of civilisations and religions, will shrug his shoulders in scorn at the folly of any one who ventures in public print to raise even the mildest protest against a horror a thousand times more horrible than that which, in the youth of the world, haunted like a nightmare the imagination of mankind.

The impact of this article, which included all the details of Stead's various exploits, was electric. By the second afternoon of the campaign, demand for the paper had grown to such an extent that Northumberland Street was rendered impassable by a great crowd of 'gaunt, hollow-faced men and women' eager to profit from the sensation. Vendors were seen offering the paper to an entirely new class of reader with placards derived from Stead's eye-bulging crossheads, which included: 'Why the Cries of the Victims are not Heard', 'Strapping Girls Down', 'I Order Five Virgins' and 'A Child of 13 Bought for £5'. The City Solicitor was so appalled by these unprecedentedly lurid banners that he fined twelve barefooted boys for displaying them near St Paul's Cathedral, even though, as Stead indignantly retorted, this was completely illegal. Such things, the editor observed, were 'common enough in Vienna, but in London such a high-handed outrage on the freedom of the Press seemed impossible'. Provocatively, Stead dared this official to take him on directly, promising that he would be able to 'personally vouch for the absolute accuracy of every fact in the narrative'. This would have unfortunate consequences, warned Stead, for numerous 'prominent public men' and even 'Princes of the Blood' – an almost unbelievably bold reference both to Gladstone and the Prince of Wales.[129]

Not everyone in the government was willing to take these threats seriously, but the outgoing Home Secretary Sir William Harcourt (who had proposed the latest version of the Bill) took the opportunity of privately asking Stead to cease publishing. To this moderate plea, the editor replied with characteristic urgency: he would not relent until *his* measure had been put onto the statute book. This almost royal contempt for 'mere' politicians was outdone a short time afterwards when Stead lectured the new incumbent, Sir Richard Cross, that he must either praise the *PMG* unreservedly in the House of Commons or dare to bring criminal proceedings against him. As ever, there was to be no middle course.[130]

Stead spoke with the authority of a journalist on a roll. For three days and nights his basement presses rattled without pause until the supply of paper – which had to be replenished with suitably garish (pink) rolls from the rival *Globe* – finally gave up. By this time copies were changing hands for up to twenty times the sale price of one penny via enterprising salesmen who had never known such fierce demand. More dishonest entrepreneurs took to making pirated copies, often with crude illustrations to excite the curiosity of even the most uneducated species of browser.

The most popular – or, rather, infamous – character depicted in this 'infernal narrative', as Stead fairly described his screed, was the ingenious 'Minotaur of London', who is believed to have inspired Robert Louis Stevenson's novel *The Strange Case of Dr Jekyll and Mr Hyde*, written in the same year. 'Here in London,' wrote Stead, 'moving about clad as respectably in broad cloth and fine linen as any bishop, with no foul shape or semblance of brute beast to mark him off from the rest of his fellows, is Dr. ———, now retired from his profession and free to devote his fortune and his leisure to the ruin of maids.'[131]

Although this man was said to have required a 'quantum' of at least 'three virgins per fortnight', his existence is hard to believe. The Reverend G. P. Merrick, who had investigated prostitution in London for many more years than Stead, had apparently never heard of him. As the writer Hugh Kingsmill long ago opined: 'It seems impossible to credit Stead's revelations, unless one is willing to accept the hypothesis that the Minotaur of London was the Rev. G. P. Merrick himself'.[132] But veracity was not all that mattered to Stead: the importance of his cause outweighed any such considerations. He was willing to use any tactic to ensure that vulnerable young women were given adequate legal protection, even if this led him to stretch the truth or to use some rather indelicate language. Comparing the legal position of women with that of game and fish, he asked seriously: 'Why not let us have a close time for bipeds in petticoats as well as for bipeds in feathers?'[133] A few days later he went on to publish an article signed by 'A Saunterer in the Labyrinth', which seriously advocated polygamy as a solution to the evil of child prostitution.[134] Such lapses threatened to undermine Stead's standing with the likes of Cardinal Manning and General Booth, who cautiously supported his agitation.

If his language and comparisons were often inappropriate, Stead certainly succeeded in dismissing fears that the new legislation would 'outrun public opinion'. When fellow campaigners started to demand that the age of consent for women be raised as high as twenty-five, Stead unexpectedly morphed into a coolheaded man-of-the-world by observing that such measures would deny a living to women who had already succumbed to 'the dreadful calling'. Although by no means an unreasonable sentiment, such remarks further alienated Stead from his natural defenders.

Little did Stead know his real problems were only just beginning.

CHAPTER 7

IN THE DOCK

Bosh! ... Prosecute me?
W. T. S., interview in *North Eastern News* (July 1885)

Stead's decision to expose the hypocrisy of elite society's sentimental attitude towards childhood predictably invited a barrage
of criticism. W. H. Smith, who was both a senior member of the
Cabinet and the owner of Britain's largest chain of newsagents,
responded to the flood of complaints he received at the outset of
the campaign by pulling the *PMG* from newsstands and compen-
sating subscribers with copies of the *St. James's Gazette.*

That paper – still under the direction of the *PMG*'s founding
editor, Frederick Greenwood – was in the vanguard of a substantial
cohort of publications that denounced Stead's series as 'the vilest
parcel of obscenity that has ever been issued from the public press'.
Even its famous contributor Lewis Carroll denounced Stead for
polluting the minds of the innocent, invoking (apparently without
irony) the words Jesus had used to denounce those who tempted
the 'little ones' into sin: Stead should be thrown into the sea
with a 'millstone hung around his neck'. Other indignant readers
sent in vivid accounts of servant boys and maids leering over the
'disgusting' contents of the *PMG*, which had excited an unhealthy
interest 'below stairs'. With scarcely less condescension, Greenwood
described to a friend how he had seen grown men attempting to
hide what they were reading as they travelled home on the suburban railway. 'How queerly ashamed they look,' he wrote, '... decent
folk ... will not take that sort of thing into their homes.'[135]

Such outrage was shared even by Stead's own contributors. The
celebrated literary critic Edmund Gosse, who wrote occasionally in

the *PMG*, vowed never again to associate himself with the newspaper that had stooped so low as to publish 'the Romance of the Brothel'.[136] Practically Stead's only ally on Fleet Street was his young reviewer, George Bernard Shaw, who offered to sell 'as many quires' of the paper as he could carry. But even he would later turn against the editor. 'Nobody ever trusted Stead,' he wrote, with some exaggeration, to Frederic Whyte, 'after the discovery that the case of Eliza Armstrong ... was a put-up job, and that he himself had put it up.' In his satirical play *Pygmalion*, written shortly after Stead's death, Eliza Armstrong would be resurrected as Eliza Doolittle; a no less tragic victim of misplaced philanthropy.[137]

Stead's colleagues were hardly more sympathetic. Of all of them, his assistant editor Alfred Milner was the most furious; though Stead – to his credit – always maintained him to have been supportive during the crisis. The truth was that Milner had taken the campaign as an opportunity to escape to the comfort of his Oxford college for a few days, from where he tendered his resignation. He rather insensitively requested that the three-month period of notice stipulated in his contract be waived under the circumstances. Even if Milner was being truthful when he claimed not to have actually read the offending articles, he knew well enough that his chief had realised his vaunted principle of 'frank brutality' to the utmost.[138]

All this mattered little to Stead, who was greatly enjoying the instant fame that his stunt had bestowed upon him and his cause. He even went so far as to actively court criticism, praising 'our friends the enemy' for doing so much to shatter the 'conspiracy of silence' that had formerly shrouded the entire subject of sexual criminality against children.[139] This strategy was initially preferred to siding with the religious and philanthropic leaders who cautiously offered him their support: Stead was consciously restyling himself as an evangelical pariah, alone 'ringing a tocsin in the belfry of the world'.[140] Nevertheless, Stead did not yet expect, or in truth desire, to find himself summoned before a magistrate for breach of the publishing laws. As he confidently explained to Henry Norman of the *North Eastern News*:

> Bosh! ... Prosecute *me*? I wish with all my heart they would, and
> they know I do ... prison is really the only place where I shall be
> able to get any rest for a long time. But I shall not be prosecuted ...
> if they do so there will be at once a hundred times more publishing,
> and all the names implicated will come out besides.[141]

The only problem was that Stead had not merely offended the
propriety of the Victorian household: he had also committed a
serious crime by unlawfully taking a child away from her parents.
About this, Stead showed practically no concern, transferring all
responsibility for Eliza Armstrong to the leaders of the Salvation
Army, who, for their part, could only operate under the assumption that the child was completely destitute. They treated her well,
although Catherine Booth was rightly concerned that Jarrett (who
had only been in command of Eliza for a few days) claimed to love
the girl 'like a mother'.[142] This led to an awkward separation of
the pair at the Army's headquarters in Paris during the course of
which the lame woman rather cruelly told the child that she had
not been sent into service after all, 'but for something much worse'.
A girl who had been out selling copies of the organisation's magazine with Eliza later recalled that she 'hung down her head, and
seemed to feel it'.[143]

Eliza's two-month stint as a servant at the home of Mrs Combe's
brother at Loriol-sur-Drôme was scarcely happier, not least because
Mrs Combe thought it best to reveal practically nothing about
the child's extraordinary history. She merely wrote cryptically
to her brother that he should try to see the *PMG* because 'you
will see something in it that will astonish you'.[144] As this would
have been practically impossible in the south of France, Eliza was
subsequently treated, as Mrs Combe had requested, no more sensi-
tively than any other 'handy and active' helper. To make matters
worse, the letters that Eliza was occasionally allowed to write to
her parents were not forwarded, but used as good copy for Stead's
articles. This provided Stead with a touching piece of childish verse
intended for Eliza's mother, which he 'quite unnecessarily' (said

Bramwell Booth) ran at the foot of the 'Lily' story.[145] It was to be his undoing.

When these letters were not responded to, the child understandably became even more distraught than she would otherwise have been. Sleeping on a bed of leaves in the dilapidated old cottage in which she was lodged, Eliza would often cry herself to sleep at the thought of never seeing her parents again.[146] Whether or not this was overstating her case (or, rather, that of her parents) against Stead, it cannot be doubted that her ordeal and new surroundings would have greatly traumatised a girl whose travels had hitherto been limited to a school trip to Richmond, where she had seen the River Thames for the first and only time in her life.

While Eliza was enduring these hardships, Stead carried on at Northumberland Street with an intensity unmatched by any of his previous campaigns. For weeks on end the newspaper scarcely treated another topic, much to the annoyance of Milner (roped back to the office in spite of his resignation) who complained to Cook that 'Stead talks, writes and thinks nothing else but of his virgins'.[147] True though this may have been, it is not entirely fair to say that Stead always did so in a sensational or overexcited manner. One of his more hard-headed leaders on the subject advocated 'complete legal liberty for voluntary immorality between adults contracting on equal terms, so long as they are no nuisance to the neighbours'.[148] Notwithstanding this classic Liberal approach, Stead responded to any attempt by persons in the outside world to dissent from his proposals for legislative reform with a level of frenzied indignation that hardly did justice to his cause. Not even his former editor, John Morley, was spared. When he voiced concern in the House of Commons that the evidence of very young girls could not be accepted under the strictures of English law, Stead responded with a leader in which he wailed: 'If a child is too young to know the nature of an oath, let her be outraged with impunity.' For this reason it is unsurprising that Stead's one-time friend and colleague, with typical lexical dexterity, privately denounced him as a 'cockatrice' – a mythical snake hatched from a hen's egg.[149]

A more unpleasant confrontation for the editor, at least on a personal level, was the one he was having with his wife. If Stead had intended his campaign to regain Emma's respect, he had failed miserably. Not only had she hardly seen her husband in weeks (a time in which she had been seriously unwell) she now endured the infamy of being married to a man commonly known to have stalked about in brothels. This led one unkind acquaintance to warn her that 'no man who was faithful to his wife could engage in the work he was doing', which she duly passed on to her husband with an angry note. A colleague who saw Stead shortly after reading this message remembered him, even sixty years later, 'sobbing as only a man can'. Stead's response appears to have been to publish a letter in the newspaper from John Wesley to his wife during a marital crisis of their own, in which the eighteenth-century evangelist reminded her that 'no one was ever forced to love another'. This was a gesture highly characteristic of Stead since it associated him with yet another one of his heroes. It may have worked, too, for in the end Emma 'stood nobly by him'.[150]

Another important relationship to be put under strain by the campaign was that with his employer, Henry Yates Thompson. This was partly because the heightened demand for the paper (circulation touched 100,000) had sparked a malicious rumour that the 'Maiden Tribute' was a ruse designed to replenish his depleted finances. Though this may be a far from shocking conclusion in the light of modern practice, at the time it was virtually libellous, since it was considered unseemly to treat a newspaper (as Stead put it) merely 'as a money producing machine'.[151] For this reason it must have been excruciating for the owner to hear himself berated in Parliament (to which he aspired) as a shameless profiteer. One MP captured the atmosphere particularly well when he observed: 'Just recently a newspaper, failing in its circulation, and having a great difficulty to maintain its own in the world, thought by a very sensational report to regain its circulation.' Another member rejoined by comparing Yates Thompson to the Roman emperor said by Tacitus to have charged his subjects for going to the lavatory on the basis that 'money does not smell':

> '*Non olet!*', said the smug proprietor ... as he shovelled tens of thousands of pounds into his pocket. '*Non olet!*' he repeated, as he galvanised into life this wretched journal that was falling to pieces.[152]

Stead denied this charge until his dying day, emphasising that the scheme actually *lost* the paper money, since both subscribers and advertisers, as Frederick Greenwood had predicted, took their business elsewhere. Though this contains a strong element of truth, it would be mistaken to accept Stead's blanket denial of pecuniary interest. Stead had been reminded on several occasions by Yates Thompson that sales needed to be improved, and he would only have been doing his job if he had attempted to achieve this by unconventional means. No one could deny that the inflated circulation that accompanied the sensation brought in plenty of extra revenue, nor was there any doubt that there was a hot demand for the 'bowdlerized' special edition of the 'Maiden Tribute' put together by Cook in mid-July. There were also numerous foreign translations – paradoxically boasted about by Stead in his ostensibly moralising commentary – which certainly gave the newspaper much publicity, even if the profits accrued in the hands of others.

The editor's impartiality is also called into questioned by the financial arrangement he made with Yates Thompson at the outset of his investigation. This stipulated that Stead's expenses, amounting to about £400 (initially shared by Josephine Butler and Bramwell Booth), would only be repaid if the inquiry resulted in material that would be deemed worthy of publication. If this in itself is not enough to justify accusations that the revelations were not wholly disinterested, a previously unpublished letter from Yates Thompson to Stead in the wake of the agitation decides the matter conclusively. This referred to '£1,000 which was an advance to you ... on the profits of the Maiden Tribute which may very likely be nil'.[153] Although this does not dispute the fact that the campaign might have lost the proprietor money in the long run, it is no longer possible to deny that both men had expected there to be a substantial return. Nowhere in Stead's voluminous writings on the subject did he ever confess that his most famous campaign brought him a boon equivalent to a year's salary.

In any case, Stead's undoing was fast at hand. It began when ragged copies of the infamous issues of the *PMG* began trickling into the slums of Marylebone, probably for the first time ever. Up to this point, Mrs Armstrong had been kept quiet by Nancy Broughton, who responded to her friend's frequent enquires about her daughter by showing her reassuring letters from 'Mrs Sullivan' (almost certainly written by Jarrett), which claimed Eliza to be well and happy in her new situation. But, upon seeing the offending journal, a neighbour recognised the child's verses resulting in her mother becoming 'the scandal of the neighbours' who supposed her to have sold her daughter into prostitution. A spectacular row subsequently took place between Nancy and Mrs Armstrong on 11 July, to the great amusement of a crowd of jeering onlookers.[154]

In the wake of this dramatic incident, Mrs Armstrong went to report the abduction of her child to the local police court; the whereabouts of which she knew from her previous run-ins with the law. Unsurprisingly in the light of their vast social differences, the magistrate took a dim view of her predicament and admonished her for the 'gross negligence' of allowing her daughter to go off with an unknown woman. Nevertheless, an investigation was rapidly begun, not only by the police, but also an early scandal sheet, *Lloyd's Weekly Newspaper*, which specialised in the proceedings of the criminal and divorce courts.

Mrs Armstrong chose not to mention the *PMG* in her statement, but it must have been evident to anyone who had read the recent scoop that her story sounded uncannily familiar. The following day the editor of *Lloyd's*, Thomas Catling, printed a prominent article entitled 'A Mother Seeking a Lost Child', which subtly repeated many of the details of the 'Maiden Tribute', differing only in its description of the plaintiff as 'a poor but apparently respectable woman'. One of the paper's reporters subsequently took Mrs Armstrong to the cottage in Winchester from where 'Mrs Sullivan' had posted her the reassuring letters, but they found the place deserted.

When Stead saw this article he realised that one of the central findings of the 'Secret Commission' was about to be challenged by his rivals. But, undaunted, he saw no harm in printing a small notice of the complaint made at Marylebone police court the following day. It seems that his desire to fuel the moral panic that was sweeping the capital about the safety of unaccompanied children outweighed any concerns he might have had for his own protection. He did, however, have the foresight to ask his pre-selected collection of churchmen and statesmen to make a private inquiry into the veracity of his findings. They were encouraged in this line by Cardinal Manning, who was 'literally denounced by Catholics' as a result.[155] Rather hopefully, Stead also implored Gladstone to contribute, with the consciously impertinent public utterance that he 'must surely care as much about the systematic ruin of English maidenhood as he cared about the outrages inflicted upon the women of Bulgaria'. Understandably he was rebuffed: Stead's decision to launch his campaign on the first day of Lord Salisbury's interim Conservative government was seen by many as an attempt to shame the late Liberal regime for failing to pass the Act.

The proceedings of the so-called 'Mansion House Committee' were kept from public view, but glimpses of its inquiry were leaked to the press, not least by Stead himself. Like many conscientious citizens at the time, the panel largely disapproved of the editor's methods, but could not help acknowledging that he had provided the necessary impetus to clamp down on a tangible social evil. When they issued a statement that his findings were 'substantially true', they specifically emphasised that they had not been interested in determining the accuracy of every particular; an oversight which led some critics to wonder why they had bothered to convene at all. When Mrs Armstrong was brought before them in evident misery on the last day of their investigation, they dealt with her summarily, though one insider later claimed that they had realised at that moment that the 'Lily' story had been a fabrication. Stead, who had been lurking in the gallery at the time, later dismissed the mother's performance as 'a maudlin kind of crying', and did nothing to facilitate the desired reunion of her with her child, or even to introduce himself as 'the Chief Director'.

But Mrs Armstrong was clearly a highly determined woman and, with the help of Inspector Borner of Scotland Yard, took her petition directly to Bramwell Booth, principally because his organisation was believed (incorrectly) to have masterminded the whole operation. This put the Salvationist in an awkward position. On the one hand he did not want to 'betray' his friend; on the other, he could hardly risk jeopardising his father's life's work in defence of a crime about which they had known little. Nevertheless, Booth showed complete faith in Stead, which may explain why he was 'at first rather rough' with his distressed and emotional visitor. When she enjoined him to return her child, he shrilly retorted, 'Have you £100?' in reference to the money he had allegedly spent on her deportation. To this, Mrs Armstrong responded by observing that she was 'only a poor woman', which not even her fiercest critic could deny. Booth's hopeful solution to the impasse was to offer her double the girl's wages if she would let the matter drop. In the hope of making her choice easier, Booth emphasised that the child was happier than ever and bizarrely offered to show Dr Heywood Smith's certificate to the attendant inspector as evidence. This ploy did not work and Mrs Armstrong was sent away with the rather patronising advice that she should discuss the matter with her husband before letting him know if they 'really' wanted their daughter returned.

It took the couple four days to compose a response (almost certainly written with the assistance of reporters sent over by Greenwood and Catling) explaining that they were grateful for the kindness that Booth had shown to Eliza, but that they thought it 'impossible that you could send a child into a foreign country without the consent of her parents'. Booth failed to acknowledge this correspondence, since his father feared that returning the child would 'add colour' to the accusations levied against them. Instead, Booth rather hopefully suggested to Stead that he insert something in the *PMG* the next day to the effect 'that we took charge of Eliza Armstrong having rescued her ... from a terrible fate'. But Stead had no intention of getting bogged down in what he grandly called the 'hubbub' surrounding the child. The same day that Mrs Armstrong had begged Booth to return Eliza, Stead had written in rapture to Madame Novikov: 'What a time we are having. It is really most wonderful.'[156]

Stead's confidence was inflated by the findings of the Mansion House Committee, which led him to make a final 'appeal to the people' with the immodest claim that Parliament would soon bow down to public opinion 'as the Muslim before the revealed will of Allah'.[157] Much to the annoyance of his enemies, Stead was not wrong. Just two days later the Home Secretary began an emergency debate on the Criminal Law Amendment Bill by frankly observing that its objective was one which had 'stirred England from one end to the other'. This naturally provoked ripples of dissent from MPs, who were aware that the Home Secretary's lips had been prompted by the upstart editor. One backbencher expressed this forcefully when he attacked the government for 'riding upon a storm created by ... a public journal'. Cross coolly retorted to this by observing that opponents of the Bill would 'have to answer to the public and their constituencies'.[158] After an unusually hurried debate, the Bill was sent up to the House of Lords, where it was immediately passed before being submitted to the Queen for royal assent. This, too, was given with the utmost promptness. According to Stead, who had long conversations with his old ally Reginald Brett about gossip at the palace, Queen Victoria 'read the *Pall Mall* every night & sympathized very keenly with ... the "Maiden Tribute" & Co.'[159]

Less indulgent observers noted that the moral panic sparked by Stead's revelations had prevented the Bill from being properly debated. These worries were legitimate. In the heat of the moment one overzealous MP (allegedly to make the new law appear 'ridiculous') had proposed the reintroduction of flogging for sex offenders, while another speculatively motioned that 'gross indecency with another male person, shall be guilty of misdemeanour'. Although the first of these amendments was rejected, the latter took hold, making homosexuality between men illegal in Britain until its repeal in the 1960s.[160]

Stead was uncritical of these excesses; indeed he took the passing of what critics and supporters alike called 'Stead's Act' as an opportunity to launch a 'new crusade' designed to purge the nation of its vices. Stead did not outline the full details of this ambitious side project, but its objective was clear: to inspire 'a purer moral life'.[161] It was at this point that Stead's critics became even more outspoken, observing that the cause had become the monomania of one *The Times* denounced as a 'self-elected guardian of morals'.[162] Even the socialist visionary William Morris refused to offer his support on the grounds that 'a Puritan revival' would do little to alter the real, social and economic, causes of prostitution.[163] Unperturbed, Stead went on to address a crowded auditorium at St. James's Hall, heedless of the advice of friends such as Bramwell Booth, who suggested that a low profile might be desirable in light of the counter-campaign that had been launched against them.

The wisdom of such warnings was vindicated when Stead was confronted with cries of 'Armstrong!' as he proceeded to berate his audience for doing 'all manner of excellent and eloquent things and then you go home and won't do a single cursed thing – not one'. Stead's response to these hecklers was assured: 'I will tell you about Lizzie Armstrong,' he said, '...[w]e took that child from a place that was steeped in vice, from a mother who has admitted that she was going to a brothel', before adding somewhat implausibly that 'no suspicion or shadow of a thought of anything wrong crossed that girl's mind'.[164] This was the first confession of what was by now a very open secret; one which threatened to cast a shadow over the great demonstration of purity that Stead and his supporters had arranged to take place in Hyde Park the following day.

The truth was that the 'game was up' for Stead. Booth had already got wind of a police expedition to Loriol (during the course of which Mr Armstrong was twice lost in the labyrinth of Parisian brotheldom), and decided that the safest thing was to bring Eliza home. The two men clearly disagreed over the issue, for the Salvation Army was 'conspicuous in its absence' at the Hyde Park rally, which Stead consciously gave a quasi-revolutionary feel. According to Stead, no fewer than 100,000 concerned parents from the lower ranks of society turned out to hear him denounce the shameful practices common among the rich. Amid a forest of banners and placards, Stead was delighted to see a wagonette of little girls bearing the sign: 'Must the Innocent be Slaughtered?'

Appearing on a temporary platform erected within sight of Sir Richard Westmacott's controversial nude of Achilles, Stead began by explaining that his wife, who sat in silence behind him, had requested that he 'speak no more' – but Stead could not resist this opportunity of practising his oratory. After expressing his disbelief that a 'humble Tynesider' such as himself could 'have such a reception', Stead told his audience, to 'loud and enthusiastic cheering': 'If you are not stirred to action ... then you are unworthy of the name of men and women and you deserve to rank among the meanest and the most degraded of your kind.'[165]

While Stead was haranguing from the podium, his private detective Mussabini and a friend, Mr Thicknesse of the Society for the Protection of Minors, were busily trying to arrange the return of Eliza to her parents before anyone actually got arrested. That morning Stead had been prompted by Catling to give these men a letter to deliver to Mrs Armstrong, as well as an undisclosed sum of money for her trouble. The letter stated that Stead understood 'for the first time' that she would like her child to be returned, and that she should come to Cambridge House for 'half an hour' the following afternoon to see that her daughter was safe. Thicknesse allegedly added in a verbal instruction that she 'must say nothing to the police' about this arrangement, but Mrs Armstrong immediately informed Inspector Borner when he called shortly afterwards.[166]

The ensuing reunion was evidently a painful one for Emma Stead, not least because her husband, fearing recognition by Eliza from their time in the brothel, chose to absent himself from the house. Her role was made even harder by Stead's solemn request that she should prevent the child from leaving their home at all costs. But Emma ultimately decided to spare Mrs Armstrong the indignity of pleading for her daughter. Evidently she secretly disapproved of her husband's recent behaviour, for she told her unlikely guest, woman to woman, that it had been 'an unusual thing' for him to have the girl medically examined. Conscious that the present situation was far from ideal, she left the reunited pair to share a tearful embrace alone in the dining room, and led the police inspector and assorted guests into the garden.

During the subsequent lunch, Mussabini made various suggestive remarks about how well Eliza was looking but in the end there was never any doubt that she was going back to the slums with her mother. The only remaining humiliation was for Mrs Armstrong to sign a receipt, put together by Thicknesse upstairs, acknowledging that her daughter had not been subjected to 'outrage'.

Although Stead was disappointed that Eliza had been returned to her parents, he was naive in thinking that this was the end of the matter. While he and his wife were packing their bags for a much-needed holiday to the Swiss resort of Grindelwald, the Armstrongs wasted no time in petitioning the treasury solicitor to take up their case for the abduction of their daughter. Writs were subsequently sent out for the arrest of Stead, Jarrett, Booth and their accomplices, which Stead heard of, to his apparent delight, just as he and his wife reached their destination. From a mountain-side post office, Stead composed a short telegram which was immediately published in the *PMG* under the provocative heading, 'A Welcome Prosecution'. In this communication, the editor boldly claimed 'sole responsibility' for what had taken place, professing his satisfaction at the opportunity 'of publicly vindicating the proceedings of the Secret Commission'. In truth, he shared some of his wife's anxiety, possibly entering a period of depression which was only thinly disguised by the excitement of the trial.

In the run-up to his appearance in court, Stead launched a 'Defence Fund' which he later claimed to have swelled to an impressive £6,000 (equivalent to half a million pounds today). This claim, made at a time in Stead's life in which he attempted to recast the incident in a more favourable light, was almost certainly exaggerated. No official record of donations was actually made: in a notice to 'would-be subscribers' Stead explained that he would not accept even a sixpence unless it could be treated 'as if it were my own private pocket-money'.[167] Whatever the eventual value of the fund, Stead decided not even to retain a barrister. Like his hero Martin Luther at the Diet of Worms, he would appear defiant and alone before his accusers. This greatly distressed Booth, who generously offered to share his expert legal team of Sir Charles Russell, QC, and the future Home Secretary, Henry Matthews, QC, MP. But it was no use. At a meeting in chambers shortly before the trial, Matthews became so fed up with Stead's willingness to aggravate the situation that he declared: 'Oh, Russell, I cannot stand these people's thirst for being martyrs.' Incandescent with rage, Stead shot back 'like lightning': 'No! You will never be one.'[168]

Stead took this sentiment with him into the preliminary hearing before the magistrate, Mr Vaughan, at Bow Street police court on 9 September. Somewhat swept up by the excitement of the proceedings, which attracted a violent mob outside the court, Stead did not properly understand that this was not the place to launch an elaborate justification of his actions. In one scene, fairly described by a reporter from *Lloyd's* as 'ludicrous in the extreme', Stead attempted to deliver a long speech about his noble motives, not realising that they were immaterial to the initial hearing before the magistrate. Scarcely had Stead uttered the words 'conspiracy of silence' than the judge stopped him, demanding to examine every page of his statement before it was allowed to be read. Glancing over each sheaf as Stead continued with his high-minded defence, each one was individually rejected until the last section, which concluded with the sentence, 'mine was the guiding brain and this the directing hand which alone is responsible for what was done'.[169]

The nobility of these words was in part undermined by the often unfeeling way in which Stead presented the chief witnesses for the prosecution, who in fairness he did not even know. It may have been true, as he claimed, that there was a sort of 'brothel lobby' behind them, or that they had the backing of 'arm-chair journalists' such as Greenwood and Catling, but this does not exonerate some of Stead's harsher statements. Much of what he had wanted to say (and controversially did say in an 'Extra' entitled 'Mr Stead's Suppressed Defence') built upon the line he had taken in the immediate wake of the St. James's Hall meeting. The most objectionable part of this was his justification of the intrusive medical examination on the grounds that it was necessary to make sure 'that a little harlot had not been palmed off upon us'.[170] How such considerations truly promoted his cause is not entirely clear. It was also highly questionable for Stead to assert that the period of the 'alleged abduction' had been 'the happiest period in the existence of the child Eliza – one upon which she will look back with regret in the midst of the surroundings into which she has been plunged'. At the subsequent High Court trial it was revealed that Stead had not even questioned Eliza about these surroundings or even of the character of her parents. To this legitimate line of questioning, the editor sheepishly responded: 'It never crossed my mind that they had been kind to her.'

Mr Vaughan was unsparing in his criticism of Stead. In his opinion, the editor had shown a tendency towards 'self-glorification', however 'praiseworthy' his motives may have been. More damagingly, Vaughan concluded that Stead had probably committed various statutory offences in the process of getting 'together materials for the concoction of that deplorable and nauseous article'. Without hesitation he sent the case up to the Old Bailey, where Stead, Booth, Jarrett, Mussabini, Combe and Mourez were to be tried before Mr Justice Lopes on the dual charge of abduction and physical assault. Vaughan was tempted to refuse bail, but ultimately allowed them to be set free for an unusually large sum of £100 each.[171]

In the weeks before his trial, Stead engaged in a brief international lecture tour, culminating with an impassioned speech on the 'State Regulation of Vice' to a gathering of likeminded reformers in Antwerp. His intention was not only to convey his importance to the world but also to highlight the fact that he had launched his crusade in the manner of a father defending his child:

> Supposing my daughter is being outraged by a brute in human form, and I am standing by watching him, and my daughter is screaming for help, and no help is near but my hand. If, whether with pistol or bludgeon or dagger, I can slay that man and send him to a dishonoured grave and to an eternal hell, do you think I would not commit that crime?[172]

Such reasoning did not spare Stead from the horror of his trial at the Old Bailey, at which his principal witness, Rebecca Jarrett, gave way under the harsh prosecuting of the Attorney-General, Sir Richard Webster. Humiliated before her friend Nancy Broughton and twice threatened with assault by Mrs Armstrong, she confessed that the 'purchase' of Eliza had not been exactly how it appeared in the story. Stead, who was visibly shaken by this disclosure, responded by observing that 'her memory seems defective', before confessing with embarrassment that 'three weeks had elapsed before I wrote the article, and during that time there had been a Ministerial crisis, and I had been visiting brothels, and drinking champagne and smoking, which I was not used to, and was very excited, and therefore I may have confused some of the statements Jarrett told me'.[173] Several of Stead's admirers have claimed this to have been a valiant attempt to spare Jarrett from imprisonment, but the reality was surely that he finally had to admit that neither Rebecca's story, nor his own discoveries – sadly commonplace as they were – had been enough for a truly shocking campaign.

In the face of defeat, Stead, whose appearance in court was described by a friend as 'slovenly and shabby', was not entirely magnanimous. He chided the Attorney-General for wasting the government's resources in prosecuting such an upstanding individual as himself, while real criminals such as 'the Minotaur' (whose identity was not revealed) were still at large. His treatment of Mrs Armstrong was also quite unpleasant: Lopes had to warn him on several occasions that he could not refer to her as 'a drunken woman' simply because she had been fined for disorder. Denied this liberty, Stead's ultimate proof against the mother was almost comic: her failure to take him 'by the throat' for abducting her child could be explained no other way 'except the promptings of a guilty conscience'. More likely, she was not as graphically aware of the dangers posed to children as her interrogator, who in many ways planted in the public imagination the deep-rooted fear of paedophilia that endures to the present day.

Before the judge's summing-up Stead made one last plea to the jury, in which he frankly stated that he had taken 'the only steps which from my experience as a journalist I knew would ... enable Mr Attorney-General to amend [the] law into something like decency'. This last line of defence was ultimately his most honest. Like a medieval king, Stead had operated under the assumption that 'necessity knows no law'. It was, however, going too far to claim, as Stead and Booth would in later years, that they were tried under the Criminal Law Amendment Act; they were prosecuted for abducting Eliza under Section 56 of the Offences Against the Person Act (1861). Moreover, Stead's later boast that he had only been convicted due to the 'technicality' that he had not obtained the consent of Eliza's father (a legal defence to the charge), rather than that of her mother, was not entirely accurate: the father's consent would also have been invalid had it been obtained by misrepresentation.

Another favourite anecdote of Stead's in later life was that he would not have gone to prison if he had decided to expose the fact that Eliza was an illegitimate child and so had no protection under the law (her parents, it was to emerge, had married after her birth). This was another half-truth. A child born out of wedlock was only more vulnerable to the extent that a man or woman purporting to be its parent would not usually be prosecuted. That would have made little difference to the outcome of the case. Not even Stead's proud claim that he had willingly sacrificed himself to spare Eliza this trauma was wholly accurate: it was actually Booth's lawyer, Sir Charles Russell, who had pointed out to him that it would be outrageous to attempt to disprove the child's legitimacy after all her family had been made to suffer.[174]

Lopes conducted the trial with the authority and discernment that befitted a respected member of the bench. But his evident hostility towards the author of the 'filthy and disgusting' articles made the jury's decision a foregone conclusion. 'If this sort of thing was to be allowed', he lectured them,

> you would no longer be governed by fixed law; but would be subjected to all sorts of caprices, and have the law constantly violated in order that persons who entertained certain ideas might carry out what they supposed to be a good object.[175]

The foreman of the jury returned the verdict of 'guilty' with a rider that Stead's actions had led to a salutary improvement in the law, notably in the raising of the 'age of consent' for girls from thirteen to sixteen, where it has remained up to the present. Shortly afterwards Stead was tried along with Jarrett, Mussabini and Mourez in the same court for drugging and physically assaulting Eliza. Again found guilty, Stead was sentenced to three months in jail; one more than he had been led to believe by a mystical 'premonition' he claims to have had while he sat writing letters in the dock. Stead was apparently on the verge of pointing out this anomaly to the court when Lopes revealed that his period of imprisonment would be counted from the beginning of proceedings, which left him with just over two months to serve.[176]

Evidently, Lopes had been partly sympathetic to his cause after all: Bramwell Booth was acquitted. Jarrett and Mourez, however, were sent down for six months to Milbank women's prison, the latter with hard labour, during the course of which the duped old abortionist died a wretched death.

CHAPTER 8

RIGHTEOUS IMPRISONMENT

It is not often that a man can look back upon his conviction and sentence as a criminal convict with pride and exultation. Such however is my case...
W. T. S., 'My First Imprisonment' (1886)

Stead's introduction to prison life began on the final day of his trial when he was led through a series of cold iron doors in Newgate, the ancient remand jail beneath the Old Bailey, 'silent as the grave'. Plenty of journalists had been punished in this way before, but almost none had faced the added indignity of being sent to a common felon's prison like Coldbath Fields, which (improbably) crested Mount Pleasant in the county of Middlesex. It is a remarkable fact that Stead managed to turn this ostensible disaster into the defining moment of his life, celebrating the anniversary of his conviction each year by travelling to work in his prison uniform and reinventing himself as the philosopher-king of his trade. As ever, he made some notable enemies along the way, and many of their criticisms were not entirely unjustified.

Stead and Mussabini were transported to Coldbath with their former accomplices, Jarrett and Mourez, in the prison's Black Maria, a huge hearse-like omnibus used to shuttle convicts from the court to the location of their incarceration. Communication was limited by the design of this contraption, which placed each detainee in a cramped pigeonhole, barely high enough for an average-sized man to crouch. Nevertheless, Stead claimed in his cheerful and provocatively entitled memoir *My First Imprisonment*, that he and his fellow convicts were in high spirits, with the exception of Mourez 'whose indignation on being removed after sentence was almost ungovernable'. In all probability, their collective mood was rather gloomy, not least because of the 'parting yell of execration' delivered by the mob; a chilling reminder of the trouble – and, in the case of Bramwell Booth (whose uniform had once been almost torn off him), physical harm – that had marred each day of the trial. One can only take Stead at his word that 'poor Jarrett' was consoled by his righteous opinion that 'she deserves the punishment for the many bad deeds she had done in her life'.[177] Her and Mourez's experiences in Milbank women's prison served as a harsh redemption.

The jail to which Stead and Mussabini were transported had a reputation for strictness, austerity and total lack of modernisation. A labyrinthine building, it was thought by one prison inspector to have 'a curious George the Third air about it', while earlier reformers had likened it to the French Bastille. Entering through its massive portal, the new inmates were shunted into a dank octagon-shaped reception hall, which even the love-thy-neighbour Stead likened to a 'human cesspool'. Silence was nominally maintained by a stern warder who sat on a narrow podium at the front, but this did not prevent a 'wild-looking larrikin' asking the humbled editor if he knew 'how much them wot was in the Armstrong case has got?' After proudly explaining that the two of them were 'them wot was in [it]' and revealing their sentences, another convict expressed the popular opinion that they had 'got off cheap'. It is possible that Stead and his friend suffered some form of abuse from these men, since Stead later wrote that although he enjoyed cordial relations with most of the other felons, there were 'one or two exceptions'. As this was practically the only time that late-Victorian prisoners were allowed to mingle with one another, it is hard to see when else these 'exceptions' could have been encountered.

The indignity of being herded with this rabble into the suitably cold (but allegedly clean) baths, which preceded a medical examination and a rough trimming from the prison barber, cannot have been lost on the editor. Though he later emphasised how well he had been treated by his custodians, his first night alone in

Coldbath must have been among the most miserable of his life. His claim to have welcomed his bare plank bed as an 'old acquaintance' on account of the articles he had written in support of imprisoned Irish Home Rule agitators, as well as his assertion that he 'felt thoroughly glad to be alone after all the turmoil', cannot disguise the fact that he must have been extremely uncomfortable and depressed about his predicament. For a garrulous and incessantly active individual, the prospect of spending two months in such conditions, unravelling thick, tar-encrusted rope for eight hours a day with nothing but bread and gruel for nourishment, must have seemed a punishment almost too great to bear. Not even the joy of martyrdom can have entirely compensated for these physical hardships.

Thankfully for Stead, he did not have to wait long for a lifeline. Almost as soon as he entered his cell, a group of influential female activists spearheaded by Millicent Fawcett (the widow of a prominent blind Liberal MP much admired by Stead) began to lobby the government for his release. 'More women love me than ever now,' exulted Stead in a cheerful letter to Madame Novikov marked 'burn this'.[178] In just a few days, these women were said to have gathered a phenomenal petition of over one hundred thousand signatures, which they planned to submit to the permanent under-secretary to the Home Office, Godfrey Lushington.

Lushington, though later a visionary advocate of penal reform, had little sympathy with the prisoner's cause and refused even to meet the delegation that managed to force its way into his offices. Echoing the view of the Home Secretary, Sir Richard Cross, he wrote that Stead's 'good motive' was too much 'mixed up with rash fanaticism and literary vanity' to be deserving of any special exemption. But the Conservative Prime Minister Lord Salisbury was more sympathetic. Writing through the medium of his secretary, Henry Manners, he overruled Lushington's advice by expressing the view that he was 'not only willing, but anxious' to take Stead from his present position to that of a 'first-class misdemeanant' 'without further delay'. His correspondent, clearly piqued, could only agree in bitter compromise that 'Jarrett of course is out of the question'.[179]

The difference between the status of a common felon and that of a first-class misdemeanant could hardly have been greater, and came as a godsend to the depressed editor. Having only spent two nights in the squalor of Coldbath, Stead was transferred to Holloway Gaol (not then a women's prison) where he served out the remainder of his sentence in a state of comfort that would scarcely have been matched by a modest country inn. 'I have ever been the child of fortune,' Stead later wrote, 'but never had I a happier lot than the two months I spent in happy Holloway'. Despite his incarceration, he was free to wear his own clothes, purchase exotic food and employ a poor fellow inmate to make up his bed and fire in the mornings. He was even allowed to continue editing his newspaper on condition that he did not refer to his sentence or imprisonment and sent no correspondence after 8pm. 'Loulou' Harcourt, whose father had first proposed the Criminal Law Amendment Bill, was only exaggerating slightly when he complained of Stead feasting on '*pâté de foie gras* and other delicacies ... his room full of flowers'. Stead's own description of his cell – the 'pleasantest room imaginable' – was hardly less luxuriant. Disturbingly, in the light of the name he had given to Eliza Armstrong in his articles, he took particular delight in a posy of lilies 'forced into premature bloom', which had been sent to him by an admirer.[180]

It was in this environment that Stead came as close to enjoying the high spirits that he claims to have characterised his entire prison experience. Shortly before his transfer he had been found by Yates Thompson, who came to lecture him on the necessity of winning back their lost advertisers, in the depths of depression. As Stead admitted to another friend: 'I, discredited as I am by the breakdown of Jarrett ... can no longer take the high line I used to.'[181] Generously, however, Yates Thompson denied that he was a 'discredited journalist' and declined, apparently for the third time since the trial, his resignation. '*God keep you from being melancholy*,' he implored.[182] But even in Stead's new spacious accommodation, which one visitor supposed to be 'two rooms knocked into one', he could not prevent events in the outside world getting him down. Most pressingly he was put in a difficult position with regard to Madame Novikov, who wanted to meet his wife for the first time – a plan that failed to win the support of Emma to such an extent that she asked her brother-in-law, Herbert, to pen a curt rejection.[183] 'This troubles me far more than gaol,' the editor wrote angrily to his former lover.

Yet pride was undoubtedly the order of the day. When Madame Novikov detected traces of arrogance in the martyr-like notices that had appeared in the paper, Stead boorishly sent her a cutting from the *Methodist Times* likening him to Jesus. This revealing action cemented an idea in Stead's mind that would last for the rest of his life: that he was not merely a votary of Christianity, but that he was the very embodiment of Christ himself. Writing to his entire family, Stead articulated the tenets of his megalomaniac 'new faith', which he proceeded to forward to less enthusiastic recipients including Cardinal Manning and Catherine Booth:

> Do you know what I think Jesus Christ would do if He came now? He would go to church and chapel ever so many times and listen, and no one would speak to him. He would look to see who sat round Him and He would see no ragged people, no thieves, no harlots, only respectable people. And He would hear all these respectable people singing hymns to Christ, and giving all the glory to Christ, and then after standing it a long time, Jesus would stand up some day in the middle of the church and just say two words, 'Damn Christ!'[184]

His point was clear: he was the only true Christian in London. Such was Stead's self-adulation that when John Morley came to see him at about this time he found his former colleague 'comfortable and lively – not to say exalted'. In his memoirs, published some thirty years later, Morley damningly recalled how Stead had asked him who he considered to be the most important man in the world. 'I could only find one answer' Stead unblinkingly continued, '– *the prisoner in this cell.*'[185]

It was in this regal, even divine, mood that Stead set to work on his most famous article on the subject of the press: 'Government by Journalism' for the highbrow *Contemporary Review*. The essay was practically unique in not only being signed but also written largely in the first person, with the obvious implication that Stead had become a 'celebrity journalist' *avant la lettre*. He began by stating that 'Government tends ever downward', from kings to noblemen to parliaments, each one resigning power to the next as the people become 'more and more impatient of intermediaries between themselves and the exercise of power'. In the 'newspaper age', contended Stead, the logical progression was for this mantle to descend to the newspaper editor, whom he memorably dubbed as 'the uncrowned king of an educated democracy'. Just to be sure that readers were aware he was referring to himself, Stead again brought to mind the rushed passing of the Criminal Law Amendment Act, the appointment of General Gordon and the sending of armies 'hither and thither' from the editorial sanctum at Northumberland Street. Such an editor, claimed Stead, would 'have to think twice, and even thrice' before changing places with the Prime Minister, let alone 'a second or third-rate Cabinet Minister'.[186]

As was so often the case, the backlash provoked by Stead's boasting was all the more severe for the fact that his assertions were partly true; not to say worryingly far-sighted. The aged Matthew Arnold was perhaps the most famous enemy of this 'New Journalism' (as he contemptuously dubbed it), despite acknowledging the 'generous instincts' of the 'clever and able man' who had invented it. In his essay 'Up to Easter', which Arnold wrote specifically to dampen Stead's fame, he objected to the investigative component on the grounds that it relied insufficiently heavily on facts: 'It throws out assertions at a venture because it wishes them true; does not correct either them or itself, if they are false; and to get at the state of things as they truly are seems to feel no concern whatever.' In essence, he saw 'government by journalism' as akin to his other *bête noire*, democracy, as being 'feather-brained', just as rule by aristocracies was 'selfish' and that of the middle class 'narrow'.[187]

Although Arnold was scornful of Stead's vision, the inmate of Holloway actually had ideals that were almost as lofty as his own. It was not the journalist's business, protested Stead, to write 'twaddle ... about the dresses at the last Drawing-room or the fashions at Goodwood', but to lift 'the minds of men, wearied with daily toil and dulled by carking care, into a higher sphere of thought and action than the routine of the yardstick or the slavery of the ploughshare'. Pandering to elected governments no less than to public opinion was also rejected, since Stead believed it to be an editor's duty to mould them both. Well could he have told journalists of any era that 'as a profession, our ideal is deplorably low'.

When Stead was not busy writing this article, he applied himself to a massive volume about 'the last six months of my life', for which he asked the office manager, Henry Leslie, to find a publisher.[188] The outcome of these enquiries was not entirely successful, as no major firm was willing to run the risk of publication; in desperation Leslie even resorted to trying the 'crotchety gentlemen' who printed religious works, but to no avail. Though this may be regretted, Stead found a no less competent propagandist in the person of Benjamin Waugh, founder of the National Society for the Prevention of Cruelty to Children, who wrote an excessively laudatory short biography of his friend, which nourished Stead's self-image as a hero. 'His love of me and his care for me passed the love of women,' Stead later wrote. They were to each other 'as Jonathan to David'.[189]

The rest of Stead's time in jail was naturally given over to the newspaper, but it can be doubted if he actually wrote 'every leader since I have been in here', as he told Madame Novikov. Cook had certainly written the leading article on the day of the verdict, 'The Sentence – and After', in which he claimed the paper to find 'no fault whatever' in the outcome of the trial, despite testily adding that 'the judge was actuated by some vindictiveness in his sentences'. To avoid being stripped of his new privileges, Stead mollified such accusations in future and devoted nearly every leader to appear while he was in jail to the coming election, as well as his latest hobby-horse: reform of the Church of England. Yates Thompson thought the latter subject a particularly good ploy to win back their lost readers and advertisers, but Stead's primary choice for straying into this tangled thicket was that he thought it a 'good joke' to write to bishops and cardinals on notepaper proudly headed with the name of the prison in which he was incarcerated.[190]

Stead took time out of his busy prison schedule to write to Gladstone, then between his second and third terms in office, to offer 'whatever journalistic services the *PMG* can render'. But the Grand Old Man was not disposed to write to Stead at Holloway. Instead, he sent a brief note to their mutual acquaintance, Reginald Brett, stating: 'If conscience and conviction should bring the *P. M. Gazette* and myself upon the same lines at a critical moment, I would be very glad.'[191] Gladstone may have been thinking of the issue of Home Rule, upon which the coming election was likely to be decided. Stead had great sympathy for this cause, but rejected extremists at both ends of the spectrum who preferred either coercion for Ireland or total separation from Britain. Since Gladstone had associated himself with both alternatives at different stages (partly to assuage the multitude of opinion within his party), the editor was not willing to give absolute support to the Liberals at the election, contributing, at least in part, to their failure to win a working majority.

Power in the 1886 parliament was therefore held by Charles Stewart Parnell's Irish Party, which Stead hoped would force the Liberals to embrace the doctrine of Home Rule with the proviso that Irish MPs would still sit at Westminster. As this was what Gladstone was ultimately, and disastrously, bullied into proposing – partly by way of a series of ingenious 'leaks' printed in the *PMG* – it is little wonder that Gladstone now hardened his heart against his former disciple. For embracing the doctrine of Home Rule, his party was driven from office for all but three of the next twenty years. This led Gladstone to conclude that although Stead had been 'a very decent fellow indeed when he had his little paper in the North', 'London [had] turned his head'. He could not believe that after all he had done for him, Stead now proposed to call the tune. 'Clever!' he once snapped in response to a warm testimonial from Cook, '– yes as clever as the devil! A very nasty newsman to deal with is Stead.'[192]

These comments, made during the course of a weekend party at Gladstone's country seat, Hawarden Castle, towards the end of 1895, reflected more than the abysmal outcomes of the general elections of 1885 and 1886. Whatever damage Stead may have done to the Liberal party was compounded a hundredfold by the new line he took regarding the private morality of office-holders in the wake of his triumphant release from prison on 18 January. Almost immediately Stead seemed to jettison his old maxim 'liberty for vice; repression of criminality' in favour of a far less indulgent creed. This not only served as an effective path back to righteousness, it was also a cunning way for Stead to bring Yates Thompson an 'immense return'. 'We are not going Maiden Tributing [sic] any more,' he wrote apologetically to his proprietor; indeed, he was going to do 'something splendaciously [sic]' to give 'the silly world some other label to paste against my name than that of criminal convict'.[193] This surely explains why Stead, for the first time, began to show a great interest in what he had previously dismissed as the 'disgusting details' of the divorce court. This break with precedent would wreak havoc with the careers of two of the most eminent politicians of the day: Sir Charles Dilke and the leader of the Irish party, Charles Stewart Parnell.

The tragedy of the Liberal statesman Sir Charles Dilke began shortly before Stead went on trial, when a relatively unimportant Liberal MP, Donald Crawford, filed for divorce from his 23-year-old wife, Virginia. By the dubious logic of the Victorian divorce court, it took little more than the husband's declaration under oath that his wife had admitted to infidelity for a decree *nisi* to be issued, which would have made their separation absolute after six months if there were no challenges. Had Crawford (or, rather, his wife) cited her real lover, the good-looking army captain Henry Forster, as co-respondent, the matter would scarcely have caused more than a ripple of 'tabloid' sensation in papers such as Catling's *Lloyd's Weekly Newspaper* and the *News of the World*. But to implicate Dilke, one of the most eminent politicians of the time – with the added revelation that he had taught his alleged lover 'every French vice' – was calculated to create the maximum embarrassment, forcing even the notionally highbrow *PMG* to take up the story. Matters were made immeasurably worse for Dilke by the fact that Mrs Crawford held a personal spite against him: he had been her mother's lover. Perhaps because of this, as well as the gossip of another woman with an animus against the co-respondent, a Mrs Rogerson, details were known about Dilke's questionable house off the Tottenham Court Road where he had taken actual lovers, but never Virginia. These factors meant that Dilke could only defend himself from her spurious accusations by revealing details of his personal life that would have ruined his career regardless of the outcome of the trial.[194]

Stead had a strong personal interest in removing Dilke from the Liberal fold. This was partly because he saw him, like Dilke's close friend, Joseph Chamberlain, as caring more about his personal career than the welfare of the party or the country. When these ministers had tendered their resignations from the cabinet in mid-1885, scuppering Gladstone's first attempt to introduce conservative Home Rule for Ireland, Stead had accurately prophesied: 'These gentlemen will only be too glad to compel the whole of their colleagues to share their position'.[195] Chamberlain would later, as a member of the Conservative Party, become the only politician in British history to split both major political groupings.

Yet Stead engineered the innocent man's destruction with such skill that he could later speak gravely, if tendentiously, of acting entirely in the 'public interest' – a phrase not yet in common usage. As the editor of a Liberal paper he could hardly be seen to hound a man from office who many believed to be the party's greatest future leadership hope. Nor could he confess that one of the reasons why he wanted to ruin Dilke might have been to repay a personal slight he had received as the enthusiastic young editor of the *Northern Echo*. In response to a political 'catechism' that Stead had intended to send to every voter in County Durham, Dilke wrote to him with a refusal to subsidise the project as the document would most likely go 'into the wastepaper basket at once'.[196] Stead, who believed the pamphlet to have swung the result of the election, clearly enjoyed turning the tables. Now it was he who could affect blithe superiority.

The Crawford divorce case first appeared in the pages of the *PMG* on 8 August 1885, under the bold (and hitherto avoided) headline 'A Great Social Scandal'. The paper gravely intoned that efforts to 'hush the affair up' had been unsuccessful, with the obvious implication that the details must now be aired before the public. Naturally Stead's ordeal at the Old Bailey supervened at this point, but the editor arrived back from prison just in time for the preliminary divorce hearing at the beginning of February. Here the judge granted the decree *nisi* even though he concluded that there was 'no shadow of a case' against Dilke for committing adultery. This suggested to those unfamiliar with the ingenious methods of legal separation devised by the wealthy that Mrs Crawford had committed adultery with the co-respondent, but not he with her. Dilke's predicament was made considerably worse by the bad advice he took from Chamberlain and his lawyer (who foolishly referred to unspecified 'indiscretions ... [that occur] in the life of any man') that he should not submit himself to the humiliation of cross-examination.

This gave Stead the upper hand. Digging up reports of speeches that Dilke had made to his Chelsea constituents prior to the election, Stead discovered that the MP had pledged to make a 'detailed reply' to the accusations made against him. The editor concluded that Dilke's passive role at the sensational trial, and subsequent silence, indicated his guilt clearly enough. Just four days after waxing indignant about the 'appalling nature of the charges', Stead regretfully informed his readers that, as there had still been no official denial, Dilke should resign his seat immediately.[197] This was another new departure in journalism. As Stead put it, elected officials had no right to make 'indiscretions' in their private lives: if the 'charges' against Dilke were true then he was 'a worse criminal than most of the murderers who swing at Newgate'.[198] Stead's only concession was mischievous: if Dilke insisted on his innocence then he should appeal to the Queen's Proctor (an official with a quasi-judicial function) to 'sift the facts to the bottom'. Reluctantly this was the course that the politician chose. The consequence was that Mrs Crawford became the most infamous witness in the history of the divorce court, and Dilke's career was ruined forever.

The level of Stead's malevolence in these actions can be gauged by his foreknowledge that Dilke could only prove his innocence by indicting himself for his other breaches of the moral code. Stead's (unpublished) claim that he had amassed evidence against Dilke from his horde of brothel-keepers can be dismissed as completely implausible. Stead even had the cruelty to note that it was rather unfortunate that the Queen's Proctor was a well-known Conservative and so was unlikely to be sympathetic to a politician with a history of championing republicanism. Justifying his actions in later years, Stead claimed that Lady Dilke had come to him in tears, wishing that she had not tried to interfere with her husband's 'intrigues', and that 'Dilke's solicitor' – supposedly his friend and lawyer, George Lewis – had admitted Dilke's culpability. In fact, Lady Dilke had only married Sir Charles after the initial accusation had been made, and Lewis was not Dilke's solicitor, but Crawford's. The defendant was the first, though certainly not the last, politician to be ruined by a sex scandal worked up by a hostile newspaper editor.

The story has an even more unpleasant aspect. Shortly before opting for the ill-fated second trial Dilke had begged Stead to desist, agreeing to tell him 'everything' (as he had Cardinal Manning) in return for more sympathetic treatment. According to the irrepressible Loulou Harcourt, Stead listened gravely to the story of how Dilke had had an affair with Mrs Crawford's mother, Mrs Eustace Smith, but responded nonchalantly that the older woman was no more than 'a common whore' and would be of no interest to his readers. Stead much preferred the story of the innocent 'girl-bride', who described herself as having 'milkmaid' looks. Her marriage represented what he took to be one of the worst features of upper-class society: the effective 'sale' of young women to husbands old enough to be their fathers. Further to his discredit, Stead also took a personal shine to the young woman who had brazenly described the particulars of her alleged romps, including 'three-in-a-bed' sex with Dilke and his maid, Fanny Grey (which had never taken place, although Dilke did have an affair with this servant, making things very awkward for him at the trial – he had her sent away). Stead went to great pains to get Virginia to write for his paper over the course of the next few years and might have even contemplated an affair with her himself. During a later spiteful campaign to prevent Dilke returning to Parliament as the representative of the Forest of Dean, Stead hastily asked one of his many female acquaintances to return all his letters, lest they be used against him in some way.[199] Refreshingly, Stead's seemingly hypocritical standpoint was not shared by the constituents, who duly returned the former Member for Chelsea and burned effigies of the malignant editor on their village greens.

The case does much to discredit the illusion that Stead was free from the double standards that pervaded his society. At the same time as making his thundering denunciation of Dilke, Emma Stead, complaining of her husband's intolerable 'close love of women', checked herself into a clinic suffering from what would probably now be diagnosed as depression. Confiding to Madame Novikov in another letter that he asked her to destroy, Stead lamented that his wife 'attributes all her sufferings to you and Miss Friederichs [the "Prussian Governess"]'. 'She refuses any longer to be my wife unless it all ceases,' he wrote.[200] This appears to have precipitated another one of Stead and Novikov's periodic bouts of non-communication, but Stead may well have been embroiled in further intrigues, not least with an attractive young socialist called Annie Besant, whom he met at this time.[201]

Annie was the unhappy wife of an Anglican vicar who had banished her from his home and taken custody of their daughter.

As a 'woman wronged', she appealed directly to Stead's innate sympathies, but it is hard to see why he became so attached to her other than the fact that he took delight in her company. In politics as well as religion they had almost no common ground, while it can be doubted whether her early contributions to the *PMG* were particularly accomplished – a far more talented female writer, Beatrice Webb, was apparently treated, after some initial encouragement, with contempt.[202] What may have particularly interested Stead in Annie was her reputation for publishing (with her friend, the controversial MP Charles Bradlaugh) a banned pamphlet in the late 1870s entitled *The Fruits of Philosophy*. This was a candid manual for young women who wanted to enjoy regular sexual intercourse without submitting to the unwanted burden of pregnancy. As Stead was at the time denouncing his enemies for treating adultery as a mere 'hygienic necessity', their alliance seems – to use Stead's description of Annie's earlier dalliance with Bradlaugh – 'not savoury'.[203]

As in the case of Hulda Friederichs, Stead attempted to channel his passion for his muse into a worthy cause: in this case the plight of the unemployed, whose numbers had increased substantially during the economic downturn of the mid-1880s. But it appears that Cook was the true author of this campaign, and that Stead only took it up when Annie congratulated him for various articles that had appeared in the *PMG* while he was on a short break with his wife at Keswick. Upon his return to the office, Stead threw himself into the new sensation with unchastened zeal. At the suggestion of William Morris, he and Annie founded a 'Law and Liberty League' to encourage unemployed men to take to the streets during several tense weeks which culminated in a demonstration at Trafalgar Square on 13 November 1887, known at the time as 'Bloody Sunday'. Though this event was not as gory as its name would suggest, Bernard Shaw and H. M. Hyndman later blamed Stead for recklessly encouraging a confrontation with the police in which one man was accidently trampled to death by a horse and Robert Cunninghame Graham MP had his head cut open by a baton.[204] True or not, Annie was delighted with the momentum that the editor had given to her cause and did not mind that Stead (on Yates Thompson's orders) had not actually been present on the fateful march. Her letters to him after this time invariably begin 'My Dear Sir Galahad', which suggests extreme familiarity almost as much as her dark warning that 'I have not worked with any man in close intimacy who has not fallen in love with me'.

In the wake of these exchanges, Annie and Stead launched a half-penny weekly called *The Link*, which lasted until their relationship petered out around the end of 1888. This publication was set up on the same principles as the newspaper that Stead had dreamed of in another article for the *Contemporary Review*; this time under the no less immodest title of 'The Future of Journalism'. Editorial material was to come directly from a large network of 'earnest men and women', organised into 'Vigilance' or 'Ironside Circles', who were to inquire into wrongdoing by 'police, landlords and ordinary citizens' much in the manner of modern investigative journalists. It was a farsighted and ambitious plan, but Annie probably shared the reservations of her old friend Charles Bradlaugh, who feared that the antidemocratic structure of the 'Circles' would expose innocent people to surveillance, blackmail and conspiracy. Nevertheless, the feelings that Annie and Stead clearly had for one another provided the glue that was necessary for the project to continue with only minor hiccups, such as when Annie – perhaps more playfully than tactlessly – addressed Stead as 'My Dear Head Centre', an unfor-tunate reference to the terrorist cells of the Fenian Brotherhood.

The affair ended when Stead regained his Puritanical self-control and took account of the effect that his escapades were having on his wife's health. This came as something of a shock for Annie, since she had clearly been encouraged by Stead's flirtatious manner and mystical talk of their 'political and spiritual marriage'. When he found her crying in his office one afternoon she was prompted to send him a note explaining that 'when a woman is very tired and very lonely and cares much for anyone she is apt to be a baby'. She may have wanted their relationship to be more than one of political alliance or, perhaps, sexual gratification. When Annie frankly told

Stead that she was in love with him, she was apparently rebuffed. But her subsequent reaction sheds much light on the kind of relationships that Stead nurtured with the attractive young women with whom he claimed to work as an equal: 'I have stupidly let myself slip into allowing you to be different from anyone else to me,' she wrote, 'and so to monopolize me that all the rest of my friends have become more or less shadows. That is what hurts me.'

Such incidents suggest that there was a direct connection between Stead's personal life and his frenzied 'purity' crusading. Yet T. P. O'Connor was almost certainly going too far when he warned that if Stead 'had been allowed to go on, he might have established something like a domestic espionage over the homes and habits of the men and women who sinned against his code'.[205] Two of his closest political allies, Reginald Brett and the leader of the Whigs, Lord Hartington, were well-known philanderers, the former also being a self-confessed pederast. Stead seemed to care nothing for these 'peccadilloes', not simply because they were the acts of friends and of relatively minor significance, but because they were never publicly unmasked. Despite his unattractive streak of self-righteousness and hypocrisy, Stead rarely led campaigns designed to expose what he viewed as personal immorality; it was only when sordid details were already out in the open – and denied – that he called for the destruction of 'sinners'. This is what put him in an awkward position in the case of Charles Stewart Parnell, whose illustrious career he was to shatter soon after the first phase of his destruction of Sir Charles Dilke was coming to its end.

For over a decade Parnell had been the hero of his nation; the one man who could unite Protestant and Catholic behind the cause of Home Rule, which he turned from being an extremist fixation to a realistic constitutional programme. There were, however, two troubling issues that his supporters had to accept as the price of his brilliance. The first was that in the early 1880s he had been associated with the radical Land League, whose most extremist fringe, the Invincibles, had murdered two English officials in Phoenix Park, Dublin. The second concern was that he was known to be having an affair with Katherine O'Shea, the wife of a political nonentity whom Parnell had recently gifted a safe parliamentary seat, much to the disgust of his senior followers.

Stead knew of these rumours, but was not sufficiently within the privileged Liberal sphere to accurately gauge their precise truthfulness. Nevertheless, when a shady journalist called Edward Caulfield Houston tried to sell him letters purporting to link Parnell with the Phoenix Park murders, he showed a level of discretion that would have been untypical were they said to be from, for example, Sir Charles Dilke to Virginia Crawford. Apparently believing them to be genuine, Stead refused to buy them and immediately set to work on a defence of Parnell that was so blunt and uncritical as to undermine his later claim of impartiality. His response to their publication in *The Times* on 18 April 1887, under the notorious headline 'Parnellism and Crime', was not that all the facts should be 'sifted to the bottom', as in the case of Dilke, but that the newspaper's editor, George Buckle, should be 'bundled off incontinently to the Clock Tower' – an arbitrary punishment for those who insult members of the House of Commons.

No such defence was offered to the statesman whose career he had so recently destroyed. This was despite the fact that Parnell was accused not merely of adultery, like Dilke, but of condoning cold-blooded murder. In Stead's warped moral perspective the former was clearly judged to be the graver offence. This led him to accept Parnell's unsworn denial as uncritically as Gladstone's solemn proclamation that '[t]he burden of proof lies on those who make the charge ... [otherwise] they are wanton calumniators and should be shunned as pests to society'. Stead made no call for Parnell to sue for libel and clearly shared the view of another prominent supporter that '[h]is emphatic denial of the authorship of the letter was as good as if he had made it on his oath'. Legal action was only taken a year later, by Parnell's friend Frank O'Donnell, but the trial was inconclusive as the plaintiff – again much like Dilke – refused to be cross-examined, fearing that matters immaterial to the case would be delved into. When this precipitated a belated official inquiry,

Stead did everything he could to avoid being called as a witness and privately worried that the Irish cause would be damaged irrevocably by the Special Commission's disclosures. In the end it was not and Stead celebrated the 'not guilty' verdict by lauding his hero as a man 'who has fought the good fight, who has conquered his foes, and awaits with tranquillity the laurels of victory'.[206]

Sadly, Parnell's enemies would not let their man go. Just days after the inquiry ended, his fate became even more sinisterly linked to that of Dilke when Captain O'Shea filed for divorce citing the Irish leader as co-respondent. It was as though the sword of Damocles had finally fallen, yet no plan had been devised as to what was to be done. While the Unionist press revelled in scandal, Stead and his Liberal confreres committed little in print either for or against their champion. Those who knew the facts with certainty, such as the well-connected editor of *Truth*, Henry Labouchere, thought it best to go on as if nothing had happened; but Stead was clearly still relatively naive about the nature of the Parnell–O'Shea connection. Although he had, in May 1886, placed a subtle notice in his paper entitled 'Mr Parnell's Suburban Retreat', which mentioned the house in Eltham where the affair was carried out, Stead was clearly in two minds about the whole matter, as was revealed by his subsequent action.

Stead's first suspicion appears to have been that Parnell was, indeed, 'guilty'; but, as yet, he had no intention of letting his inscrutable principles end another promising career. Writing to William Walsh, the Archbishop of Dublin, in January 1890, Stead suggested that the 'next best thing' to proving Parnell's innocence was for him to 'cease conjugal relations with Mrs O'Shea, say *peccavi* [I have sinned] and publicly confess his sin'. Despite forgetting that he was writing to a Catholic primate, Stead correctly surmised that Mrs O'Shea's divorce and subsequent marriage to her lover would do little to discredit Parnell's reputation in Ireland – although he contradicted himself a few days later by confidently telling Brett that the English would be the most tolerant subjects of the Queen. Stead's comment to Brett may have been based on the fact that he had no intention of 'going for' Parnell as he had Dilke, thus sparing him a similar fate. If so, Stead grossly overrated his powers to topple or prop up statesmen who sullied his professed ideals.[207]

What turned Stead suddenly and harshly against Parnell was the result of a perfectly innocent misunderstanding. After being confronted by one of his disgruntled allies, a young MP called Tim Healy, the Irish leader had promised that he had done nothing for which Captain O'Shea could not continue to treat him 'as a gentleman'; by which he meant (as was true) that the affair had gone on with her husband's knowledge and consent. Through his friend Michael Davitt, who occasionally wrote in the *PMG*, Stead was reassured that Parnell had not had any improper relations with Mrs O'Shea, which he apparently believed. Just one month after his man-of-the-world letter to Archbishop Walsh, he resumed their correspondence by noting that he was now 'quite certain that he [Parnell] is going to come off with flying colours and that the whole thing is to break down'. In a 'Character Sketch' of the Irish leader, published just as the crisis was reaching its climax, Stead indulgently compared Parnell to the kind of schoolboy who is always accused of evil because he is so perfect, and scarcely mentioned the looming divorce trial of the O'Sheas.

Although Parnell had never actually dared enter into friendship with Stead, the editor felt personally betrayed when the obvious fact of his culpability was revealed at the divorce court the following November. Gladstone suddenly found himself overwhelmed by a torrent of letters from the outraged editor, who was appalled by Gladstone's apparent willingness to stand by their old ally. With revealing honesty, Stead stated that Parnell's relationship with Mrs O'Shea was to him no more 'venial a fault as taking an extra glass of brandy'. What disgusted him was that *he* had been duped by this 'thorough-paced dissembler' into believing that he had been falsely accused. More to the point, Stead practically admitted his jealousy: Parnell, he said, was

> like a man who gets his butcher to secretly sell him sausages in a world where it is forbidden to eat meat on a Friday.

Gladstone appears not to have honoured this communication with a response. At length, when it became clear that Parnell was unlikely to resign as Irish leader, Stead grandly brought their intermittent friendship to an irrecoverable close by declaring that he would now 'most unwillingly' go on the warpath.[208]

Stead spoke on behalf of what *The Times* half-jestingly called 'the Nonconformist conscience': a force that would rapidly destroy the promising links that had developed between the Liberal and Irish parties. But he did not go nearly so far as his old acquaintance Hugh Price Hughes, who thundered in the columns of his *Methodist Times* that the Irish were 'an obscene race utterly unfit for anything except a military despotism'.[209] It is perhaps revealing of the kind of power that Stead believed himself to wield that he simply wrote to Gladstone, much as Cromwell might have to Charles I: 'I know my Nonconformists well, and no power on earth will induce them to follow that man to the poll, or you either, if you are arm-in-arm with him.'[210]

Yet in public it was always Katherine O'Shea whom Stead held personally accountable for the whole regrettable business. Almost in total contradiction to his hitherto worshipful attitude towards womankind, Stead compared her to White Fell, the rapacious female werewolf invented by the catchpenny novelist Clemence Houseman. In the aftermath of the tragedy Stead rhapsodised:

> Tall she was, and very fair, graceful as Diana, and radiant with the beauty of strength; but in her eye there shone at times an awful light, and those whom she lured to kiss her by the hearthstone she subsequently devoured in the field.[211]

Like so many who place the female of the species on a pedestal, Stead was liable to become unpleasant when he realised that the robe of irreproachable innocence and purity was not always donned willingly, or with merit.

CHAPTER 9

LAST YEARS AT
NORTHUMBERLAND STREET, 1886–89

I shall either crown an edifice or come a final cropper.
W. T. S. to E. T. Cook (April 1888)

In the years after his triumphant release from prison, Stead's high spirits gradually waned as he became ever more obsessed with the peccadilloes of statesmen and the pursuit of extra-marital happiness. In the course of this descent, many of his most influential friends began to desert him, particularly when they realised, as Morley told Chamberlain at the height of the Dilke scandal, that he could be controlled no more than the 'north-east wind'.[212] Such pragmatic considerations were echoed even by the editor's most loyal supporters, who felt him to be substituting his distinctive brand of New Journalism for pettiness and insularity. Bramwell Booth expressed this view tactfully when he regretted that his friend might have 'become a great power in the nation on the side of important reforms' had he not 'preferred to plough a lonely furrow'.[213]

The situation was particularly bleak for Stead at the office, where the hitherto devoted staff and loyal proprietor felt increasingly alienated from their unpredictable helmsman. The improvement in revenue that Stead had promised to Yates Thompson had not materialised in spite of his recent exploits. Matters were made worse by the launch of a new evening rival, the *Star*, in 1888, by T. P. O'Connor and his rising protégé, Henry Massingham, which rapidly set journalism in a new direction by influencing government via a mass readership rather than by directly appealing to ministers. Though Stead's attempts to stem this tide were not wholly ineffective – including the introduction of competitions, campaigns against alleged miscarriages of justice, innovative cartoons and overseas reporting – he was no longer in harmony with the spirit of the age. His latent conservatism prevented him from catching the wave of Fabian socialism that would make the press a vigorous and exciting force for the remainder of his life and well beyond.

Part of the problem was rooted in Stead's erratic manner of finding new staff writers. Unlike his more successful competitors, he gifted jobs mainly to those whom he liked, or thought most needy, rather than the most able. This was partly due to his (not unjustified) belief that the 'best qualified' applicants – typically Oxbridge men who saw journalism as an easy route into politics – did not value the work sufficiently for its own sake, nor would they be likely to look up to him as an editor. Never was this more clearly demonstrated than when a good-looking and intelligent young graduate 'who thought he wrote verses' turned up at the office in search of a job one day in the summer of 1887.

The visitor, Edmund Garrett, would almost certainly have become a famous literary figure had he not devoted the best years of his life to journalism and died at the relatively early age of forty-two. He came fresh from his final examinations at Cambridge where he had been President of the Union and an accomplished classicist. But with impoverished parents and several unmarried sisters to maintain, he had no prospect of embarking on the carefree existence of the majority of his peers. In such circumstances, he might have felt entitled to court favour with the famous editor by mentioning that he was the nephew of the noted women's rights activist, Millicent Fawcett, who had helped Stead in the wake of his conviction. But Garrett appears not to have stressed this propitious connection. As a result, the editor barely disguised his unwillingness to interview the caller, whom he thought looked too pale and bookish to be a journalist. 'I had the good fortune never to be at a university,' he said unconvincingly, as he threw his feet onto the mantelpiece with a studied regal air.[214]

When Garrett realised that Stead had little interest besides patronising him, he cleverly took command of the situation by quizzing the editor on his journalistic creed. Upon his return to Cambridge later that evening, Garrett set to work on a long article entitled 'An Interview with the Editor of the *Pall Mall Gazette*', which he sent to Stead the following morning. This amusing and cunning ploy impressed Stead far more than Garrett had managed to in person. Of all its most telling passages, none was a truer reflection of Stead than: 'I take my impressions on the moment; the logical defence is rather an afterthought.' It explained why he had run into difficulties with the parents of Eliza Armstrong as much as why he had initially been cool with his brainy young interlocutor, whom Alfred Milner instantly hailed as 'the new Stead ... with all his virtues and none of his faults'.

Almost every young male writer to call on Stead in this fashion found him similarly prejudiced. Even his remarkably able sub-editor and future biographer, James Robertson Scott, recalled Stead being irritable when he showed up with an impressive article – highly flattering of Stead – for *Sell's Press Dictionary* some time in 1888. For the entire time that his guest was talking, the editor 'stalked about [his office] ... beating his legs with a long-handled clothes-brush', apparently fully consumed with removing some stain from his typically worn-out trousers.[215]

Prospects were much brighter for the emerging class of female journalists, to whom Stead became a profligate patron. One of these young ladies, the 'plump' but pretty Marie Belloc, was introduced to him by Cardinal Manning just when his relationships with Hulda Friederichs and Annie Besant appear to have been coming to their unhappy conclusions. Despite Marie having almost no journalistic experience, Stead showered her with commissions, including a trip to Paris to assist in the writing of an 'Extra' at the unprecedentedly high salary of £10 per week – rather more than Robertson Scott's meagre 6*d.* per hour back at the office.[216] Proof of the unprofessional nature of their relationship is indicated by the complaint of Stead's assistant, the pious and long-suffering Edwin Stout, who objected to the pair kissing in the office – an almost unimaginable liberty by the moral standards of the 1880s.

In later years Stout would muse in a private letter to Robertson Scott: 'I fancy [Stead] was a bit afraid of me, I knew so much. This kind of thing [affairs?] is calculated to knock one's heroes off their pedestals.'[217]

But Marie was not entirely selfish with her influence: she successfully persuaded the editor to give some work to her feckless older brother, the future poet and author Hilaire, who was then making his first forays into the field of letters. Reluctantly Stead took him on as a glorified errand boy. A typical sample of the young man's fairly extensive correspondence with Stead reads: 'I have been round the bicycle shops in Holborn ... I should advise you to choose between Messrs. "St. George" and "Manchester".' Such was Stead's inability to recognise uncommon potential that Belloc hardly ever referred to the two years he spent under the famous editor's wing. He once commented dryly to a friend, in reference to Stead, that he simply 'did not understand him'.[218]

Similar stories are numerous, as when the future Sir Robert Donald (one of the most esteemed journalists of the early twentieth century) was set to work stuffing envelopes in 'a vacant building a few doors down from the office', manned principally by 'beery out of work clerks'. Donald appears not to have forgotten the slight, since he was later at the forefront of the younger generation of writers who cruelly destroyed what remained of Stead's reputation as a journalist. Even the great political caricaturist Francis Carruthers Gould was barely recognised by Stead as one of the newspaper's most valuable assets when he began submitting his work in 1887. It was only under the editorship of Stead's successor, Edward Cook, that Gould became a permanent member of staff, beginning a relationship with the newspaper (and its successor title) that would see it through lean years.[219]

Yet Stead still had a remarkable ability to hunt down good copy from obscure places. The 'Maiden Tribute' articles – bold, brave and reckless though they were – represented this at the editor's best. But Stead had promised Yates Thompson no more cries from the gutter in the wake of his release from prison, and could offer no help to the many 'fallen women' who called at the office in the wake of his explosive campaign. In future he would fight the cause of the 'disinherited of the world' principally on the condition that they were at least fringe members of the influential group of upper-middle-class readers to whom the *PMG* was addressed. Thus began the modern tabloid campaign: an institution which thrives on the tragic misfortunes of the well-to-do.

The woman for whom Stead rendered this valuable service was Mildred Langworthy, the duped wife of a Manchester cotton millionaire. Young, beautiful, intelligent, but lacking friends, few visitors to Northumberland Street could have wafted more easily into the editorial sanctum. She brought with her a story of lust and deception that excited Stead to such an extent he spiked nearly every news story for over two weeks, during which time he published her 'strange true story of today' in the form of a gripping novelette spanning seventy-five richly embellished chapters. It was another innovation: the respectable *Times* and *Manchester Guardian* would not even accept advertisements concerning private injustices, let alone turn them into thrilling penny romances.

Mildred claimed to have met her husband, Edward Martin Langworthy, in the conservatory of a fashionable Parisian hotel, where she had been charmed by his smooth talk and courteous manner. Though she and her chaperone had politely declined to visit his motor yacht, the *Meteor*, the young pair were clearly interested in one another, since Mildred returned to Paris some months later to see him again. Their swift courtship improbably ended when Langworthy took her back to London to see Gilbert and Sullivan's *Patience*, after which he immediately proposed. By the editor's devious Puritanical logic, this was the beginning of her perdition: 'After going to the theatre it was but a step to visiting the yacht.'[220] Next could only come the inevitable 'outrage'.

This next step suitably took place back on the Continent, where Langworthy declared one afternoon that they should get married in a small Catholic church, despite the fact that neither of them belonged to that faith. Taken somewhat off guard, Mildred consented and went through an obscure ritual, without witnesses, which she immediately realised to be bogus. Rather than jettisoning the man for attempting a very serious crime, she asked if they could get married a second time, to which he apparently consented – provided it was in Antwerp, where he arranged for an equally unlawful marriage ceremony to be conducted by an American pastor. This completed, she acquiesced in his sexual advances, to which Stead alluded with revealing censoriousness: 'Whatever may be thought of the ethics of the sexual relationship,' he wrote,

> there is one point that even the most cynical debauchee admits to be indefensible. To ruin a young life, to betray maiden innocence, to triumph in the destruction of a woman's honour – that according to the ethics of the man of the world is but a venial offence. But when to seduction there is added hypocrisy, when the voluptuary lulls the conscience of his victim to sleep by the sound of prayers and holy words, and when the cruellest wrong which one human being can do to another is accomplished by fraud, cloaked beneath a form of religion, that is a crime for which even in the easy-going ethics of society there is neither palliation nor excuse.[221]

Not long after writing these considered lines, Stead entered into a long correspondence with the libertarian zoologist, Professor Ray Lankester, who commended Stead on his identification of duplicity as the only immoral aspect of consensual sex between adults. Without allowing men to sleep with women as equal partners, regardless of matrimony, contended Lankester, they 'will take it just the same – from maid-servants, from ladies of position and from the few skulking syphilised whores...'.[222] This was the kind of language that would have appalled the editor's public persona, yet Stead clearly enjoyed their exchanges and asked Lankester for a sanitised article on the subject, which duly appeared under the pseudonym 'Philanthrope'. In this piece the scientist could well have had the editor in mind when he defended 'those somewhat irregular persons who contemplate the enjoyment of life without the aid of the marriage register'. In reply Stead was almost damningly candid, printing: 'Not until sexual intercourse is absolutely severed from parentage can that difficulty be overcome.'[223] It is curious that at this point in time he was on the brink of meeting Mrs Besant, an expert on the subject.

Yet Stead's reservations about the danger of consummating his extra-marital relationships were nevertheless real, and it must have been partly due to envy that he went after Langworthy with such venom. Certainly his latest target had behaved shamefully, but on many points Stead seems to have overplayed his hand. This is clear from the outset of his epic tale, when Langworthy is introduced torturing kittens in the garden of the Lisbon hotel where he took his wife for their supposed honeymoon. His method was so cruel and calculating that it is hard to reconcile with the elegant man that Mildred evidently fell for in Paris, let alone someone who was known to encourage poor British migrants to settle on his vast estates in Argentina.

In Stead's account, Langworthy was said to have lured his feline victims with caresses and kind words before dropping a red-hot coal on their backs. He would then 'chuckle with glee at the struggles of the helpless creature[s]' as they slowly drowned in the nearby well into which they had been chased.[224] For readers unaware of his vivid allegory, Stead emphasised that Mildred was soon to share a similar fate; but they would have to buy the paper the next day to find out more – and so on until the bloated series closed some three weeks later.

The completed story, which was republished as Stead's bestselling 'Extra' of all, deserves recognition as the *locus classicus* of the maltreated Victorian woman. Nonchalantly told that her child would be illegitimate, Mildred is shut up in her cabin for two days with nothing to eat except 'Leibig's [meat] extract in Angostura bitters' and 'morphia ... dosed with mercury' – presumably to increase the chances of a miscarriage.[225] Later they sail to Buenos Aires, but upon arrival she is not permitted to land. Instead she is given £50 and a box of cloth with which to swaddle her unborn child, before being rowed over to the mail-steamer for England. Here she beds down like a tramp in 'a squalid doghole of a cabin' attended only by a young cousin who is sure she will die. She then learns that she will be able to draw £240 a year from a bank in Frankfurt-am-Main on the condition that she lives on the Continent and reverts to her maiden name. When these conditions are refused, she spends four years trying to win alimony through the courts in London but comes into difficulty, not least because Langworthy remains in Argentina. Stead recounts all of these happenings with his characteristic exaggeration, the nature of which – as well as his utter credulity of Mildred's version of events – can be deduced from the fact that at one point she learns her husband has returned to London in a dream.[226]

Though 'the Langworthy marriage' was doubtless an unhappy one, many details appear to have been less sinister than Stead supposed. All the evidence suggests that it was only because of a serious row or disclosure on board the *Meteor* that they did not wish to remain together. There was also the issue of Langworthy's mother, who was worried that her son had made a *misalliance* and made threatening noises about withholding a substantial portion of his inheritance. In any case, it appears that Mildred gave as good as she got. The image of the meek virgin 'chained helplessly to the rock to be devoured at the leisure of some hideous monster' simply does not ring true.[227] Closer to the mark was probably the editor of *Truth*, Henry Labouchere, who saw the affair as a regrettable case of 'diamond cut diamond'.[228]

Stead's obvious partiality to Mildred may be attributed to more than charitable sympathy. Described as 'brave and beautiful', she appears throughout the narrative as his embodiment of female perfection, even more so than the child 'Lily' of the 'Maiden Tribute' articles.[229] His devotion to her, if not outright love, is perhaps acknowledged by her casual demand made soon after they met for '£75 or £100 by return [post]', which was apparently forthcoming.[230] If so, she was neither the first nor the last beautiful woman to exploit the editor's weaknesses. After his death there were stories of a mysterious woman who falsely claimed to own extensive estates in Russia wringing a total of £15,000 from his all-too-willing hands.[231] There were also traces of bills for fur coats and expensive dresses from tradesmen 'informed ... that you may be in a position to forward a cheque for the [stated] amount'.[232] Evidently his wife discovered some of these skeletons and sensibly demanded that he hand over £1,000 of his improved salary of £1,200 at the start of every year. As Edwin Stout caustically observed in retirement: 'As for Mrs Stead, there is this to be said about her. She probably thought that if she did not get more money it would go to other women. I don't blame her.'[233]

With these facts in view, it is hard not to feel that Edward Langworthy and his solicitors, Bircham and Co., were somewhat unfairly treated by the newspaper. In a matter of days their private matter had become part of what Stead spectacularly called 'Satan's invisible world ... unveiled by those quick, piercing eyes, which see everything, from the secret intrigue of the palace to the obscene orgies of our pothouse Sodoms'.[234] Such language is not the kind to inspire confidence in the impartial reader, but few devices could have more effectively provoked universal outrage in the Victorian era. Even in distant Buenos Aires, where the articles were translated into Spanish and serialised in *La Nacion*, Langworthy was reviled as one of the most evil persons ever to have lived. On a visit to the city he was hissed off the platform at Santa Fé railway station by an indignant mob. In later years, Stead mused that this image 'abides with me as one of those permanent consolations with which a man can comfort himself in the days when he is depressed and disheartened'.[235]

Motivated by schadenfreude or not, Stead succeeded in winning Mrs Langworthy her alimony, which was certainly her due. This entailed a vast windfall of £20,000 plus £1,500 costs, which dwarfed the considerable sum that Stead had wrung from his readers with characteristic forcefulness: 'These funds the people of Great Britain and Ireland can provide – and will.'[236] Yet, as might have been expected, Mildred's remaining years were not destined to be happy. Her husband's life had been completely ruined, probably vindictively, and it was inevitable that he would have his revenge somehow. Years later he invited his ex-wife to dinner in Paris, only to murder her in their hotel room before taking his own life. Whether this can be taken to prove or disprove the veracity of the original case against him is moot, but Stead had certainly played a considerable part in precipitating the tragedy. The fact that he did not comment publicly on the matter when it was reported in the press suggests that he realised he might have gone too far after all.

Another famous example of Stead's 'Justice by Journalism' (as the disapproving *Saturday Review* called it, though not to Stead's displeasure) was the case of Israel Lipski, a 22-year-old immigrant Polish Jew accused of raping and murdering the wife of a neighbour in London's East End. As an editor who had only recently written of '[h]ordes of Jewish paupers' descending on London from 'their Polish breeding grounds ... greatly lower[ing] the standard of living, as well as the general moral tone', it is extremely surprising that Stead came out strongly in favour of the defendant.[237] It may have been because he saw it as a means of causing more difficulties for old enemies such as Henry Matthews (now Home Secretary), and Harry Poland, who was involved in Lipski's prosecution at the Old Bailey as well as Stead's own. There was also the interesting coincidence that the judge, James Fitzjames Stephen (an uncle of Virginia Woolf), had submitted an atheistic article to Morley which Stead had threatened to resign over soon after his arrival in London. But it is more probable that his defence of Lipski was principally a means of attacking the Conservative government as a whole, whose Irish policy continued to be a cause of resentment.

If this was the case, Stead chose a very unpromising pretext over which to launch his anti-Tory crusade. The accused had been found cowering under the bed of his victim, Miriam Angel, in a room locked from the inside. Angel was said to have had 'her chemise rolled up to her breasts' and had been killed by nitric acid which Lipski had bought from a local chemist the previous day. When the case first appeared in the *PMG* in June 1887, no foul play in the proceedings was suspected; but by the time the Langworthy saga had drawn to a close in August, the editor became more receptive to the entreaties of Lipski's barrister, John Hayward, who was working pro bono for Lipski's solicitors. It cannot have been a coincidence that Lipski's execution was due to occur at the same time the government was trying to force a controversial Crimes Bill through Parliament, much to the disgust of Stead and his Home Rule allies. As a lifelong supporter of the death penalty, Stead's cry of 'judicial murder' can only be explained as an opportunistic means of bringing about the demise of an unpopular Home Secretary, which in turn might have precipitated the collapse of the Salisbury administration.

Hayward came to see Stead on the morning of Friday 12 August, with a story of a meeting that had taken place between himself, Mr Justice Stephen and Harry Poland at the Old Bailey. It was alleged that the judge had expressed remorse about the jury's 'guilty' verdict, but Hayward begged Stead not to make any statements that could be traced back to him. Later that day, the editor ran a small notice speculating on the possibility of Lipski's innocence. Hayward was delighted when Matthews was subsequently grilled on the subject in the House of Commons, but sent Stead a note asking him not to allude to their private conversation any further. A shrewd editor might have guessed from this request that the nature of the judge's remarks had been greatly exaggerated, if not invented. As it happened, Stephen had written to his wife on the day of sentencing to emphasise that 'there was morally no doubt about it. It was exactly the story of David and Bathsheba, except that poor Mrs Angel was virtuous, and Lipski brutally murdered her when she disappointed him.' Any 'doubts' he subsequently had evaporated as soon as he read Stead's final edition splash: 'Hanging an Innocent Man – Conversion of Mr Justice Stephen'.

This gave an allegedly verbatim account of the conversation that had taken place at the Old Bailey, in which Stephen was reported to have said: 'I cannot tell you what I think. But I can tell you this, that if I were not I, I should heartily wish you success.' This would

be a very uncharacteristic turn of phrase for an eminent judge, especially one who had authored the definitive *History of the Criminal
Law of England*, a work which emphasised the independence of
the judiciary. Yet Stephen was saved from any possible embarrassment by a characteristic example of Steadean embellishment.
Upon leaving the judge's office, Hayward had apparently been told
by the senior clerk that '[t]he governor is terribly worried about
it. I've never known him so bothered about a case all the forty years
I've been with him.' As the enraged Stephen fumed in *The Times*
the morning after Stead's damning article, there was no chance that
his clerk would have referred to him as 'the governor', nor had he
been in his service for forty years. To his wife Stephen could be even
more explicit: he had been played false by 'the vile Stead'. 'Did you
notice,' he continued, 'the liar said, "in the forty years I have been
with him and on". Why, in 1847 I had not gone up to Cambridge,
and Dyke [the clerk] cannot have been seven years old.'

As ever, such details were immaterial to Stead when he had a
'higher end' in view. But it is noticeable that whereas he defended
women by reference to their good characters, such as Mildred
Langworthy and similar 'women wronged', including a Miss Cass
and, a few years later, the famous Mrs Maybrick, he had virtually nothing to say in favour of Lipski. Practically the only reason
he could think of as to why he would not have raped Mrs Angel
was that he was due to be married in a few weeks, which perhaps
reveals more about Stead's conception of matrimony than anything
else. Evidence that his campaign was primarily a ploy to destabi-
lise the precarious balance in the Tory Cabinet can be detected
in his mischievous public advice to Lord Salisbury that '[t]he
Prime Minister must know by this stage that he cannot trust the
judgment of the Home Secretary'. When Lipski later confessed
to the murder, not long after Stead had won him a week's reprieve,
the editor could only bluster beneath the ridiculous headline 'All's
Well that Ends Well' that it was 'the solitary success of a ministerial
career now fast coming to a close'.[238]

The case did more to damage Stead's reputation as a journalist than any event since his conviction. Almost every newspaper in the land echoed the Conservative *Evening News*, which crowed: 'He has during the last few years done more to degrade the Press than any man living; but in his efforts over the Lipski case, he has surely touched low-water mark.' Though it is ironic that this newspaper had formerly been edited by the infamous philanderer and blackmailer Frank Harris, who pioneered headlines such as 'Extraordinary Charge Against a Clergyman' and 'Gross Outrage on a Female', the judgement regarding 'low-water mark' was probably fair. As Stead confided to Madame Novikov (who was always attempting – usually unsuccessfully – to convert him to her Slavic prejudices):

> Lipski!!!! Alas could any human being not a Pole and also a Jew have played the *PMG* so scandalous a trick. It was a bad fall. The Respite brought me immense fame. The Confession dashed me to the ground again. And the baying of the hounds at my heels is something strange. How I am hated![239]

Stead also indicated that the debacle had put even greater strain on his relationship with his wife, writing: 'it may be that I may have to live as a hermit cut off from even contact with a woman's hand'. Something dramatic would have to be attempted or else, as he told Cook, both his career and his marriage were destined to 'come a final cropper'.[240]

✧

Stead's plan was to free himself from the strictures placed on him at the office, both by Yates Thompson and his staff, who found his latest brand of sensationalist journalism even more reprehensible than the last. A breaking point apparently arrived when Stead devoted nearly two weeks to exposing a Tory MP, Francis Hughes-Hallett, who had allegedly seduced his wife's daughter by a prior marriage. Aside from the fact that Stead had muddled the facts somewhat – the MP had actually impregnated the stepdaughter of his sister-in-law – loyal readers became exasperated with such petty crusades. Even Robert Louis Stevenson, who had apparently revelled in the 'Maiden Tribute' articles, grew sick of the *PMG* and its editor at this time. Writing to his friend William Archer in mid-October, Stevenson complained that the 'dirty dog' was up to his old tricks, and would probably continue for an interminable duration. 'He's an honest hypocrite' he concluded, '... one of the most interesting people of the time.' But Stead had become an oddity, obsessed with 'crusades' and increasingly shaky on the political subjects that interested the majority of his readers.[241]

After a few more awkward months, Stead announced at the end of April 1888 that he was going to leave Cook in sole command of the paper while he toured Europe as an exalted 'Special Commissioner'. The public declaration of this, which appeared in an interview in the *Star* (presumably because Yates Thompson disapproved of such naked self-promotion) invited universal derision. Even the man sent to conduct the interview barely disguised the comical nature of the enterprise. He arrived 'just as Mr Stead was hurtling divers goods and chattels into his portmanteau and parting instructions to his staff', expressly mentioning a strange sealskin hat – a gift from Madame Novikov – that would soon become a cause of considerable embarrassment.

Asked to clarify the particulars of his trip, Stead vaguely responded that he would be going 'wherever Providence and the interests of journalism carry me. My tour may last two weeks or eight.' But it was common knowledge that the real purpose of his voyage was to journey to Russia in order to meet his political hero, Tsar Alexander III: a sovereign known to contemporaries and posterity alike as a bovine reactionary who weakly undermined his father's reformist leanings. That this was well known is clear from an unsigned poem in the same newspaper by Bernard Shaw entitled 'A Ballad of Northumberland-Street', in which Stead was mocked as 'the Pope of Pall Mall'. After making some barbed references to Madame Novikov, Shaw lampooned: 'Oh, mighty Tsar, no Pope am I / (Though I have often thought / The berth would just have suited me; / So if I ain't I ought).'[242]

The Irishman and his friends had good reason to laugh. Arriving in Paris on the first day of his expedition, Stead realised that his international credentials were not as impressive as he had supposed. Unable to contact government ministers directly, he was reduced to seeking out an attractive young journalist named Emily Crawford, whom he had been maintaining on an inflated salary much in the manner of Marie Belloc. He was announced by her maid at 7am as an Englishman of '*un type assez original*'; but the slumbering reporter recognised the name that was scrawled on a piece of paper and had him ushered in. Shorn of his accustomed position of power, Stead admitted the real reason of his visit: Yates Thompson was going to 'chuck' him unless he could prove himself to be a competent political journalist, thus getting the proprietor back 'at my feet'. Sympathetically, Emily agreed to help, but only on the condition that Stead ceased 'the praises he bestowed on my unworthy self' – almost certainly a reference to her visitor's amorous overtures. After mumbling a few words in agreement, Stead sulked on a bench on the Champs-Élysées while she rushed around various government departments organising interviews, some of which came to pass, in spite of the French ambassador in London cabling that the 'Special Commissioner' was 'dangerously indiscreet, and feared [even] by his friends'.[243]

What followed resulted in a lifelong animus against the editor, but it is likely that Emily's real grievances were personal and therefore omitted from the poisonous 'obituary' that she published just a few weeks after Stead's tragic death. In this article, she mauled her erstwhile friend for being inappropriately attired for his meeting with Prime Minister Charles Floquet, which she had personally arranged. As she recalls,

The appearance of Mr Stead appalled me. He forgot to take off a worn-out sealskin cap. His yellowish-brown tweed suit, ill-cut, ill-fitting and untidy, shocked in a room remarkable for its harmonious

elegance and eighteenth-century tone and lightness of colour...
The cap gave the wearer the air of a dog-stealer. A propitiatory
smile completely bared two rows of peculiarly set teeth. With these
same eyes, so beautifully blue when he was airing his [spiritualist]
Borderland musings and looking so much the seer, entirely disap-
peared. He might have been a poacher, who saw an opportunity to
snare a pheasant, for all that was craftily mischievous in his character came out in his countenance.

But Stead evidently impressed his host, who subsequently
telephoned the Foreign Minister, René Goblet, to secure him a
follow-on interview. According to Crawford's account, the editor
then betrayed her by printing a 'flaming article' on the European
situation which did not uphold the gentlemanly convention that
nothing was supposed to be revealed about such meetings; a great
inconvenience for an overseas reporter of any kind. In fairness,
Stead actually published a fairly insipid essay, which tried overly
much to bolster the French government's doubtful claim that it
did not seek to avenge the country's humiliating defeat in the
Franco-Prussian War twenty years previously. Even in his interview
with the bellicose demagogue General Georges Boulanger, Stead
allowed his peaceful inclinations to dull his journalistic perception,
writing – not, as it turned out, without prophecy – that he was 'not
a man for coup d'état'.[244] Stead also expressly stated that his meeting with Floquet was 'a conversation between gentlemen, not ... an
interview between a journalist and a public man... Hence I can say
nothing.'[245] In this light, Emily's complaints seem quite mysterious
unless they are viewed in the context of the editor's other suspect
relationships with female journalists.

The workings of Stead's mind at this time may be deduced
from the pair's subsequent visit to the famous Salon. In her savage
pen portrait, the younger journalist recalled Stead 'unconsciously
revealing all that was best, and anything but best, in his nature' as
they stalked among the artworks. She may have been referring to
an attempted pass, though it is equally possible that she took the

initiative and was rebuffed. In any case, the first article that Stead dispatched after this encounter, which gave unusual prominence to 'the nudities at the Salon', suggests that his thoughts were not entirely focused on European politics. When he called briefly on the journalist and future Prime Minister of the Republic, Georges Clemenceau (who refused to be interviewed), shortly afterwards, Stead could only remark how strange it was that the Frenchman had a copy of the Venus de Milo in his office – 'a divinity not usually encountered in the editorial sanctum'.

These unusual observations were dutifully given prominence by Cook – a real art connoisseur, who went on to write Ruskin's authorised biography – but it must have been troubling to give so much space to the 'Special Commissioner' while good copy was left unused in the sub's basket. Nevertheless, Cook succeeded in using his two months in control of the paper to begin a series of reforms, strongly resisted by Stead, which clearly had the backing of the proprietor. These included the introduction of sports report-ing, a daily gossip column (entitled 'Tittle-tattle for the Tea Table') formulated by Morley's nephew, Charles, and some discursive arti-cles on women's fashion.

Unaware that these changes had been effected, Stead travelled on to Russia via Berlin, where he paused briefly at the bedside of the new Emperor, Frederick William III, who was stricken with throat cancer. Here Stead penned a long and somewhat tedious descrip-tion of the sovereign's ailments, apparently based on little more than a five-minute 'confidential' chat with his English doctor, Sir Morell Mackenzie. It was scant consolation for missing the oppor-tunity of interviewing Otto von Bismarck, who was trying vainly to maintain the system of alliances which had ensured German dominance of the Continent for the previous generation. According to the state papers, Stead's request to see the Iron Chancellor was refused on the grounds that he was an 'over-bearing, conceited bad mannered brute' – a slight the editor would avenge on his return to England with a savage anonymous article in the *Contemporary Review* entitled 'The Bismarck Dynasty'.[246]

Yet Stead was not entirely out of steam. Arriving in St Petersburg in the latter half of May, he bore letters from the Tsar's top officials, presumably secured by Madame Novikov, which excused him from the demeaning formalities obligatory for foreign visitors. In his exalted eyes he was there on a special diplomatic mission to negotiate an informal treaty between Britain and Russia, protecting Germany from invasion from her Western neighbour, France. Even in the most grandiose phase of his 'government by journalism' a few years previously, Stead had never before written with such confidence that 'it was high time that the press should have ambassadors too'; a comment which tacitly explains why his articles toned down his fears about potential French aggression. As one historian has justly observed, his well-meaning newspaper diplomacy involved 'an odd mixture of high politics and low comedy' – a fitting description of his entire professional life.[247]

The epicentre of this phase of his voyage was Princess Catherine Radziwiłł, an exiled Polish socialite who was introduced to Stead by Madame Novikov at the Hotel d'Europe – a palatial venue rented in the 'season' by an array of minor European notables. That year the party included the beautiful, but still completely unknown, Maud Gonne, who would later become famous as an Irish patriot and the muse of the poet William Butler Yeats. She was there on her own secret mission on behalf of her lover, the right-wing French politician Lucien Millevoye, to forge an alliance between France and Russia, freeing the way for the invasion of Germany should the opportunity arise.[248]

Yet when Stead met this rival 'diplomat' at the behest of their hostess – who was eager to discover why this strange Englishman was in Russia – he completely forgot about the purpose of his visit. Years later his companion recalled how the 'curious' journalist had spoken to her not about the precarious international situation, but about his 'sex obsession'. 'Obsession', she wrote, 'is the only word to describe it.' Though Maud claims that this 'made him rather repellent to a girl who hated such talk', it is likely that she knew exactly how to charm her rival and thereby scupper his plan to forge ties between St Petersburg and London.

According to Maud, she soon received from Stead a 'very foolish and very amorous' letter, which conveniently found its way into the hands of Madame Novikov – allegedly because she had ransacked Gonne's apartment, although this seems unlikely. When Stead burst into the Irishwoman's room after a sleepless night the following morning, she told him 'laughingly, to comfort him and sooth his vanity, if not his love: "You have nothing to complain of; you should be very happy; you have made a Russian conquest, much better for you than an Irish one, and the lady must love you very much. Isn't jealousy a sign of love? My compliments."' The truth was that Maud had played a very cruel, but ingenious, trick to destroy the editor's connection with the only person who could secure him entry to the Tsar's palace.

For a few days the situation seemed dire for Stead. In desperation he called upon the British ambassador, Sir Robert Morier, in the hope of securing his desired introduction. The veteran diplomat's refusal to offer any assistance was unsurprising. Not only did Morier have a very low opinion of Novikov and her circle, he had recently written to a friend that the *PMG* was 'an indispensable daily record of the temperature in the lunatic asylum to which my country is reduced'.[249] This may explain why Stead's early dispatches to Cook lacked the inside scoop befitting a 'Special Commissioner' – they included an uninspiring discussion of railway timetables and a second-hand account of the hunting adventures of a 'Mr George Littledale of Wick Hill, Bracknell'. Stead's more enterprising plan to 'get locked up [in prison] for experimental purposes' failed to get the backing of the authorities: he had to make do with a stilted tour of a model penitentiary.

Luckily for Stead, he managed to recover the situation by making up with the Grande Dame; an essential prerequisite to meeting her biological kinsman. Though his methods of persuasion are not known, Stead may have used language that had worked with the princess before: 'Perhaps you still like me a wee little bit – eh

Olga? & I like you more, much more than a wee little bit.'[250] She apparently responded with the same telling playfulness that would accompany the republication of his special articles as [*The*] *Truth About Russia* upon his return: '[O]ne can never fall out with you ... naughtiest of men.' Indeed, she pulled out all the stops in securing him his much-desired audience, despite the fact that Alexander had never before agreed to be interviewed by a journalist.[251]

The meeting took place on 24 May at the Imperial Palace at Gatchina, where the editor was promised a fifteen-minute discussion 'about the weather' in recognition of his services on behalf of the Russian cause in Britain. Predictably Stead was not willing to have such impositions placed on him, not even by an emperor. But there is no question that he had become, as he admitted shortly after his release from prison, 'less unhesitatingly impudent ... in tackling notabilities'.[252] In contrast to the vituperation of his early days (when Admiral Fisher recalled his friend 'tackl[ing] a Prime Minister like a terrier a rat'), Stead began the meeting on bended knee, asking Alexander 'forgiveness for all the injuries we have inflicted on your country'.[253] Stead then explained that he wanted to know the Emperor's policy 'so as to be the better able to defend it', even to the extent of asking what his reaction would be to various hypothetical impasses, such as the building of British fortresses along the Dardanelles. Stead's unpublished notes make excellent reading:

> Well, only let me know. For see how it would go. If I believe that you would allow it, I discuss it as possible, and perhaps the English would come to regard it with favour. Then after public opinion has been educated to accept this solution, you say no, we cannot have the Dardanelles. What happens? All is spoilt, and everyone says: 'Confound these Russians, they will take everything and agree to nothing', and all we have said will be quoted against you, and I shall be made a fool of.

In effect, Stead was offering himself as a semi-official spokesman for the Imperial regime – a bizarre position for a journalist who had made his name as a protector of the downtrodden. Pushing the bounds of equality to even greater limits, Stead agreed with a sentiment the Tsar had mumbled in broken English about the need for Russia and Germany to remain on friendly terms: 'Yes, that is always my policy,' Stead grandly concluded, 'Germany and Russia allies, and England friends of both.' With that he drew the interview to an abrupt halt, supposedly because he believed himself to be keeping the Empress from her lunch. This unconscious breach of court etiquette (the Tsar, not his guests, was required to signal the end of an audience) again threw Madame Novikov into a rage, which she calmly put into print a few years later: 'The Emperor was so amused,' she wrote, 'that he went to the Empress and announced that he had just been dismissed.' For Morier, the whole affair was simply 'monstrous'.[254]

Stead was not at all bothered about this little storm. In his loving two-volume biography of his Russian friend he later wrote: 'I knew nothing about that. I only knew when I saw the Tsar smile that I had been an idiot for my considerateness.' Stead may have been put at his ease by the fact that his corpulent host had casually lit a cigarette from a candle on the table during the course of their forty-minute 'conversation'.[255]

Even for Stead, the success of this meeting was qualified by the fact that he was forbidden by journalistic convention to refer to it in print. This may have been why he had the inspired idea of writing his final articles as 'Special Commissioner' from the home of the only other Russian universally known to his readers: the novelist Count Leo Tolstoy. How Stead arranged a visit to his estate at Yasnaya Polyana remains a minor mystery, but it is known that he had written various letters to the author praising his fiction – perhaps revealing as much of Stead's paradoxical tastes as his secret love of the controversial works of Emile Zola and Henrik Ibsen. Like Stead, Tolstoy was at this stage of his life a religious mystic, whose equal love and loathing for sex was a great motor for his prolific output.

According to Stead, the pair passed a few genial days 'sally[ing] forth together over field and forest, drinking in the glad sunshine, and exulting in the beauty and glory and melody of spring'; but it is unlikely that they could communicate with ease. Tolstoy may have been a superb linguist but he was not a noted conversationalist. Their most meaningful recorded discussion involved the editor – in his favourite guise – pressing his host as to whether it would be justified to strike a man on the verge of sexually assaulting his attractive teenage daughter, Tatiana. After initially demurring, the famous pacifist agreed that it was the one instance in which violence might be justified.

For most of Stead's time at Yasnaya Polyana it seems that the novelist was working hard at repairing an old pair of boots, a favourite recreation during these years. This gave Stead the opportunity of writing his lengthy dispatches to Cook from the same desk upon which *War and Peace* had been written, which led Stead, slightly unimaginatively, to adopt 'War or Peace?' as his title. This series was prefaced by an expansive account of his rambles through the woods with his host, culminating in the tragic, and apparently real, destruction of a peasant village by fire. Taking this as the starting point of his political discourse, Stead compared his enemies in the press – notably the fervently Russophobe *Times* – to 'boys who play with matches', putting the lives of the public at risk with their irresponsible articles. Yet he was slow in coming to his conclusions and somewhat repetitive in outlining his arguments. He also seemed to forget that he was the man who had boasted of sending Gordon to Khartoum, not to mention that it was he who had caused the famous 'naval scare' of 1884. 'The Armed Peace', Stead now wrote,

> sits like a vampire at the bedside of the people, draining the life-blood while they sleep... Sooner or later, and sooner rather than later, they will rush to war rather than wait to be slowly suffocated by the sheer weight of their armour.[256]

For all its prolixity, his prediction was farsighted; perhaps too much so for Cook, who complained that the editor-at-large had already provided enough material to fill thirty-five fat newspaper columns. With the consent of Yates Thompson, he instructed the sub-editor – presumably Robertson Scott – to reproduce Stead's latest instalments in small type in a narrow section at the foot of the front two pages of the newspaper. It is likely that he did so without realising that he would inadvertently be administering another slight to the Tsar as well as to Stead: Morier railed that the Emperor could not be expected to read the product of his interview with 'three extra candles and a magnifying glass!' For this reason there was a great row upon Stead's return, which Cook, a reserved man, records in his diary:

> Crisis at the *P.M.G.* begins. Stead back on Saturday. Travelling straight through had seen nothing of the way we dished up his articles till he arrived at Queenborough. Blackguarded me strongly – disobeyed his express orders – was equivalent to dismissing him from the editorship – was he editor or not, etc.?[257]

Poor Cook. Not only had Stead given him permission to run the paper on his own terms, he had also sought the consent of Yates Thompson to present Stead's articles in the novel manner. But Cook did not attempt to row with Stead. Like his future protégé, the influential political commentator J. A. Spender (known to the Liberal Prime Minister Sir Henry Campbell-Bannerman as 'Chairman of the Cabinet'), Cook knew that arguments with pacifists could easily descend into violence. So he agreed, 'in his usual curious, nonchalant way', said Stead, to the editor's absurd demand that the offending articles be reproduced in full. This was a course of action that Stead acknowledged, or even boasted, to his readers as being 'absolutely unprecedented in the history of Modern Journalism'. Cook responded to the incident by sending Stead a polite epistle explaining that 'there is a wide distinction between quarrelling with my use of discretion and denying that I had any right to use discretion at all' – a telling acknowledgment that Stead's judgement was no longer considered, if it ever had been, unimpeachable by his staff.[258]

For Yates Thompson the situation was even more serious. Returning from his annual sojourn on the Continent on 25 June, he was appalled to be confronted by Stead's leader, which was no less than a public denunciation of the running of the paper in his absence. This immodestly justified the republication of 'War or Peace?' on the grounds that the articles would 'have a serious effect upon the public opinion of the Continent', before hysterically denouncing his employer and his deputy editor for their levity, even to the extent of drawing attention to particular articles published in his absence. 'If the journalist has no higher function than the vigilant chronicling of parochial small beer,' railed Stead,

> and the smart writing up of the twopenny halfpenny banalities of the whippersnappers of party, then we admit that a discussion of the length of a ballet girl's skirt and the record of the slang of the lobby or of the betting turf must exclude all attempts seriously to bring before the citizen of the modern State the conditions and the forces governing the great world in which Englishmen still love to dream they play a part.

This article broke one of the cardinal rules of journalism: internal disputes are never to be aired before the world. But it is worth considering that it was not the rude and barbarous Stead who championed the light journalism that would soon make the likes of Alfred Harmsworth a fortune: it was the cultured products of elite public schools alongside whom he worked.

Be this as it may, Stead's hopes of remaining editor of the *PMG* were fast evaporating. Immediately after reading Stead's scolding article, Yates Thompson came to the office in a mood to throttle his lieutenant, but Stead had already left for the day: the atmosphere at Northumberland Street had become intolerable. Swearing in front of the secretaries in their confined 'hutches', the bookish proprietor asked Cook: 'Why in the world couldn't Stead have waited, instead of being so utterly discourteous and lacking in consideration?' For the editor's remaining eighteen months at the office the two men never saw eye to eye, nor was Stead invited to Yates Thompson's dinner parties, in spite of Mrs Yates Thompson's apparent desire to include him. More seriously, Stead's salary was reduced from £1,200 to £1,000 'to make an impression on me' and to deter him from further 'playing tricks'.[259]

The main reason that Stead was allowed to keep his job was his consent to Cook's plan to alter the paper's bespoke appearance, which had remained practically unchanged since the high-minded days of Frederick Greenwood. In the owner's opinion, this format was 'God-forsaken, mean [and] inconvenient', not to mention outdated and unattractive to the advertisers to whom they were increasingly beholden. When the matter was broached during a rare editorial conference, 'Stead at first sulked and said nothing' before declaring his objection to the *PMG* 'becoming like any other paper' – by which he probably meant the advertisement-crammed *Star*. With the support of Cook, Leslie and Stout behind him, the indignant Yates Thompson hurled back that the *PMG*'s 'chief difference from other papers was that we have never paid [i.e. made a profit]'.[260] Reluctantly Stead accepted the proposed changes, which greatly enlarged the paper's front page and submerged his daily leader in a sea of soap and theatre advertisements. Stead, who believed that a good newspaper should fit snugly into a man's jacket pocket, also had to put up with the reinstatement of Cook's 'whippersnapper' political gossip and sports reporting.

Stead's acquiescence in these reforms was purely practical: he had a large family to support and was in no position to cast off in a new direction. But he made no attempt to hide his true intentions from his colleagues, who were evidently exasperated by his increasingly disdainful attitude towards their profession. On one occasion Stead told Cook that his latest 'premonition' was that he would leave the *PMG* in the middle of 1889 to edit his own paper, which he grandly proposed to call 'The New Times'.[261]

Stead's disenchantment with the kind of journalism he had unwittingly invented was well demonstrated at the end of August 1888 in a leader which denounced 'The Blood-Thirst of the Day' just twenty-four hours before the first victim of 'Jack the Ripper' was found mutilated at Whitechapel.[262] Throughout the course of the ensuing three-month newspaper sensation Stead refused to revise his opinion that graphic descriptions of violent crimes should not be printed in newspapers: the murders rarely featured on the front page. When they were discussed, it was invariably to highlight the hypocrisy of the same 'arm-chair journalists' who had previously denounced the 'Maiden Tribute' campaign. Calling for a 'Court of Conscience' made up of newspaper editors, Stead attacked his rivals for bringing out special editions 'drip[ping] with gore ... almost as "creepy" and revolting as the gashed and mangled corpse[s] of the murderer's victim[s]'.[263] Oddly, however, Stead hypothesised that the killer was a philanthropist intent on drawing attention to the appalling conditions of life in the East End, much as he had himself. Of course, no evidence links Stead to the murders but since 'Jack the Ripper' was said to have had a bushy red beard, much like Stead's, it is surprising that his name has never been put forward in the wild speculation about the killer's true identity.

This may be because the recorded details of Stead's private life are so startling as to require no flights of fantasy whatsoever. Nowhere was he more candid about such matters than in a rare surviving diary entry, written just a few months after the 'Ripper' first struck. This explained how Stead's wife had suddenly announced to him that she wanted a sixth child (supposedly 'to give the ovaries a rest'), bringing to an end their lengthy period of sexual abstinence. This provoked the editor to pen a thoughtful discourse on the seriousness of bringing another child into the 'battlefield' of life, which rapidly turned into a sickly account of his sexual proclivities and anxieties. 'I do not like to write of these matters,' he wrote, before continuing: 'Intercourse limited to twice a week with emission in the hand rather than in the vagina [and] the withdrawal taking place just before the supreme moment never did me any harm.' Strangely, Stead did not explain what he had done when his wife was unresponsive to his carnal yearnings in the past, presumably because a discussion of women besides Emma would have been too private even for his remarkably uninhibited diary. But it is perhaps revealing that Stead expressed a preference for *coitus interruptus* on account of '[t]he pleasure ... [being] rather greater than when the emission takes place in the vagina'. He went on to explain that indulging in sex more frequently than 'thrice or four times in the week' caused his hearing to be impaired by 'apparent wax formation in the right ear'.[264]

The passage has baffled every chronicler of the great Puritan's life. Only Robertson Scott among his early biographers, somewhat bravely, dared include it on the grounds that it was in keeping with his subject's 'character and temperament'. As he wryly observed, Stead would not have minded its inclusion if he was still 'sensible of what is going on in the world, as he believed he would be'.

Modern writers have been less sympathetic. At the very least they have taken it as vindication of the 'sex obsession' referred to by Maud Gonne, which Stead's acquaintance, the sexologist Havelock Ellis, believed to be the 'motive force ... of many of his activities'.[265] Others have drawn on it to hypothesise that behind his knight-errantry, Stead was secretly a chauvinist and a selfish lover, too. Neither of these theories are particularly fair. One of the least commented on features of the entry is actually the amount of interest that Stead showed in his wife's enjoyment of their love-making; a consideration which probably would have surprised his contemporaries more than his decision to write about such matters in the first place.

> [My] desire increased with years rather than diminished, and the last twelve months I worshipped my wife with my body, as the prayer book has it, more than ever before. She also was responsive and affectionate. With her also the pleasure was far greater than when she was first married. (For me it was immeasurably so). Nor could we say positively that the interruption did her harm. It did not interfere with her satisfaction. Rather [it] enhanced it.

Happy though this reconciliation may have been, the brief rekindling of the couple's romance did not outlive the birth of their penultimate child, Jack, the following year. This unfortunately took place while Stead was on an overseas assignment, which led Emma, for the first time since their marriage, to neglect her husband's birthday. Stead was greatly upset by this but he was made even sadder by Emma's subsequent request that he should henceforth sleep in their eldest son's room. 'A shadow of great darkness can be felt,' wrote Stead in self-commiseration, 'entirely unconnected with the paper but nevertheless intimately concerned with all that makes life and work possible.'[266]

Marital problems compounded Stead's ongoing difficulties at the office. His desperate attempts to regain the high circulation of early 1885 had failed. His gamble in going to Russia had achieved nothing. He had 'been humiliated' and '[f]rom the very pinnacle of success' been 'hurled into the abyss of failure'. Old scruples began to falter: Stead briefly contemplated going into partnership with a millionaire who kept a mistress and admitted to visiting prostitutes. Still, Stead remained confident that 'God will find the cash and provide me with the work necessary'.[267] In a sense he was correct. It would not be Tsar Alexander or any of his other unlikely new acquaintances – including Pope Leo XIII and the diamond millionaire Cecil Rhodes – who would 'unshackle' him from his dependency on Yates Thompson. The man of the hour was to be an old school friend with whom he had had almost no dealings since childhood. Though Stead viewed this as a great triumph, it was, in fact, the beginning of his demise.

CHAPTER 10

VATICAN, LONDON

Before founding the Review I went to Rome to see what chance there was of the Pope undertaking my task. Finding there was none, I did it myself.
W. T. S.'s personal inscription in *The Pope and the New Era*

On 4 April 1889, Stead had one of the most important meetings of his life. He could hardly have anticipated its significance. Arriving from the broiling diamond fields of South Africa, a scarcely known English adventurer called Cecil Rhodes had asked a friend to put him in touch with a man who could help drum up support for a Royal Charter for his formidable mining business: the South African Company. This would free his hand to open mines all over a vast expanse of territory north of the independent Transvaal Republic, later to be renamed Rhodesia (modern Zimbabwe). For all his influence as an editor, Stead was a far from obvious choice of ally. Yet as was so often to be the case in the 1890s, Stead would be wooed – or seduced – by a person with whom he seemed to share little common ground. It would be the first of a number of curious relationships, with women no less than men, which would lead Stead ever further from his original calling: from newspaper editor to magazine proprietor, staunch Liberal to fanatical Imperialist, and ardent Nonconformist to obsessive spiritualist and potential convert to Roman Catholicism. That it would end in a total nervous breakdown is perhaps unsurprising. The remarkable thing is that the logical dénouement was postponed for so long.

Stead claims that he had no great desire to meet the diamond king. 'I had expected nothing – was indeed rather bored with the idea of meeting him,' he later wrote. This was not entirely

accurate. Only two weeks before their introduction by Sir Charles
Mills, chairman of the influential South Africa Committee, Stead
had denounced Rhodes and his allies in the *PMG* as a 'pack of
unscrupulous concessionaires', greedily amassing private fortunes
under the patriotic flag of Empire. Stead's opinion can hardly have
been altered by Mills's subsequent attempt to bring the two men
together at a dinner party at which both Rhodes and Stead's mortal
enemy, Sir Charles Dilke, were to be present. Stead had declined
this invitation, but a more sedate lunch was arranged to take place
at South Africa House instead. This would be the setting for one of
the strangest interludes of Stead's career.

During the meal, Stead and Rhodes eyed one another with
caution. Outwardly they were remarkably alike. Both came from
pious provincial backgrounds (Rhodes was the son of an Anglican
vicar) and were noted for their carelessness of dress and, on occasion, of speech. More importantly, both men sincerely believed
that they were forces for good in the world, for whom conventional
law and morality need not always apply. But their dialogue was at
first reserved. It was obvious that each wanted something from the
other: in the case of Rhodes, support for his precious charter; for
Stead, the 'rich white witch' whom he believed would finance 'The
New Times'. Only after the plates had been cleared, and Mills had
discreetly withdrawn, were such matters broached with candour.

Rhodes was an expert at this kind of negotiation. Having identified Stead as a vain man he gratified him by representing himself
as one of his disciples. '[N]o sooner had Sir Charles Mills left the
room,' wrote Stead, 'than Mr Rhodes fixed my attention by pour-
ing out the long damned up flood of my ideas.' Any reservations he
had about 'concession hunters' and 'the *soi-disant* imperialist, Mr
Cecil Rhodes' evaporated as he heard the 'Gospel According to the
Pall Mall Gazette' virtually parodied to reconcile him with his new
friend's plans for ill-fated Matabeleland. Rhodes's contention that
he had met with Stead's leading articles 'everywhere' when looking for diamonds in South Africa would have tested even a child's
credulity. His claims that he had unsuccessfully attempted to visit

Stead while he was in prison and that he had been quietly present at the Exeter Hall meeting celebrating his release were scarcely more believable.

Yet Stead was won over. He particularly warmed to his new friend's idea of founding 'a Society which would be to the Empire what the Society of Jesus was to the Papacy...'. For several hours, said Stead, they 'talked on and on, upon very deep things indeed'.[268]

Rhodes had judged his man astutely. Shameless bribery would not have been effective with Stead. Yet their final agreement – for all its lofty talk of promoting the 'reunification of the English-speaking peoples' – was scarcely better than the corrupt methods that Rhodes used to secure the support of more cheerfully immoral editors, such as Frank Harris of the *Fortnightly Review*. He offered Stead a huge 'free gift' of £20,000 as a 'nest egg' to go towards the newspaper that he apparently supported, if only in principle. '[Y]ou must never say who gave [the funds] to you,' Rhodes coyly insisted, '...say an old man gave it to you.' Though Stead claimed to combine 'the cunning of a serpent with the innocence of a dove', he appears to have had no idea he was complicit in a rather shady deal. He immediately wrote to his wife with the enthusiasm of a 'lovesick schoolgirl': 'Rhodes is my man! ... He is full of a far more gorgeous idea in connection with the paper than even I have had... It seems all like a fairy dream... How good God is to me.' Stead added, perhaps not untypically, that he would not be returning home that evening.[269]

Although Stead initially claimed not to want Rhodes's money, his latest confrontation with Yates Thompson led him to request an instalment of £2,000 the following day. To the amazement of Cook, who had been away at the time, Stead had some months prior vilified a defendant in a divorce trial without even glancing at the law report. This led to the paper being sued for libel and saddled with damages of £1,250 – 'a curious instance of Stead's zeal minus discretion defeating itself', Cook dryly recorded in his diary.[270] Aware that this was potentially a sacking offence, and sure that Rhodes would provide the cash, Stead calmly announced to Yates Thompson that under the circumstances he would foot the bill. He kept the identity of his benefactor secret by making Rhodes's cheque over to Brett before getting the latter to pay a new one into his personal account. This added to Stead's mystique: no one connected to the paper could work out how he had managed to raise the money.

Partly thanks to the support of the *PMG*, Rhodes was granted permission to annex Matabeleland on behalf of the British government shortly afterwards, and returned to South Africa to pursue his tandem career in politics and business with a growing fortune at his back. When he was elected President of Cape Colony the following year, he continued to use Stead as his unofficial spokesman in England, notably with regard to playing down (accurate) reports that he had used machine-guns to defeat the defiant warriors of the Ndebele. Yet their friendship remained almost entirely one-sided. Rhodes's favours to Stead, such as appointing Edmund Garrett as editor of his South African newspaper, the *Cape Times*, early in 1895, were largely self-serving. Less useful proposals, such as Stead's idea of touring the world in advance of attempting to found his own newspaper, were invariably rebuffed with nicely phrased objections. But Rhodes knew how to keep Stead onside, and clearly had some genuine liking for him. In 1891 he made the grand, though ultimately meaningless, gesture of appointing him second trustee, after the first Baron Rothschild (1840–1915), of his fifth will. As long as he did not die suddenly, this was a costless method of 'squaring' a useful ally who would prove almost fanatically loyal until the final breach came at the time of the Boer War ten years later.

This situation was tantalising for Stead. He had unexpectedly befriended one of the richest and most up-and-coming men in the world, yet he had come no closer to founding his newspaper. He had 'no signpost', and was psychologically removed from his work at Northumberland Street. Fortunately, his last major news story at the paper, the Dock Strike of August 1889, suggested an improbable exit.

The strike was the first case of 'industrial action' by unskilled, non-unionised labourers, and therefore had huge implications for the future of Liberal capitalism. Stead was sympathetic to the dockers' modest demand for an extra penny in their hourly wage, but he emphasised the futility of withdrawing their labour to secure this objective. Stead's view was indicative of how much more conservative he had become since the days when he had encouraged Annie Besant and the Social Democratic Federation in the weeks leading up to 'Bloody Sunday' two and a half years previously. His stance was broadly similar to that of his friend Cardinal Manning, who implored the men to go back to work while at the same time asking the shipping companies to redistribute their profits more paternalistically. Though this was only cautiously supported by the strike leaders, including the future cabinet minister John Burns (whom Stead met at this time), it proved effective. As a result Stead began to think seriously about the potential of the Catholic Church as a force to resolve the problems facing the modern world. More hopefully, he wondered if the Pope might replace Cecil Rhodes as the financier of his fledgling newspaper.

This was one of Stead's most absurd ideas, but Manning clearly approved of his plan to travel to Rome to interview Leo XIII on the subject in mid-October. Ever since the days of the 'Maiden Tribute' campaign, the aged cardinal had considered Stead to be a potential convert to Roman Catholicism, and hoped this might be his final act outside the Church. This was not far-fetched. In his idealisation of women, his deep suspicion of male vice and his thirst for absolute knowledge and power, Stead had Catholic leanings. Yet, as both the Rev. Stead and General Booth had already discovered to their disappointment, Stead would not easily submit himself to institutional authority, no matter how benign. His trip to Rome was not a spiritual pilgrimage but a voyeuristic examination of an institution that attracted him in spite of his evident loathing of its teachings and trappings. In essence it was a brilliant piece of self-promotion: his articles were syndicated by 'more than a dozen leading papers in England, Ireland, Wales, Scotland, the United States, and Australia', which Stead fairly considered to be a more significant fact than anything written in his dispatches themselves.[271] As a staunch Nonconformist, naturally predisposed to view the Catholic Church with suspicion, if not visceral hatred, he had hit on an excellent formula to generate the maximum possible sensation. His 'Letters from the Vatican' were to pave the way to his new journalistic home, though not quite in the manner he had anticipated.

It was unfortunate for Stead that his wife was due to give birth during the period he was to be away. Emma's evident displeasure was exacerbated by the news that her husband would be taking Marie Belloc as his interpreter: a choice that was no more practical than it was troublesome – though a Catholic, she was not an expert Italian speaker. Yet Stead appears to have had one of the most pleasant trips of his life. The difficulty of telegraphing a long article to London every two or three days was nothing for a man with his mania for writing and inexhaustible fund of ideas. His collected dispatches, published on his return as *The Pope and the New Era*, proved to be one of his most successful books, despite the fact that a large portion of the press had by this time banned any appearance of his name from their pages. The Catholic journal *The Tablet* practically dismissed it in a sentence: '[T]he grammar ... is certainly marvellous.'

Stead's series began at the end of October with a characteristically grandiloquent – and consciously flawed – attempt to assert his impartiality. Comparing himself to Joshua leading the Hebrews into war against the Canaanites, Stead half-seriously explained that no one would rejoice more than himself if the armed stranger blocking his path – the Catholic Church – replied that he was 'with us', as Jehovah proved to be in the Bible. The questions he wanted answered were threefold: was the Church ready for power to transfer to 'the English-speaking peoples'; did it have a workable alternative to socialism; and was it prepared to accept the emancipation of women, which Stead believed would cause the 'most sweeping revolution ever achieved on this planet'. Stead also wanted to know if the Pope recognised the importance of journalists in doing God's work. This was perhaps the only one of his questions to be definitively answered, albeit negatively. 'The Press!' scoffed a senior Dominican sharing the editor's carriage on his way to the ancient city, 'Rome has never used the Press and never will'.

Over the course of his three-week stay, Stead would hear this sentiment repeated often. Although he naturally claimed to resent it for undermining his project, it strengthened his self-image as a wounded friend of the papacy. In truth, Stead must have been aware that his audacious language could not have won him the support of even the most sympathetic of the Pope's officials. In one of his published letters he summed up his views succinctly: 'Less incense and more newspapers, fewer masses and more leading articles, and at least one live editor for every half-dozen cardinals – on those lines much may be done.' Leo predictably declined to give him an audience; a slight which unleashed a steady stream of disgruntled letters to Manning that bewailed Rome as 'a sink of idolatry and atheism'. At this point it seems likely that the Cardinal quietly, and no doubt humorously, dropped any residual hope that his friend might be about to enter the Catholic fold. 'You must not write like a dare-devil,' he warned. 'Do not lecture the Pope, nor recount "rebuffs" which, after all, may be like the buffeting of His Master, by Divine permission and for a greater good.'[272]

The advice, though sage, was only partially taken. Stead harangued the Curia on all subjects about which he cared. He insisted, for example, that instead of demanding temporal power the Pope should simply relocate his entire operation to '[t]he centre, the capital, and the mother city of the new world' – London. Even when Leo promulgated his famous social democratic encyclical, *Rerum Novarum*, two years later, Stead believed that the papacy had not fully grasped the nettle. The core of his objection – surprisingly in light of his public advocacy of chastity – revolved around the Church's teachings on sex. Its 'exaggeration of the virtues of celibacy,' wrote Stead, 'is simply lamentable; and if it were strong enough it would probably deem it necessary to burn me at the stake as it burned Giordano Bruno...' It would be interesting to know what Emma thought of this observation, or her husband's regret that the Catholic clergy have 'never known the joys nor suffered the sorrows which make up a great part of the higher life of the ordinary man ... [including] how he may please his wife'. Probably she would have been revolted: her husband was staying alone in a hotel with an attractive 'modern' young woman with whom he had been known to enjoy overfriendly relations in the past. While the pair was gallivanting around St Peter's, she was literally left holding the baby.

Stead returned to London in mid-November disappointed, but not entirely demoralised. Shortly afterwards, on the fourth anniversary of his conviction for abducting Eliza Armstrong, a representative of the *Methodist Times* found him in 'exceedingly high spirits' as he sat down for supper at Cambridge House 'dressed in prison garb'. This was always going to provide good 'copy' for the newspaper, but the cheerful interview, which hardly touched on any of his inner worries, was not an accurate reflection of the situation. Stead's trip to Rome had been fairly unsuccessful. Not only had he failed to secure investment for his newspaper, he had not even succeeded in interviewing the Pope, a feat that more diplomatic journalists would achieve with comparative ease.

Yet Stead still understood the newspaper game. To loosen the purse strings of a sympathetic millionaire he had to maintain his reputation as something out of the ordinary. In all probability he wrote much of the *Methodist Times* dialogue himself: rivals in the press would later claim that Stead demanded privileges in interviews which he never allowed to his own 'victims'.[273]

The man who ended up providing the money for Stead's project sat oddly beside Cecil Rhodes and Pope Leo. He was a humble fellow Old Silcoatian called George Newnes, whom Stead knew only vaguely in spite of their common provenance. Newnes was a few years younger than Stead and had made his first fortune out of a soft furnishings and stationery empire, which allowed him to open a profitable vegetarian restaurant in central Manchester in the late 1870s. His flight into journalism was equally unforeseeable.

Each week he used to amuse his wife with a collection of anecdotes culled from the halfpenny newspapers. She thought the idea so good that she implored him to start a weekly newspaper along the same lines. In October 1881 appeared its first number: *Tit-Bits from all the most interesting Books, Periodicals and Newspapers in the World* – or just *Tit-Bits*, as it was known. Though the title had a cheeky anatomical connotation, its contents were scrupulously purged of any hint of impropriety. The first issue included a variety of snippety articles including 'A Strange Hobby', 'Curious Epitaphs' and 'How Our Queen was Wooed'. Within hours the entire print run had sold out. It was the kind of journalism that would soon make Stead's allegedly 'feather-brained' New Journalism seem absurdly heavyweight.[274]

Stead wrote to Newnes at the start of December 1889 with three ideas sketched on the back of an envelope. The most appealing to Newnes's reductive mind was for a monthly magazine offering 'time-saving reading which represents the scattered wisdom and opinion of the civilised world'. Just as *Tit-Bits* had been successful with its amusing stories from the penny press, Stead envisaged a magazine in which all the best articles of the monthly reviews would be 'boiled down' and discussed for the benefit of a poor but aspirational readership.

It was not a bad idea. Current affairs magazines were expensive but numerous and still of immense cultural significance. Touchingly, Stead thought what a blessing such a compendium would have been to him when he was growing up in Howden or working at the counting-house in Newcastle. But a new generation had emerged since then – the products of the free board schools – whose hopes and dreams were considerably more mundane than his own had been. As Newnes lectured him, such readers did not care for the kind of journalism 'which directs the affairs of nations ... makes and unmakes Cabinets ... upsets governments ... [and] builds up Navies'. They simply wanted 'a little fun and amusement'.

This prophetic warning did not prevent Newnes from adopting the inspired title, the *Review of Reviews*, in place of Stead's practical but highly unimaginative preference of 'The Six-Penny Monthly'. Newnes may have been inspired by an aside made by Thomas Carlyle, who, sixty years previously, chanced upon a magazine of the same title at the Leipzig book fair. But Newnes was an unpretentious man – 'there was nothing about him that was larger than life, not even his dreams', says his biographer – and he generously claimed the idea to have been Stead's. His aim was simply to appeal to men and women for whom publications such as the *Contemporary*, *Fortnightly* and *Quarterly* reviews were bywords for boredom and expense.

Stead wasted no time in enthusing to Yates Thompson about this new departure, allegedly under the misapprehension that he would, like Morley, be able to combine two editorships. But the proprietor was unmoved. 'I may as well say now,' he curtly replied to Stead's dramatic announcement of his plans, 'that I don't ... see the least prospect of ... going shares in the Editor of the *PMG* with Mr Newnes of *Tit-Bits*.' His contempt was almost tangible. Even Stead recognised that 'there was some farce' in the situation, but he was reassured by a stream of supportive letters from '[The leader of the House of Commons, Arthur] Balfour and some twenty other big people' to whom he had written with his scheme.[275]

This put Edward Cook in an awkward position. On the one hand, he coveted the editorship of the *PMG* for himself, but on the other he was still Stead's loyal understudy and refused to accept the top job if it meant a breach with his former mentor. Stead seems not to have appreciated his reserve. Over the course of several tense days there were a series of violent rows at the office, in which Stead unfairly accused Cook, no less than Yates Thompson, of conspiring against him. By the middle of December, barely a week since his first letter to Newnes, it was agreed that Stead would have nothing more to do with the paper as of 1 January 1890. In deference to Stead's wishes, Yates Thompson agreed to overlook the three-month period of notice stipulated in his contract so as to leave 'no ragged edge'.[276]

But Stead now waivered. After vacating the office for just a couple of weeks to put together the first issue of the *Review of Reviews*, he wrote a 'long sentimental letter' to Yates Thompson lamenting his imminent departure. This appealed directly to the proprietor's amenable wife Dolly, who persuaded her husband, against his better judgement, to retain Stead as 'Political Director' under Cook's editorship. This arrangement was evidently resented by the staff, for the next morning – New Year's Day – Stead had what appears to have been a lover's tiff with Miss Friederichs on Waterloo Bridge. 'Oh,' she exclaimed upon seeing him striding briskly along, 'so you've not gone, but are coming back to undermine Mr Cook's authority?' Her fears were not unjustified. Cook was soon complaining to Yates Thompson that the new arrangement was inoperable on account of his 'long subordinate position and Stead's intrinsic weight'. Matters were not improved by Stead's evident willingness to lord it over his former staff: Cook resented him 'receiving people, making appointments [and] using the big room', even if he generously acknowledged some 'very useful' editorial hints. The office manager, Mr Leslie, was blunter: 'The man's vanity,' he told Cook one afternoon, 'is odious.'[277]

It would only be three weeks until Yates Thompson was given a second excuse to discharge Stead. In an interview for the *Star*, Stead was believed by his proprietor to have given the impression that he was still in control of the paper. This was perhaps an overreaction, since the offending line only referred to Stead coming 'hot from the editorial room at the *PMG*'; but the existing situation clearly had to end. Though he would remain in touch with Cook for the rest of his life, Stead wrote very little more for the *PMG*. Without him, the paper became a good deal 'more steady' (as one wit observed) and gave support to the Liberal party in a far more slavish manner than before, much to the delight of the party managers (although Yates Thompson would never get his coveted baronetcy). This change in tone was matched with a more general calming of the environment at Northumberland Street. Whereas Stead had followed the publication of the day's first edition with 'a whirl of callers and ... a frantic lunch with a clattering company',

Cook retired to his office 'with a sigh of relief' to reflect on higher matters than newspaper editing.[278] Within two years the paper would be sold over his head to supporters of the Conservative party, perhaps justifying, belatedly, Stead's long-held distrust of his proprietor.

While these events were unfolding, Newnes assembled a skilled group of journalists from the *Tit-Bits* office, located a few hundred yards further up the Strand at Burleigh Street, to assist Stead in producing the first number. The most notable member of this team was a young journalist named Arthur Pearson, who, as founder of the *Daily Express* and other successful titles, would soon become one of Britain's most successful newspaper entrepreneurs. He had secured his first job working for Newnes as a highly original prize for a competition featured in *Tit-Bits*, and had quickly worked his way up the organisation from errand boy to office manager. But Stead appears to have had little appreciation of his drive or ability: Pearson left the *Review of Reviews* within only a few months to found his own magazine – the hugely popular *Pearson's Weekly*. Before doing so, however, he did the older man a considerable service, which the latter never properly acknowledged. Apparently on his own initiative, Pearson travelled to America to launch an *American Review of Reviews* edited by Dr Albert Shaw, a college professor with a great talent for journalism. This publication, as well as the subsequent *Review of Reviews for Australasia*, proved to be far more profitable than the British title. Stead's passive role in their formation is indicated by the fact that the editors of these subsidiary magazines had practically no contact with him: they even resented his interference and complained that they were used as little more than cash-cows to subsidise his follies. For the next two decades Stead would need almost constant reminding that selling his overseas shares would risk bankruptcy. Despite the best efforts of his business manager, Edwin Stout, he could never make the *Review* profitable.

The first issue, published at the beginning of January, gave a clear, if primitive, indication of Stead's continent-striding aspirations. It ran to seventy-two sparsely illustrated pages, wrapped in a blue cover depicting the world surmounting a newspaper. Even Robertson Scott had to concede that from an artistic point it was 'deplorable'. But it suited Stead's purposes. Some years later he would reject a fashionable art deco design (which would have perfectly captured the spirit of *fin de siècle*) on the grounds that it was insufficiently serious. Such earnestness may have been one of Stead's greatest strengths, but it was also his downfall. In the era of Oscar Wilde and the Roaring Nineties, the magazine-reading public did not know what to make of such pious entreaties as Stead's plea in the opening number 'To all English-Speaking Folk'. In a strange blending of Cecil Rhodes and Pope Leo, he explained that he wanted his *Review of Reviews* to be

> to the English-Speaking world what the Catholic Church in its prime was to the intelligence of Christendom ... with affiliates ... [and] correspondents in every village, read as men used to read their Bibles.

For a small magazine put together at a few days' notice in a back office of *Tit-Bits*, this could only have invited ridicule. But Stead was deadly serious. The problem was, predictably, that he could not stick to the original plan of simply summarising the best essays in the leading journals. This was only partly because rival editors shared William Archer's criticism that the magazine was a 'Vampire Review', which would die as the periodicals upon which it fed vanished. Most actually agreed, after a few hesitations, that the project would be a good form of advertising for which Stead paid them over-generously. The *Review*'s Achilles heel was that the all-powerful editor was free to pursue his passing crazes, fads and eccentricities with no effective force to stay his hand. Campaigns for 'Imperial Penny Postage' gave way to 'Reading Material for Workhouses' and, finally, 'Baby Exchanges' for women who could not conceive. While the best editors were discovering the inexhaust-ible popularity of the short story, Stead contented himself with summarising entire books and three-volume novels, many of which were far from current or even of general interest: the 'Book of the Month' for February 1891 was Aristotle's *Treatise on the Constitution of Athens*.

Other features of the *Review* were equally startling. Each number began with a lengthy and idiosyncratic summary of current affairs entitled 'The Progress of the World'. This flitted between events on the fringes of the Empire to provincial 'purity' (anti-prostitution) campaigns, in which Stead took a personal interest. There was also a detailed 'Character Sketch' of a leading personality or institution, usually written by Stead himself, again with a strongly personal flavour. In the first couple of years alone he featured Cardinal Manning, the *Pall Mall Gazette*, John Morley, Olga Novikov and a host of other supposedly influential friends and acquaintances, whom Stead generally discussed in the first person and even included extracts from their private correspondence. Such material usually occupied about half of the magazine; the rest was given over to 'reviewing the reviews', including French, German and Scandinavian titles. There was also an exhaustive index of every English periodical.

The book of the month in the first issue was more contemporary than Aristotle's *Treatise*, but to call it contemporary was an exaggeration. Lady Georgiana Fullerton's *Ellen Middleton* was over forty years old and long forgotten, although an obscure journal had recently republished a review of it by a young William Gladstone. The book tells the story of a woman who accidently pushes her half-sister down a ravine to her death and is consumed by guilt, since she has no impartial friend to whom she can unload her secret. 'I longed to kneel before Him,' the protagonist bemoans, '...in deep prostration of spirit, and lay all my sorrows, all my sins, all my difficulties at His sacred feet.' This appealed directly to Stead's instinct as a journalist. Taking 'Vatican, London' as his telegram address, and posing as a 'level-headed friend', Stead invited his readers to write to him with a 'horrid secret which poisons their existence'. This 'Practical Suggestion' for a 'Lay Confessional' went some way towards fulfilling Stead's desire to make his paper the 'father confessor, spiritual director, moral teacher [and] political conscience' of the world.[279] Yet rather than heralding the first advice column, Stead solemnly swore never to publish anything that was sent in, and that he would pass on any problems that he felt unqualified to deal with to a genuine priest. The same lack of business sense was revealed by his disregard of advertisements: he hoped to do away with them completely once the circulation was sufficiently high.

Sidney Low, who had replaced Frederick Greenwood as editor of the *St. James's Gazette* in 1888, made light of Stead's scheme by publishing a spurious 'confession' from 'a matron' describing herself – in characteristically Steadean language – as 'the embodiment of womanly tenderness and compassion'. As a little girl, he mocked, 'she' had caused a disturbance at the zoo by feeding a 'blue-nosed money' a lozenge. '[T]he once peaceful monkey-house had become a pandemonium, and through my agency', 'she' sighed.[280] Other critics were even more scathing, denouncing Stead for prurience and sham religiosity; charges that he would sternly deny. The reality was probably somewhere in between. One of Stead's young helpers in the early days of the *Review* recalled the morning's post-bag as

> always an adventure... Lots of madmen wrote to Stead ... writing to him week after week, year after year. Every sort of madman, but the sexual maniac was the most common. There were the men who had committed the Whitechapel murders and gave in full their reasons for the crimes; there were men who would tell you of their nympho-maniacal symptoms; there were women in the same boat; there was one man who told in detail how he had seen nothing for it but to get rid of temptation once and for all, and then proceeded to narrate how he had done so with a shilling penknife.[281]

It is not clear what Newnes made of these developments, but he was evidently reassured by the good sales: 30,000 copies were sold in the first nine days alone. Even so, there was a difference of temperament between the two men that would make their partnership as unworkable as Stead's had been with Morley. 'Have had no writs at present,' Newnes nervously joked a few days after releasing the maiden issue. He did not realise that being hated, sued and prosecuted was part of Stead's *raison d'être*. Bernard Shaw put this well in a letter to Cook shortly after his replacement of Stead at Northumberland Street: 'Get rid of the infernally friendly terms you are on with everybody,' he lectured. 'Everybody says you are a very nice fellow. Everybody always said Stead was the damnedest scoundrel and hypocrite. You have a tremendous chance. And you are throwing it away because you wish to behave as a gentleman.'[282] Tellingly, Newnes would soon part company with Stead in order to join forces with Cook, whom he appointed editor of his new Liberal organ the *Westminster Gazette*. It turned out that the softly spoken public school boy, not the garrulous fellow northerner, proved to be the preferred editor of the self-made newspaper baron from Derbyshire. His only gripe, apparently, was that Cook was not often known to smile.[283]

The dissolution of Stead's partnership with Newnes took place no less rapidly than it had been consummated. Perhaps taking advantage of a flu pandemic which had incapacitated most of his staff (and from which he too was suffering), Stead penned a vicious 'Character Sketch' of *The Times* for the March issue. This called the newspaper's editor, the 35-year-old former All Souls Fellow George Buckle, 'a young and ineffective man', and insinuated that he took 'public opinion' to be no more than the musings of a 'single, shrewd, idle clergyman, loitering about in places of common resort...'. 'How innocently archaic is this!' howled Stead. More controversially, Stead speculated that the losses incurred by the newspaper as a result of the forged Parnell letters were as high as £100,000; which was not inaccurate, but largely founded on hearsay. His opinion that 'the *Thunderer* was no more' and that the paper would soon collapse did not prove to be correct. Even his friend and solicitor George Lewis warned that he would have to remove various key passages if he wanted to avoid yet another appearance in court.

After he had read the article in proof, Newnes rushed over to see Stead at the office he had rented for him in Great College Street – coincidently, or not, next door to Marie Belloc's home. He warned that the damages 'could be enormous if indeed it did not land you back in Holloway, with me in the adjoining cell'. He had not intended the magazine to be so outspoken and begged Stead to reconsider the wisdom of publishing the article. Since Newnes had already been overruled on two matters of lesser importance (the printing of scores of letters from famous well-wishers and the introduction of the controversial name of Annie Besant into the paper's pages) he expected his demand to be heeded. But Stead simply looked him coolly in the eye, apparently without a glimmer of humour, and explained that *The Times* article was 'nothing' compared to what he planned for the future. When Newnes pressed the issue, Stead grandly rose from his chair, and, with an air of finality declared: 'Then it becomes a question as to whether we ought not to separate.' Newnes was taken aback, but was clearly also partly relieved at the opportunity to free himself from such a liability. He suggested that if Stead preferred to have things his way, he should get one of his 'rich friends' to buy him out for a 'fair and reasonable' price. Stead instantly agreed, but soon afterwards sent Newnes a self-pitying letter resenting his 'sudden end' to their agreement. It was too late.[284]

From a financial perspective this was easily the worst decision of Stead's life. Within twelve months Newnes would found the acclaimed *Strand Magazine*, which fast became one of the most profitable and popular journals of all time. Stead's praise for the 'peculiar genius' of his former proprietor was undermined by his sneer that the *Strand* was 'quite safe against suggesting forbidden speculations' and did not 'provoke its readers to too great exercise of thinking'. In truth, Stead was extremely hurt, if not jealous, of his missed opportunity. This must have been all the more insufferable for the fact that Newnes's most famous contributor,

Arthur Conan Doyle, had formerly been a freelancer for the *Review of Reviews*. It seems that Stead had not recognised the potential of the inventor of Sherlock Holmes, for he used him solely as a minor medical authority, second even to the jobbing scientist-cum-novelist, Grant Allen. At the end of his first year editing the *Review*, Stead had suggested that Conan Doyle travel to Italy to investigate, sympathetically, the supposed cancer cures of the eccentric Italian 'electrohomeopath' 'Count' Cesare Mattei, who boasted of owing 'his higher education to a duel and his medical knowledge to his neighbour's dog'. Conan Doyle, who had recently written a serious examination of Dr Robert Koch's work on the tuberculosis bacillus, chortled that such an enterprise would allow 'the greatest man of science' to be followed by 'the greatest quack in Europe'. 'Stead glared at me angrily,' he recalled years after, 'for it seems that the Mattei treatment with its blue electricity and the rest of it was at that moment his particular fad...' The great Conan Doyle would not trouble that editor again – ever.[285]

The problem of where Stead was to find the money necessary to buy Newnes out proved hard to solve. He confessed that to his 'uninstructed mind' it was incredible that after only three months of publishing the magazine could be worth so hefty a figure as £12,600, which was the value placed on it by Newnes's accountant. Raising such a large sum of money, however, was only the beginning of Stead's difficulties. His decision to part from Newnes also meant losing the valuable *Tit-Bits* staff and the facility of printing and distributing cheaply through the magazine's Burleigh Street office. Luckily for Stead, Lewis's hard bargaining with Newnes allowed this profitable arrangement to continue until the appearance of the April issue. 'You used to speak of Providences,' observed Newnes with a chortle. 'I believe that the fact of Mr Lewis not coming to terms with me is a providence for you. Because as long as I am connected with the *Review of Reviews* it will make money, and *that* after all with a family man must be of some value.'[286]

This situation lasted until May, when Stead made a deal with General Booth for a secret loan of approximately £10,000 at 5 per cent interest, secured by a life insurance policy. This made clear that if Stead died the magazine would be worth practically nothing: a consideration Stead had rightly pointed out to Newnes.

Booth's offer was not wholly unreasonable and there is every reason to suppose that Stead was still on friendly, if not intimate, terms with the Booth family. Their organisation continued to protect Stead from further charges by paying off the Armstrongs, whose legal representatives periodically intimated that they would bring fresh charges relating to the abduction of their daughter. Perhaps as a mark of gratitude for this, as well as for the timely loan, Stead enthusiastically offered his assistance in writing the General's famous book on urban poverty, *In Darkest England and the Way Out*, which he, a little self-interestedly, called 'the Book of the Month, nay, the Book of the Year' when it appeared in October 1890.

Booth's initial proposal had been modest: he asked if Stead could provide him with a 'literary hack' to 'lick' his overlong manuscript into shape while he tended to his wife, who was dying from cancer. Since this was by no means a complicated request, it must have been greeted with some surprise and anxiety when Stead shot back, with characteristic solemnity, that the work was 'too important' to delegate to anyone but himself. Instead of merely editing Booth's text, Stead proposed to begin afresh on the grave understanding that he would maintain his anonymity and would always bow to the General's wishes. '[I]f you desire to advocate, let us say,' said Stead, 'polygamy, as a means of social regeneration I will obey you implicitly, and put a chapter in praise of polygamy into the book.' All that Stead demanded was the freedom to denounce such 'deadly heresy' after publication.[287]

Needless to say, *In Darkest England* did not contain a chapter on polygamy. The book's title, derived from the travel memoir *In Darkest Africa* by the swashbuckling explorer Henry Stanley, gave an accurate indication of its tone and content. In the guise of a noble savage, Stead depicted London as a vast malaria swamp, where gin palaces served the 'River of the Water of Death' for seventeen hours out of every twenty-four. Men toiled for a pittance or had no work at all, while their wives and daughters slipped easily from match-making into prostitution – the 'only career in which the maximum income is paid to the newest apprentice'. This vision of 'Modern Babylon' was by now long familiar to Stead's readers; but, just to make sure that his involvement was not missed, Stead surreptitiously inserted the entire text of what he called his 'famous leader', 'Is It Not Time?', as a means of autographing his handiwork.[288]

The most curious feature of *In Darkest England* was the proposed 'way out'. This drew rather coldly on contemporary ideas of imperialism and social Darwinism, which were clearly attractive to Stead. The poor, he proposed, were to be retrained as farmers and transported to the furthermost reaches of the Empire. Those unwilling, or unable, to make such a voyage were to be put to work in special Salvation Army workhouses, where living standards were to equal those of 'a London cab-horse' (Stead dismissed the 'gaol standard' as 'utopian'). Disturbingly, Stead and Booth added that the 'residuum' – those deemed incapable of reform – should be cordoned off from the rest of humanity. They had no more right to breed, or to live in freedom, than a 'mad dog'.

More in line with Stead's earlier ideals, the author envisaged vigilantes be hired to hunt rapists and absentee fathers to force them to pay maintenance; if they would not, Stead proposed to divulge their wrongdoing in the press. It was this element of the scheme which particularly enraged the aged Thomas Huxley, who denounced the book's 'Sicilian mafia' principles in a series of irate letters to the editor of *The Times*. He particularly took the author to task for misappropriating – and misunderstanding – the theory of human evolution. Booth's scheme, claimed Huxley, promoted nothing more than 'autocratic Socialism' masked by a 'theological exterior'.[289]

Huxley was clearly using *In Darkest England* as a means of attacking his *bête noire*, the Salvation Army; but he was perfectly aware that his old editor was the real author. Not only was he familiar with

Stead's journalistic style, his friend James Knowles, who edited the fashionable journal the *Nineteenth Century*, wrote to inform him that the book 'was written and boomed by that most accursed of all Iscariots': Stead's 'hoof-prints', he claimed, were on every page.[290]

Huxley's reticence in revealing Stead's authorship may have been an act of courtesy. Equally, he may have feigned ignorance as a means of making an unreserved swipe at his old acquaintance. In any case, there was little need for Stead to wade in, as was his wont, when his name was briefly mentioned by Huxley in a cutting aside about the Armstrong trial published in *The Times*. '[S]eeing that my name has been brought into this,' Stead disingenuously protested in his reply, generously published by Buckle the following day, '... may I ... give the most unqualified denial to the statement as to the alleged admission on [Bramwell Booth's] part of falsehood?' His correction was semantic: '[i]n short', Huxley accurately summed up the day after, Booth 'did not say what was wrong; but he did what was wrong'. This spat achieved little, but it drew further attention to Stead's connection with the controversial pamphlet.

To his colleagues Stead was even more willing to disclose his involvement. 'You will recognize my fine Roman hand in most of the chapters,' he boasted to Alfred Milner, now working at the Ministry of Finance at Cairo. Yet when Cook, quite fairly, pointed out in the *PMG* that the 'vivacious touch of a well-known journalist' could be traced 'in page after page, and phrase after phrase', Stead exploded with rage. There is little doubt that he believed Cook to be highlighting the absurd nature of his narcissistic ravings in the *Review of Reviews*. Here he described the author – supposedly Booth – as being 'as earnest as John the Baptist, for now and then the aboriginal preacher reappears crying aloud, Jonah-like, messages calling men to flee from the wrath to come'. He was a 'saint', the only man in London 'who would discover Jesus Christ if he came again'. The temptation to reveal Stead's 'open secret' must have been intense.

Although sales of the book were encouraging – 10,000 were sold on the first day alone – General Booth was furious to discover the extent to which Stead had embedded his identity in the text. His fears were realised when Stead began to make claims upon the sum of £40,000 which had been donated by enthusiastic supporters of their scheme during the first few weeks. 'You may say "Is not the Book mine; are not its profits mine, and may I not do what I like with my own?"' Stead menacingly wrote to him in January 1891. 'But ... the public will be, rightly or wrongly, surprised, to use no stronger term, if the profits accruing from the sale of a book published to promote a certain Social Scheme, are not devoted to ... the salary of the Director General of the Social Scheme' – evidently Stead himself.[291]

Many of Stead's less intimate friends encouraged him to take legal proceedings against anyone spreading 'lies' about his involvement, especially that he had received a loan from the Salvation Army (which, of course, he had) in return for writing the book. His nonchalant dismissal of this suggestion reveals much about Stead's ability to dissemble. He would not, he told one friend, sue for libel even 'if it were stated that I had killed my grandmother and eaten her'.[292] Such language succeeded in saving Stead (and the Salvation Army) from embarrassment, but with hindsight it raises serious doubts about some of Stead's no less emphatic denials. The most notable of these regarded his relationships with women, which hereafter became an even bigger feature of his life than during his youth. Though Stead always swore blind that his extra-marital relations were chaste and proper, many of the women themselves were notoriously promiscuous, none more so than 'Daisy' Brooke, the lover of Stead's old nemesis, Edward, Prince of Wales.

CHAPTER 11

MY LOVELY LITTLE DAISY WIFE

I am told that there is an awful article in here about me, I dare not open it...
Edward, Prince of Wales, to Lady Brooke (July 1891)

During the St Leger race week of September 1890, Albert Edward, Prince of Wales was entertained by a wealthy ship-owner at Tranby Croft, a large country house some miles outside the Yorkshire city of Hull. It was to become the epicentre of one of the most damaging scandals in the history of the Royal Family. A fellow guest, Lieutenant-Colonel Sir William Gordon-Cumming, Bt, of the Scots Guards, was accused by their host's son Stanley Wilson and a collection of onlookers of cheating at baccarat, an illegal and unskilful card game played for high stakes. The Prince, who sat as banker and had apparently noticed no foul play, rashly compelled the officer to sign a secret pledge never to play cards again. When the incident became public a few weeks later, Gordon-Cumming, protesting his innocence, sued Wilson for slander.

The looming trial evoked unhappy memories of the last time the Prince had been embroiled in an ugly legal case. This had taken place in 1870, when a 29-year-old Edward had 'voluntarily' denied having an affair with a noted society beauty, Harriet Mordaunt, at her divorce trial. Few doubted that the Prince – an infamous womaniser and adulterer – was lying. But the judge concluded that Mrs Mordaunt was 'insane', thereby invalidating her testimony.[293]

The press at the time of the affair had abided by an unwritten code that members of the Royal Family were not to be criticised too severely. Edward might be caricatured as a bounder or a fool, but it was considered unacceptable to question his moral fitness to reign. By the early 1890s, however, high-minded newspaper editors such as Stead were beginning to dispense with such antiquated courtesy. It had become possible to ask, as Stead did in a leading article marking the Queen's Golden Jubilee in 1887, whether the monarchy would even be able to survive the accession of the 'fat little bald man in red'. Clubland gasped. A new era had begun.

The latest scandal provided Stead the perfect opportunity finally to chastise the Prince in unreserved terms. Amazingly, however, he chose not to do so. Destroying the careers of 'mere' politicians such as Sir Charles Dilke and Charles Parnell, it appears, was one thing; savaging the heir to the throne was quite another. Like many journalists, both before and since, Stead seems at heart to have been a repressed toady. Given the opportunity to enter into the Establishment, he seized it with alacrity.

It says much about Stead in middle age that he heard the details of the scandal while staying at Eastnor Castle, the stately home of Lady Henry Somerset, whose brother-in-law had been a guest at the ill-fated party. His hostess was one of a number of jilted society ladies whom Stead met through his diligent and highly respected solicitor, George Lewis. Lewis had first approached Stead at the height of the 'Maiden Tribute' agitation demanding that none of his clients be implicated by the paper's sensational revelations. No doubt with the same kind of diplomacy that would work so well for Cecil Rhodes, Lewis explained that he and Stead had a common interest. In return for protecting his clients, he would gladly provide the editor with the legal services that he would undoubtedly require.

Stead's first service to Lewis was to shield Lady Colin Campbell, who came to him, doe-eyed, in the midst of the longest and probably most graphic divorce case of all time. In the course of the public hearing it emerged that her husband, the son of a high-ranking Conservative politician, had intentionally infected her with syphilis and that she had consoled herself by seducing a series of men in their West End drawing room, including the Captain of the London Fire Brigade. The testimony of her butler, who witnessed proceedings through the proverbial keyhole, led one journalist to denounce her publicly as a 'sex goddess' possessing 'the unbridled lust of a Messalina and the indelicate readiness of a common harlot'. Stead, however, dutifully abstained from censorious comment. If her later novel *Darell Blake* can be taken as evidence, this was partly because he was taken in by her charms: the story involves an unhappily married newspaper editor who falls hopelessly in love with an attractive, promiscuous young aristocrat.

Lady Henry was a more elusive character than Lady Colin, but appears to have been no less strong-willed – or amorous. She had been miserably married to the homosexual second son of the Duke of Beaufort, Lord Henry Somerset, who proved unwilling to supply her with the fifteen children she had once expressed a desire to conceive. Inevitably, the marriage was a total failure. In 1874, she took the bold, and socially ruinous, decision of obtaining a legal separation from her husband, citing 'lack of intimacy' as a principal grievance. She went on to write articles in the press about contraception, and surrounded herself with the sexually adventurous members of the Women's Christian Temperance Union, with whom Stead would also form a strong connection. Her social shame was completed in 1889 when her husband's younger brother, Lord Arthur Somerset, was caught up in the Cleveland Street male brothel scandal – another *cause célèbre* in part handled by Lewis, and conveniently ignored by Stead.

Over the course of their weekend party, Lady Henry and her temperance colleagues implored Stead to denounce, once and for all, the Prince's infamous lifestyle. But he told them that it was 'absurd' to criticise the Prince merely for gambling, as 'that was what everybody did in his set'. Only when Stead returned to London a few days later did he succumb to the 'general expectation' that he 'must say something' about the affair.[294] This was quite believable. As the leading light of the 'Nonconformist conscience', the country looked to Stead for the voice of righteous indignation. But Stead correctly supposed that, at this stage in his career, he could probably exert more power and influence by siding with the Prince rather than opposing him. Presumably with the encouragement of the likes of Brett and Lewis (who acted as Stanley Wilson's solicitor), Stead approached the Prince's private secretary, Sir Francis Knollys, for assistance in writing a sympathetic 'Character Sketch' to appear in the immediate aftermath of the trial.

Stead began his meeting with Knollys by explaining one troubling condition of his support: he would need reassurance that the Prince's wrongdoing extended no further than 'ordinary immorality', about which he, somewhat unconvincingly, claimed to have 'never said a word'. Stead was undoubtedly aware that the Prince was a noted philanderer and habitué of the same kinds of Parisian brothels that had roused his ire so memorably in years past. But, with apparent empathy, the editor explained that he 'fully recognised' the Prince was 'quite as often seduced as he is the seducer'. He was therefore relieved that the first time he was compelled to 'go for' the Prince it concerned an issue about which he could 'honestly remain indifferent'. The only matter he wanted officially denied by Knollys was a story he had heard through his friend Annie Besant that the Prince had seduced 'a chambermaid or a governess in distressing circumstances in a Duke's shooting box, or at Sandringham'. Knollys – himself a noted womaniser – solemnly pledged that 'as to Sandringham at any rate' there was no truth in the story.[295]

This satisfied Stead. In the coming weeks he put together a sympathetic article about the Prince, which he respectfully passed on to Knollys, Gladstone and Lord Salisbury, for approval. 'I think there we did some good,' quaffed the Grand Old Man to Morley after they had made several important alterations to Stead's text.[296]

The article appeared in mid-July, exactly one month after the close of the baccarat trial. The Prince took it directly to his lover, Lady Brooke ('The Blabbing Brooke' as she was known on account of leaking the story in the first place), and said in a trembling voice: 'I am told that there is an awful article in here about me, I dare not open it...' He had little reason to be afraid. Stead's overarching theme was almost comically gentle: Edward had done nothing wrong in forcing Gordon-Cumming to sign the controversial pledge. And as for playing baccarat: it was only natural that the Prince should find much-needed relaxation at the card-table. Practically in the guise of the Prince's late father, Prince Albert, Stead suggested that Edward be given more worthwhile responsibilities than merely the 'sentry-go of monotonous and soul-wearying ceremonial'. Without more weighty duties, concluded Stead, Edward would inevitably turn to gambling, or even perhaps 'those pleasures of the senses which are apt to transform themselves into Deadly Sins'. Evidently, Stead recognised something of himself in his royal subject.

What particularly surprised, and annoyed, the new generation of journalists about Stead's article was that he reserved his most scathing criticisms for his own profession. 'It has been recognised on all hands,' Stead pompously lamented, 'that it was the news-paper which pandered to the passion of the people for gambling [with its promotion of horse-racing and the stock exchange]' – not the Prince's casual dalliance with baccarat. To condemn Edward merely for playing this exotic game, he claimed, would be like a temperance reformer denouncing champagne, while permitting the consumption of beer and spirits (an aside obviously intended to placate Lady Henry and her circle). With some force, he concluded that if the British wanted a truly popular monarchy they would have to reform their own vices before they turned upon those of their social superiors.

Stead clearly believed himself to have done an enormous favour to his erstwhile enemies at the pinnacle of society and expected to be treated on more equal terms by senior politicians in recogni-tion of his services. In some respects, at least, he would not be disappointed. Within a few months of the appearance of the article he became a regular addition to the breakfast table of the Conservative leader of the House of Commons, Arthur Balfour, while Lord Rosebery, who replaced the 83-year-old Gladstone as Liberal Prime Minister in 1894, tolerated Stead's presence while he slit open the pages of his new books in the study of his Berkley Square mansion. But Stead's famously uncouth appearance invariably upset these meetings: Rosebery's butler twice sent Stead away on the assumption that he was a nuisance caller or a madman. Although Rosebery apologised for this, and promised to 'sit in the porter's chair till you arrive', it hardly suggests that Stead's presence was particularly welcome. Privately Rosebery told Cook (a far more trusted confidant) that he always felt himself 'on thin ice' in Stead's company. Balfour was even more unwilling to get close to Stead. 'No, a thousand times No,' he responded to a request for a formal interview, ' ...[I] would as soon allow [myself] to be interviewed for the "World" or any other [lowbrow] newspaper.'[297] Nevertheless, Stead's plan had worked: his feet were squarely beneath the (breakfast) table of power.

The qualified success of this achievement came at a heavy price to the plaintiff of the baccarat trial, who looked in vain for a prominent journalist to take up his cause. His counsel, the Solicitor-General Sir Edward Clarke, had fought valiantly, if improbably (as a high-ranking Conservative politician), against the formidable defence team of George Lewis, Sir George Russell and the rising Liberal MP Herbert Asquith. But Clarke had been complacent in assuming, at least at the outset of proceedings, that the defendants would simply withdraw their accusations once they had been refuted in open court. In his mistaken view, the facts scarcely needed articulating. Gordon-Cumming, a respected solider and experienced gambler, had played a method known as 'coup de trois', whereby half the value to the stake can be added to the original amount if the winnings from the previous hand are kept on the table. All the other players understood this and made no objection to his methods. Only when the host's young son-in-law, Lycett Green, told the other guests that he had seen the officer surreptitiously raising his stakes did anyone else see a cause for alarm – primarily because they wanted to avoid a scandal. The implication was that Gordon-Cumming had been forced to sign the humiliating pledge merely as a means of sparing the Prince from any reflected embarrassment of the incident becoming public. An even more delicate matter, scarcely alluded to by Clarke, but pertinent to his brief, was that Gordon-Cumming was almost certainly having an affair with Green's young wife, Edith. He had 'taught her cards', and she had been 'very intimate' with a friend of his. This may go some way to explain the curious fact that Gordon-Cumming, along with the Prince, had been the party's joint guest of honour.[298]

Clarke's defence of Gordon-Cumming suggested that the Prince had compelled an innocent man to sign away his career and reputation in defence of his own. This brought a heap of obloquy upon Clarke, even from the judge Lord Chief Justice Coleridge, whose partial summing-up in favour of the defence was fairly judged by *The Observer* as 'a melancholy and flagrant violation of the best traditions of the English bench'.

Stead, who should have seized upon these points, dismissed the Solicitor-General's reasonable theories as 'silly' and a 'scandalous injustice' to the Prince. He must have been aware that Edward had already, in the case of Harriet Mordaunt, shown himself capable of sacrificing the reputation of a fellow subject for his own protection. Gordon-Cumming's future was no less rosy than his predecessor's. Within hours of losing his case he was cashiered from the army and consigned to forty years of social oblivion, mitigated only by the devotion of his wealthy American wife, Florence Garner, whom he defiantly married the day after the jury's humiliating verdict.

It was characteristic of Stead to turn a blind eye to impropriety that did not involve sex or adultery. Yet, as he warned Knollys, if a *third* scandal should ever impinge upon the Prince, especially involving women, he would not so willingly come to his defence. 'I have a horrible presentiment,' he told the doubtless terrified private secretary, 'that a day may come when I shall be confronted by some scandal in which a ruined woman or an injured husband will come to me, and I shall be driven, however much I dislike the task, to go for the Prince as I have gone for Dilke...'[299]

It was a typically Steadean 'prophecy': just such a storm was already in the offing.

cs

The man at the centre of this potential crisis was the dashing naval captain Lord Charles Beresford, who had recently stood down as a Conservative MP to pursue his military career. In background, lifestyle and temperament he was almost the antithesis of Stead's erstwhile ally, the more senior Captain 'Jacky' Fisher, with whom Beresford would later row bitterly. At this juncture in his life, Beresford was known principally as a popular 'man about town' and a close friend of the Prince, whose passion for beautiful women and practical jokes he shared. On one occasion he was said to have cut off the air supply to the cabin in which Edward was thought to be making love to his then mistress, the actress Lily Langtry.

In the mid-1880s, Beresford had had an affair with Lady Brooke, the well-endowed wife of his close friend Francis Greville, who was shortly to succeed his father as Earl of Warwick. 'Daisy' (as she was known to her friends) was considered to have been the most beautiful woman of her generation, and so it was only natural that she would progress from the handsome naval captain to the Prince; she would become his 'own lovely little Daisy wife'. But her good looks masked a colossal vanity. 'In my teens,' she wrote in old age, 'it came as an almost incredible surprise and delight to me to find in men's eyes an unfailing tribute to a beauty I myself had not been able to discern.' Her husband dutifully put up with the 'inevitability' that she would have 'a train of admirers'. 'I could not help it,' she wrote. 'There they were. It was all a great game.'[300]

Daisy's relationship with Beresford began in a manner typical of her libidinous weekend parties at Easton Lodge, which were suitably popular with the Prince's fast-living Marlborough House set. These occasions commenced with an informal selection by each female guest of a man – not their husband – to 'amuse' them for the duration of their stay. Lady Brooke dutifully arranged a complicated series of codes and conventions to ensure the avoidance of any notoriety or scandal: assignations, when not taking place in her Elizabethan cottage (replete with French erotic literature), had to be concluded by 6am so as not to arouse the suspicion of the servants. Yet, like so many strict enforcers of protocol, Daisy failed to live up to her own high standards. To the horror of Beresford's remarkably good-natured wife, Jeromina, she calmly announced one morning that she intended to run away with Beresford to France. 'I determined not to sacrifice Lord Charles's career to such an insane project,' Lady Charles later wrote, 'by taking him home with me on the spot.'[301]

That should have been the end of the matter. Beresford certainly thought so, for within a few months his wife became pregnant with another child. But what should have been a happy occasion provoked Lady Brooke to throw all pretence of decorum to the wind. In an angry letter to her former lover, she claimed that he had 'no right' to sleep with his wife and informed him that one of her children was his own – a demonstrably false statement. Unfortunately for Lady Brooke, however, the scandalous letter arrived while Beresford was on an overseas assignment. Worse, Beresford had instructed his wife to open any correspondence delivered to their Eaton Square home. Lady Charles kept her adversary's letter closely guarded. Only after an exceptionally awkward holiday in Monte Carlo later that year, during which Lady Brooke 'bombarded' the Beresford villa with 'notes most unblushing' from nearby Beaulieu, did Lady Charles decide to take action. Like many women of her class, she turned to George Lewis for assistance.

Lewis informed Lady Brooke that her letter to Beresford was now in Lady Charles's possession and implicitly threatened, in suitably legal phrases, that further steps would be taken unless she ceased harassing his client. As Lady Charles later put it: 'The lady thereupon sought and obtained an Interview with H. R. H. The Prince of Wales (whom she hardly knew at the time) he being an intimate friend of Lord Charles and myself, and begged him to help "Beauty in Distress".' Her exaggeration was only slight. As an arch-manipulator of men, Lady Brooke knew only too well how to enlist the Prince's support. 'He was charmingly courteous to me,' she later wrote, 'and at length told me he hoped his friendship would make up in part, at least, for my sailor-lover's loss. He was more than kind ... and suddenly I saw him looking at me in a way all women understand. I knew I had won, so I asked him to tea.'

Presumably it was shortly after this tea party that Edward called at Lewis's home, at the extraordinary hour of 2am, demanding to see Lady Brooke's letter. As a professional solicitor, Lewis should have politely refused this improper request, but in an act justly described by Beresford as 'sycophantic servility' he acquiesced. Clearly he sensed a far more lucrative client in the Prince of Wales.

Edward was horrified by what he was shown: it was 'the most shocking letter [he] had ever read'. But to have the document destroyed, Lewis regretfully intoned, he would have to convince Lady Charles that this was the best course of action for all concerned. To this end, Lady Charles tells us, Edward paid a visit to Eaton Square 'and ordered me to give the letter up to *him*. This I naturally refused ... warning him that he had no business ... in such an affair.' Upon leaving, the Prince angrily demanded that Lady Charles send her 'ultimatum' to Mr Lewis.

Her terms were comparatively mild: she would return the letter if Lady Brooke abstained 'from coming to London that Season'. But in the world of high society this was an impossible imposition. It was also a direct affront to the Prince, since it threatened to wreck his new love affair. No doubt for this reason, rather than any higher motive, when Edward paid Lady Charles a second visit he was 'anything but conciliatory'. He told her that her behaviour had jeopardised not only her position in society, but also her husband's career. This was too much. As Lady Charles later wrote, the Prince had taken up 'the cause of an "abandoned woman" against that of a perfectly blameless wife ... for the gratification of his own private design'.

When Beresford learned about this incident shortly afterwards, he was initially sympathetic to the Prince. But when he discovered that his wife was being socially ostracised by Edward 'in vengeance for my turpitude' he loyally came to her defence. From his cabin of his aptly named ship *Undaunted* he sent the Prince a series of angry missives. The most threatening of these might almost have been written by W. T. Stead in his prime:

The days of duelling are past, but there is a more just way of getting right done than can duelling, and that is – publicity.

Coming, as it did, just a few months after the baccarat scandal, this was seriously threatening. Even Lady Charles (to whom her husband had sent his letter to forward to the Prince) thought it too strong. For this reason she passed the letter on to Lord Salisbury, who gently told Beresford that 'public opinion of our own class' would be against him. The elder statesman did not appear to recognise that 'public opinion' had come to extend far deeper than the upper echelon of society. Fortunately for the Prince, Lady Brooke was not so naive.

Almost immediately, Daisy set about arranging a meeting between herself and the famous editor. But her plan was far from easy to achieve. Stead's isolation from high society was well demonstrated by the fact that he had never joined a club, nor did he even own a dinner jacket. The only person that even superficially linked him to the Prince's circle was an eccentric monetary reformer and amateur journalist called Moreton Frewen. Daisy now sought him out.

Frewen was almost a caricature of a nineteenth-century buccaneering English gentleman. For years he had travelled the globe, speculating wildly in everything from African timber to Wyoming cattle ranches. Stead, who was almost proud of his ignorance of economics, considered him to be an unabashed libertine: a man who 'left babies at other people's doorsteps'. Yet Frewen understood his editor's foibles. When Lady Brooke asked him to dissuade Stead from taking a high moral line in the impending crisis, he replied wisely: 'But you, Daisy, would do it so much better ... [Stead] could not resist those enormous blue eyes.'[302]

His observation would be made more emphatically in later years by another of Stead's close associates, Alfred Milner, who claimed to know no man more 'susceptible ... to the most fleshy type of feminine "charm"...'.[303] This would be a happy revelation for Lady Brooke, who anxiously awaited the dinner party she arranged to take place at Frewen's West End home.

Stead would later describe this unlikely meeting as the work of 'sorrow ... the dark-robed angel that has ever brought you near to me'. It would be more accurate to say that he was immediately bowled over by her beauty and flirtatious manner. Like many strict Nonconformists of his generation, there was an element in Stead's personality that 'yearned to be corrupted'. While his fellow diners talked amiably among themselves, Stead sat, unusually quiet, admiring Lady Brooke's demeanour. When the other men withdrew, he approached her in the hope that they might have a proper chat.

Daisy appears to have taken the lead in their conversation. She began by congratulating Stead for the article he had written on the Prince, which she thought contained some 'very good advice and was very fair'. Stead was obviously flattered. But she threatened disenchantment by asking, presumably with a smile of feigned surprise, why so many people believed him to have a 'Pharisaic virtue'. This was a masterclass in Puritanical seduction, worthy of a woman who boasted descent from both Oliver Cromwell and Nell Gwyn. 'As a matter of fact,' retorted Stead, 'I never talk to anybody intimately – so as to know and understand their position – without feeling that if I had been in their place, I should probably have been much worse than they were.'[304] The implication was clear: sinners were safe from the malice of his pen so long as they kept him abreast of their wrongdoing.

It is not clear whether Stead began to look at Lady Brooke 'in a way that all women understand', but he was clearly, no less than the Prince before him, brought to heel. In contrast to her relationship with Edward, however, Lady Brooke appears to have genuinely liked Stead and took his advice that she should use her social position to help the disadvantaged to heart.

Within a few days of their meeting, Stead wrote Lady Brooke a long and excited letter suggesting that they should meet to discuss some charitable projects that he had in mind for her. When no response was forthcoming, Stead, almost exactly as he had in his courtship of Madam Novikov over a decade earlier, sent a wounded note. His beloved's response was no less encouraging than the Russian's had been: 'I fear your letter may be lying somewhere unopened,' she reassured him, '...had I received one, it would *not* have been neglected!' This was music to Stead's ears. 'Some day,' she concluded, 'I hope to have the great pleasure of seeing you again. For several words you said when we last met have sunk into my heart.'

This was the start of a lifelong friendship which would moderate the excesses in both of their characters. Stead would not only become more laidback about moral transgressions, he also began defending the aristocracy as 'splendid paupers' under threat from new taxes and the encroachment of selfish plutocrats. Lady Warwick (as she became in 1893), meanwhile, would shun frivolity and embrace social reform – eventually, to Stead's disappointment, she became an ardent socialist (albeit of the champagne variety). But her ostentatious destruction of Stead's letters to her in her fireplace at Easton Lodge precludes the same insight offered by his correspondence with Madame Novikov. One is at a loss to know whether he obeyed her stipulation that they should remain only 'real *friends*', as opposed to anything more dangerous.[305]

This much is clear: Stead was passionately in love with Lady Warwick and was regularly invited to stay, alone, for a 'quiet evening' at her Essex mansion. Sometimes she was almost giddy to be reunited with him: 'I want to see you very *very* much indeed...' she once wrote. Other occasions were no less spirited: '...you always "enthuse" me! either by your writings or your personality. I shall have to stay in London a night *next* week...' Most telling of all, perhaps, the Prince, whom Stead always called 'your Parishioner' (she was 'the priest of the parish'), became 'rather jealous' of Stead's 'influence on [her] life and thoughts!' This appears to have been largely groundless: Stead repeatedly told Lady Warwick, apparently without humour, that she should not leave the Prince but 'stick to her post'.[306]

Through Lady Warwick, Stead eventually had the opportunity of meeting the Prince. This took place at a lunch party on Tuesday

8 December 1896, at Lady Algernon Lennox's palatial townhouse
in Mayfair.[307] Stead grandly claimed in later years that he could
have met Edward much earlier had he wished, but chose not to
on account of the Prince's demand that they meet on a Sunday
– Stead 'never went up to Town on Sundays, and ... would not
make a beginning with the Prince'. A more plausible explanation
was surely that Edward was not especially desirous of making the
editor's acquaintance.

Stead left a detailed account of his rendezvous with the future
king. Few documents give a better indication of Stead's exaggerated
sense of self-importance. Though he tried to maintain his indiffer-
ence about the occasion – 'I never said "Royal Highness" as far as I
can remember' – he was clearly in awe of the royal person.

While he and Lady Warwick sat waiting for the Prince's arrival,
Stead frantically asked what would be suitable for them to talk
about. Could they discuss politics? Or his forthcoming 'Character
Sketch' of the Queen? 'Anything,' Lady Warwick replied. Could
he, then, 'sing her praises as soon as she let the room'? 'She seemed
rather amused [by this],' recalled Stead, '...[but] said she had no
doubt it would please him as much as anything I could [say].'

For a man who had recently written to a correspondent that he
was 'very much more in favour of making cases of adultery, proved
in open court, offences punishable by imprisonment than I used to
be', Stead seems to have been remarkably relaxed.[308]

The Prince arrived at ten minutes past two. He was late and had
a train to catch at half past four. This may have coloured some of
Stead's less kindly first impressions. 'He struck me when he came
into the room,' recalled Stead, 'as being slightly under the middle
height, not so stout as I had expected, very simple in his manners.
And had at first a look ... which made you have a half-impression
that he had either a slight squint, or that one of his front teeth
was awry.' Stead's many critics might have recognised this as a
convincing self-portrait: his acquaintance Colonel Brocklehurst
once described him as '[t]hat gaunt wild-looking individual, always
badly dressed'.[309]

Lunch was served immediately. Stead sat opposite Lady Warwick so that the Prince was seated at the head of the table. It is hard to believe that their conversation was easy or agreeable, but Stead's memories were favourable. 'I was perfectly at my ease all through,' he wrote. Edward, however, does not appear to have viewed it, at least initially, in the same light. His opening gambit about some heavyweight articles he had been reading in *The Times* about old-age pensions was strikingly uncharacteristic. Certainly, Edward had lately been involved in a government Commission designed to look into this controversial issue, but he had spent most of his time in the committee room drawing Union Jacks with crayons brought specially for his amusement. Moreover, as Stead would later mention over brandy, it had been a running joke in his early days at Northumberland Street that the staff 'must make room for a note or two of a lighter character for the Prince of Wales' – Morley had let slip that the Prince found their pages 'too strenuous'. With a good deal more discretion, Stead chose not to refer to the well-known fact that the Prince had ostentatiously cancelled his subscription to the *PMG* at the time of the 'Maiden Tribute' campaign.

The meal was apparently not excessive, but it was ample enough for there to have been a lobster course, which Stead and Lady Warwick followed the Prince's lead in declining. Stead once had to call the servant with the bell. The rest of the meal they were quite alone.

A topic of mutual interest was the British Empire, about which Stead spoke expansively. 'The Prince listened very attentively,' boasted Stead, '...every now and then chiming in.' It was only when they got onto the thorny subject of Russia that the Prince broke free of his unaccustomed deference.

'Ah, I don't like your Madame Novikov,' he interjected with a knowing smile. It had been Lady Warwick who had brought the Russian's name into the conversation, no doubt with mischievous intent. '...She gives herself such airs as if she had a great position and great power, and I know she has none of these things.'

It would be hard to imagine that Edward did not have the same view of his interlocutor, who instantly rushed to his old friend's defence. 'I beg your pardon,' riposted Stead, 'I have known Madame Novikov for twenty years, and she is not a bit of a humbug ... she has been the only person who has attempted to make English people understand Russia policy.' It was a defence no less applicable, in Stead's view, to himself.

After the meal, Lady Warwick, who was recovering from a fall from her horse, withdrew to rest upstairs. Stead followed her to the door asking 'in a side whisper' if it was 'going on alright?' With a firm squeeze of his hand, which the Prince must have seen – and resented – she assured him that it was going 'quite right'.

Stead now hit his stride. Accepting the Prince's offer of a large cigar, he recounted his travels around the courts of Europe; how he had met the Tsar; how Bismarck had refused to see him because he was 'a dangerous man'; how he regretted the accession of the Prince's nephew, Kaiser William II (he 'ought to have been a newspaper Editor'); how he hoped the Queen would use her influence more often to check the excesses of politicians. These, and other, of Stead's reflections were so brash that he may have invented them to please the secretary to whom he dictated his notes. Yet they have an authentic ring. At one point he allegedly told the Prince that he would 'rather have been your mother's son and heir-apparent than any king that ever sat on the English throne ... [including] Henry VII, Henry VIII, Charles I, James I, or Charles II'. To Edward's undoubted amusement and astonishment, Stead went on to remark, casually, that all these positions paled into insignificance beside that of the editor of the *Review of Reviews*: 'I think I have the best position in the Empire,' he stated unblinkingly, 'but I think that after me, you come.'

'The idea seemed rather to strike him,' Stead seriously wrote, 'but he only assented and said nothing more.'

The Prince's discomfort must have been extreme. But he knew, as well as Lady Warwick, that a show of friendship with Stead was the best possible defence against a future press attack. By appearing to admit Stead into his confidence he had 'drawn his sting' – something Stead, in earlier days, had warned his reporters to avoid. He even asked forgiveness for any former slights he might have made, to which Edward, magnanimously, replied at once that he was a 'liberal-minded man' and would hold nothing against him. Stead had hoped to 'hook and eye' the Prince, yet it seems that it was in fact he who had been 'speared'.[310]

The day after their meeting, Edward wrote a polite note to his lover declaring how pleased he had been to meet her 'remarkable' friend. One day he hoped 'to hear from you the impression I made on him'. Neither this, nor Stead's optimistic hope that he and Lady Warwick would 'share the Parishioner', would come to pass. When Edward ascended to the throne as King Edward VII a few years later, Daisy received an earth-shattering visit from Stead's old friend Lord Esher informing her on behalf of the new king that her services would no longer be required. Her usefulness to Stead was duly diminished. And he, too, had become less important to her. At the end of her long life she credited Stead for inspiring her 'middle-class period ... my Board of Guardians, philanthropic, educational, lady-gardening period'. He did not prove to have the same hold over her imagination as her later mentors, notably the socialist journalists Robert Blatchford and H. M. Hyndman, who were anything but admirers of Stead. Nevertheless, for several happy years Lady Warwick, like Madame Novikov before her, was the star to which Stead hitched his wagon.

CHAPTER 12

DON'T DEMAND A CHAPERONE

*I have just lunched with a young lady who has seen five of her relations
and friends who have appeared to her at the moment of death... She is
... about 25, and is devoted to good works; lives in Society, has a first-
class education, and is perfectly self-possessed.*
W. T. S. on meeting Miss Ada Goodrich-Freer (September 1891)

When Stead signed the lease on his new office at Mowbray
House, overlooking the Thames at Norfolk Street, Strand,
he was only a few years past forty, but was already beginning to
show signs of old age. His russet beard, once thick and flowing, had
become slightly grey and unkempt, and his once smooth, attractive features seemed to be slowly crumpling. It would not be long
before younger journalists would start referring to Stead (among
themselves) as 'Grandpa Stead'. This sobriquet arose not only in
response to Stead's increasingly shabby appearance. He invited it
himself with his continual harking back to the glory days of his
'reign' at Northumberland Street, his time in prison and other
events that had little relevance to the modern world. There was
also a growing consensus that Stead's mental powers were fading;
perhaps an inevitable result of two hard decades of continual
newspaper editing. Sides of his character that had been wisely kept
from public view by the moderating influences of Yates Thompson,
Cook and Newnes suddenly leapt to the fore.

The most striking feature of Stead's new office was that it was
staffed almost exclusively by attractive young women. This was
incredibly unusual by the standards of the time, and surprised even
the most liberal of visitors. But it was potentially logical: women
were far cheaper to employ than men, which was important

as Stead was now paying his team from his own limited resources. Stead was also adamant that his staff was entirely 'clerical and secretarial', since he optimistically proposed to undertake all editorial work himself. This proved unsustainable. And it soon became clear, when the editor enlisted the help of his old colleague from the *PMG*, Edwin Stout, as office manager, that many of these women were of little value to the magazine. 'There were heaps of women,' Stout reflected in retirement, 'who did little or nothing and considered themselves "Stead's staff".' They were impossible to fire and often paid considerable sums out of charity.[311]

Among these women, however, there was at least one incredibly talented young journalist: Flora Shaw. She had first approached Stead while he was editor of the *PMG* with a proposal to become one of his numerous overseas correspondents. All he could offer her at the time was financial cover for 'carriages and gloves', but he generously promised to view sympathetically anything that she could send from Spain, where she was apparently planning a holiday. The result was an important interview with the man General Gordon had wanted to succeed him as Governor-General of the Sudan, Zebehr Pasha, who the British had imprisoned for slave-dealing. Her article is believed to have contributed to the man's eventual release.[312] Now that she was back in London, Stead was eager to give her something else to do and offered her the considerable salary of £120 simply to review the French journals – a job that Marie Belloc, a native French speaker, had assumed would be delegated to her.

Whether there was tension between these two women is not clear, but Stead evidently had a 'particular regard' for each of them. Flora's diary refers to Stead coming to visit her at 11.30 one night and staying in her bedsitting-room until 3am 'talking, smoking and drinking tea'.[313] Nocturnal visits of this kind between a married man and an attractive younger woman would be highly suspicious even in the present: at the time they were virtually akin to adultery. Flora wrote touching letters to Stead, thanking him for his assistance and promising that she was 'improving' with her journalism. But she worried that he was working himself too hard. 'I came upon W. T. Stead trade mark so often that I said to myself sorrowfully "this cannot go on"', she wrote on reading the *Review*'s first issue. More revealingly, perhaps, Flora went on to suggest that there was some hypocrisy in Stead's idea for the 'Lay Confessional': 'You of all men to become father confessor to the universe!' she wrote, '...Excuse the good one-sided laugh I am having.' Elsewhere her letters speak of Stead 'taking too seriously what I said to you last night'. But the evidence soon peters out: by early 1892 she had fallen out with Stead – allegedly because he had printed a story in the *Review of Reviews* which she had told him in the strictest confidence. Not long afterwards she secured a job, somewhat ironically in the light of Stead's opinions, at *The Times*, where she established herself as one of the foremost women journalists of the period. 'I hope before long to go to Mowbray House to say goodbye,' she wrote in her final letter to Stead. 'You must not think that in ceasing to write to you I can forget the kindly relations which have existed between us.'[314]

Reading the back issues of the *Review of Reviews* with such information in view, many of the most banal stories featured in its pages assume a new significance. In May 1891, for example, there was an eye-catching 'Plea for Polygamy' discussing the practices of the Mormons, whom Stead frequently defended in spite of his avowed defence of the principle of monogamy. There was also the first (abridged) translation of Tolstoy's *Kreutzer Sonata*; a harrowing tale of jealousy and adultery which culminates with the murder of a young woman wrongly accused of infidelity by her husband. Stead pretentiously claimed the book to have been 'to some extent the off-shoot of a long conversation' he had had with the author when in Russia. In Stead's version, no doubt, he took the part of the blameless wife: he often told friends that he had a 'woman's mind' and identified with Otto Weininger's assessment of female sexuality in his chauvinistic *Sex and Character*. Be this as it may, Emma Stead remained anxious about the 'temptation' to which her husband daily, and voluntarily, subjected himself.

In the first months of the *Review* Stead also featured the curious *Journal of Marie Bashkirtseff*, which delineates the mind of a beautiful, vain and lonely young Russian woman who died at an early age. Though Stead made a point of dissenting from the author's view that woman is a creature only to be loved – as opposed to loving others – he nevertheless revelled in her indulgent navel-gazing. 'My body is like that of an antique goddess,' she mused, 'my Spanish hips, my small and perfectly shaped bosom, my feet, my hands, and my childlike head – of what use is it all, since nobody loves me?'

It is not difficult to imagine Stead inviting his nubile staff up the stairs to his 'sanctum' to discuss the merits of such literature. Here he sat, often in a rocking chair, surrounded by photographs and statues of all his most treasured idols and contemporaries: Oliver Cromwell, Maud Gonne, Cardinal Manning, Olga Novikov and innumerable politicians of all shades. He was always frank with his assistants but his ideal was impossibly high: 'Don't demand a chaperone' or attempt to be 'a journalist up to nine o'clock and Miss Nancy after nine', he advised aspiring 'lady journalists' – yet it was also wrong for them to be 'forward' or 'mannish'. Stead clearly wanted to be viewed as a benevolent father figure, to whom they could go with their problems.[315]

This desire to be admired by women was apparent in Stead's unusual 'Scholarships in Contemporary History', which he intimated midway through his first year editing the magazine. They were offered to women under twenty-five years of age (later extended to thirty-year-olds), who, in spite of the broad title, were examined exclusively on Stead's articles in the *Review of Reviews*. Feigning modesty, Stead claimed that he had considered extending the remit to include articles in the highbrow *Spectator* as well; but Stead concluded that the 'acidulated pessimism' of that journal was not calculated to 'excite the interest and kindle the enthusiasm' of his preferred type of candidate.[316]

Stead's motive in launching the scheme is not entirely clear. Certainly it encouraged young women to buy his journal, but it is unlikely that increased sales fully compensated for the added administrative work, most of which he took on himself. More likely it gave Stead a sense of direct contact with the kind of reader for whom he most cared. Applicants were encouraged to send him their photographs or even to make impromptu visits to Mowbray House to see him. One candidate, nineteen-year-old Edith Harper, recalls meeting Stead at a mutual friend's house in Newcastle shortly before he awarded her fourth place in the competition. Her enthusiasm about meeting the editor may be taken as indicative of the reverence with which many young female readers regarded him:

> there he was, seated at one side of a long tea-table, in a big easy-chair, surrounded by a bevy of admirers... Suddenly he seemed to become aware of my gaze fixed ... [he] jumped up ... and, coming round the table to where I sat, took hold of both my hands and exclaimed, with one of those searching glances of his which seemed to penetrate one's whole being like a lightning-flash – "Why, my dear little girl! Why did you not come and speak to me?"[317]

It was not a day that she would ever forget. Stead spoke to her without pause for almost three hours about such tangential subjects as Madame Bashkirtseff, Tolstoy's novels and female emancipation. Afterwards he took her by the arm and walked her to the station, with her mother, one imagines, reluctantly in tow. They did not part before Stead had pledged her to call on him one day in London. Some years later she would assist him in gathering material for his biography of Madame Novikov; a delicate and intimate task. But the scholarships themselves ended up being no more than cash prizes, since the Mistress of Girton College, predictably, was not interested in offering special places for young women who had won the admiration of the notorious editor of the *Review of Reviews*.

Stead clearly enjoyed the empowerment of these relationships, but he was at least as much influenced by his new friends as they were by him. Their overall contribution to his career, however, was highly lamentable: they helped to convince Stead that his psychic powers were genuine.

Though many instantly saw it as the end of Stead's reputation as a serious journalist, spiritualism was a craze with a huge following in the late nineteenth century. Like alternative medicine today, it had elements of respectability and often courted scientific investigation. Moreover, many practitioners, including Stead himself, were zealous Christians who wanted to sure up his faith in the face of the scientific advances and theories that struck at long-cherished assumptions. But there is no doubt that Stead's main impetus in this 'side show', as one sceptical secretary called it, was intrinsically linked to his unorthodox relationships with his female staff.[318]

The ubiquitous Marie Belloc held two women in the office accountable for Stead's 'conversion'.[319] One was Mrs Davidson. She was a fragile woman of about thirty, who came to Stead in desperation because the meagre fifteen shillings a week she was receiving from her late husband's family had come to an end. Marie remembered her as 'certainly the most eccentric human being' she had ever come across. At a time when it was customary for men and women to wear dark clothes in public, she was always 'clad in white', even in the depths of winter. Stead gave her a generous allowance of £1 per week, for which she felt duty bound to make the tea and generally maintain the appearance of the office. This caused some resentment among the other staff because she apparently 'gossiped about them' to Stead. All seemed to want to be the object of his undivided attention. When a potential rival to Mrs Davidson calmly announced one day that spirits could write with her hand, the latter went one better: she revealed that she had an 'astral body'.

These mysterious entities would prove to be an abiding fascination for Stead. They were considered by their advocates to be second bodies that could be controlled by the mind, either while dreaming or by conscious thought. Stead claimed to have seen one for the first time when he and his family were worshipping at the Congregationalist Chapel in Wimbledon, as they did every Sunday morning. In the middle of the service a figure remarkably like Mrs Davidson in appearance, and dressed in her usual attire, made a theatrical entrance. Stead opened the pew door and tried to hand a hymn-book to her, but she would not enter. Anxiously, Stead whispered to his wife that the lady would have to come for lunch with them, as he believed her to be in trouble. But at the end of the service Mrs Davidson could not be found – not even at the railway station, where she should have been waiting on account of the fact that, at that time, trains did not usually run during Divine Service.

When Mrs Davidson did not appear at Mowbray House the following week, Marie was instructed to check up on her. The unhappy woman was found in bed at her rundown lodgings with a doctor in attendance, who asserted that she could not possibly have been in Wimbledon over the weekend. Though Marie suggested a terrestrial explanation, Stead was convinced that he and his family had witnessed a miracle. For this, and many other irrational deductions (including a belief that the late Poet Laureate, Alfred Tennyson, had dictated to him a new poem), Stead surely earned her cutting reminiscence that he was an utterly 'credulous man, inclined to believe anything he was told' – at least by a woman.

Mrs Davidson's fellow spiritualist in the office was the daughter of an Indian army officer, who came to Stead with no greater aptitude for journalism than her counterpart. Stead was intrigued by her 'automatic writing', which involved holding a pen loosely against a sheet of paper and invoking a particular spirit to write a message 'from the other side'. For months she flirted with Stead by explaining that her deceased friend, 'Frederick', was eager to write with his hand. She told him that this apparition had seen the ghost of a distraught woman following him about the office, urgently wishing to tell him something. Desperate, as ever, to satisfy the demands of this attractive young woman and her 'spook' (as Stead always referred to spirits), he made various attempts to write 'automatically' himself, and succeeded in getting some modest sentences out of a 'Mrs D.' and the disembodied spirit of a 'Henry L.', who had apparently 'been violently opposed' to Stead during his lifetime. Though pleased, Stead was not entirely convinced.[320]

This reserved scepticism changed dramatically when Stead was staying with the members of the Women's Christian Temperance Union at Eastnor Castle a few months later. He was ostensibly in the area to oppose Sir Charles Dilke's re-election to Parliament after seven years in the political wilderness; a task for which Stead was briefly given control of a local newspaper. But Stead was easily distracted, and spent the long evenings quizzing his hostess about her allegedly brutal treatment at the hands of her estranged husband. According to Stead, this man was 'addicted to practices the pursuit of which is incompatible even with the large laxity of the English aristocratic life'. Whether this was true or not can be debated. Lord Esher, for one, believed that Stead's judgement was never worse than when it concerned the plight of a woman in distress.[321]

Also staying at the castle was a young temperance activist known only as 'Ellen'. She was the best friend, and possibly lover, of a recently deceased young American journalist called Julia Ames, who had visited Stead in the summer of 1890 with questions about the Passion Play at Oberammergau – an amateur representation of the crucifixion staged every ten years by the villagers. So enthused was Stead by Julia's company that he promised to visit the play himself, and even went so far as to publish a translation of the text. Her letters to him frequently began 'My Dear Brother Beloved', but it is unlikely that they had ever spent more than a few hours in one another's company. He was obviously captivated by what he believed to be her great beauty and ability as a journalist.

Ellen told Stead that she had seen Julia's spirit twice since her death: most recently during the course of the previous evening. She asked if he could use his new-found 'powers' to obtain a message from her departed friend. Anxious to help, Stead promised to do all he could.

Sitting alone in his room the following morning, Stead asked aloud: 'Now Miss Ames, if you are about and care to use my hand, it is at your disposal if you have anything to say to Miss Ellen.'

'Almost immediately,' Stead later wrote, 'my hand began to write, and not in my accustomed handwriting' but in that of the spirit of 'Julia'. Though Stead claimed the characters on the page to have been 'clear and distinct', Frederic Whyte – who saw the originals, since lost – tentatively suggested the scrawl to have evinced 'a mind unhinged'.[322]

'Julia's' first message to Stead was unmistakably this-worldly: Ellen was told not to worry about her hostess's plan to 'subvert' the temperance movement (she was regarded as being less extreme than her American counterparts). 'We will take care of Lady Henry,' 'Julia' eerily wrote. The veracity of this communication was 'proved' by a test that Stead immediately demanded of his new spirit friend: he asked her to tell him something he did not know already. With some exasperation, 'Julia' asked him to remind Ellen of what she had told her 'when last we came to Minerva'. Upon receiving this bizarre message, Ellen told Stead, to his obvious delight, that 'Minerva' was the nickname that Julia had given to another temperance agitator – though only a few moments before she died! Ridiculous though this was, Stead was now prepared to declare to the world that he had powers as a medium. For several hours he sat solemnly answering questions on behalf of 'Julia', which he later published in his strangest of books, *Letters From Julia*.

It is unclear whether Stead actually believed in the truthfulness of this 'gift'. His closest friends and family never doubted it. But the strong flavour of what Edmund Garrett called 'Steadese' in all the writings of 'Julia' cannot be ignored. What is most likely is that his 'automatic writing' provided a means of venting a side of his personality that was almost completely suppressed by the conventions of his era and his strong religious beliefs. It was also perhaps a symptom of mild schizophrenia, which Stead may have acknowledged in a candid interview with a representative of the *Christian Commonwealth*. 'The real self, the Ego,' explained Stead, 'sits behind, as it were, both the physical consciousness and the mind.' This almost certainly reveals that his early messages to Ellen were the confessions of a guilty lover:

Oh, Ellen, Ellen ... my darling ... you and I used to love each other with what seemed to us sometimes too deep and intense a love, but that at its very best was but the pale reflection of the love with which He loves us, which is marvellously and wonderfully great beyond all power of mind to describe. His name is Love; it is what He is – Love, Love, Love![323]

'Julia' went on to explain that heaven was filled with 'convicts and murderers and adulterers' – categories into which Stead obviously seemed willing to place himself. This was supposedly because 'crimes perpetrated in a gust of passion' were not as bad as 'the long-indulged thoughts of evil which come at last to poison the whole soul'. Though such antinomianism did nothing to alter Stead's harsh judgement of Sir Charles Dilke, it was evidently at the core of his inner being. This is at least partly acknowledged by the disproportionate anger that Stead showed to critics who accused him of expressing his own ideas through 'Julia' or when they pointed out that she was, like himself, remarkably up to date with events in the newspaper world. Undoubtedly, his skills in the art of deception were not overly impressive. 'Julia's' comforting description of life after death, for example, seems to have come straight from the pages of Rider Haggard's pulp-fiction classic *She*: '...the flame-bright One said to me, "Julia, behold your Saviour!" and when I looked, I saw Him.'[324] The only remarkable thing about Stead's spiritualism was that other people seemed willing to take it seriously.

One of the few early dissenters among Stead's inner circle was his youngest – and almost only – male employee, the future publishing baron Grant Richards. He had been given a job by Stead through the influence of his uncle, Grant Allen, who wrote a monthly 'scientific causerie' in the *Review*. Though Richards admitted to being something of a 'hero-worshipper' at the time, he never came under the spell of 'W. T. S.' This was mostly because he was 'annoyed and mortified' by the way in which he was patronised at the office. Stead toyed with the idea of dismissing him for a long time for his insubordination, but when the prospect of a better job came along Stead denied Richards the right to leave. (A young Alfred Harmsworth had suggested that Richards join the staff of his new venture – the incomparably successful *Daily Mail* – but Stead implored Richards to stay; supposedly because he did not rate the paper's chances.) The younger man was indignant when only a few weeks later Stead casually suggested that he apply to become John Morley's secretary, since he was no longer of use to him in the office. Having once been the ever-ready friend of young journalists, Stead had become a barrier in their way.[325]

Richards vividly recalled the rapid change in mood at Mowbray House following Stead's embrace of spiritualism. The office became a beacon to clairvoyants and charlatans of all kinds: Stead even had the audacity to refer, seriously, to Mowbray House as 'Mecca' and his home in Wimbledon as 'Medina'. Richards had no doubt that many of the women who came promising to nurture his talents were really out to take his money. But Stead enjoyed the reverence of these acolytes, even if it was largely feigned. The psychic investigations he conducted with them, which were often faintly sexual in nature, amused him. One evening a week, for example, he would have a clairvoyant locked in an upper room with one of his secretaries while he and a group of well-wishers would wait downstairs in the hope of catching sight of her 'astral body'. The assistant's job was to record the precise time, tone and character of all the medium's moans and sighs, which he would then compare with the schedule of what was apparently seen in the room below. These evenings would often go on – extended by genial tea breaks – until well past midnight, leaving Stead exhausted and unfit for work the following day. It became a familiar sight to see the 'chief' sound asleep on top of his desk 'without any pillow or easement'.[326]

Matters became more serious when Stead announced that he had progressed from 'automatic writing' to telepathy. He was encouraged in this line by a young woman who had published a series of ostensibly scholarly articles on crystal-gazing under the pseudonym 'Miss X.' in the *Journal of the Society for Psychical Research*;

a periodical set up by a group of Cambridge dons to examine spiritualism scientifically. After discussing these essays at length in his *Review*, Stead asked the journal's editor, the ebullient Frederick Myers, if he could have an introduction to 'Miss X.' Within days he had the prim Ada Goodrich-Freer in his sanctum discussing the spirit world. Their relationship would be long and colourful, although nearly all of their correspondence appears to have been systematically destroyed – almost certainly by Mrs Stead, who had good reason to dislike her.

Ada was the archetypal Victorian spiritualist hoaxer. Her story was that she came from a respectable family, which had cast her off when it was discovered that she had the gift of second sight. In reality she was an almost completely uneducated woman who lied about everything, even her name – 'Goodrich' was a pretentious invention. But she was well aware of her attractions to the opposite sex. In a letter to her future patron, the third Marquess of Bute, she recorded that it would be difficult for her to find a female chaperone to take her to Scotland, but there would be 'plenty of men who would be glad' to accompany her.[327]

A more disturbing aspect of her life, which has only become apparent in recent years, is that sado-masochism lay behind much of her spiritualism. This is clear from a letter written by an unnamed friend of hers, in which it was explained that Ada had asked 'if I would go and "stroke" her sometimes, as it does her good'. Though some scholars have politely suggested this to be cryptic, there can be little doubt that she enjoyed being beaten, and perhaps beating others, as a form of sexual gratification. 'I don't think that can all be flattery,' the lady continued, 'because she couldn't stand it unless it did her some good, but on the other hand she must know that I would enjoy immensely to do anything of the sort.'[328]

It is unlikely that Stead was unaware of Ada's predilections, but whether he was willing to gratify them cannot, of course, be determined conclusively. Certainly, he would not have been the first Victorian 'purity' crusader to solicit flagellation as a means of easing the sexual torment of 'rescue' work. His former hero,

William Gladstone, was well known in certain notorious back-streets for demanding similar services, which he described in his diary as 'strange and humbling' acts. When he felt that his mortification at the hands of these women had not been severe enough, he would often complete the task on his own.[329]

These kinds of practices ran deep in the springs of Victorian Puritanism, from which Stead had drunk deeply. Spiritualism, too, worked for many as a kind of sex suppressant – the new word 'telepathy' took its origin from two Greek words meaning 'distant touch'. In the person of Ada Freer, all of these discordant cultural tropes found their embodiment.

Of the few surviving supernatural communications Stead had with Ada, it is obvious that many of them were of a highly intimate character. One was plainly a Steadean fantasy. 'I am very sorry to tell you,' she allegedly telepathed to him one afternoon, 'I have had a very painful experience, of which I am almost ashamed to speak.' Stead went on to explain in some detail how a man had attempted to 'master' her in a secluded railway carriage when she denied him a kiss. In self-defence she had apparently struck him over the head with his umbrella, which she had kept, though this was now broken. When Stead sent her this unusual account of her day, she gamely wrote back that it was *exactly* what had happened, but the umbrella was hers, not his. The image of this penniless woman damaging her only umbrella so as to assure Stead of his psychic powers was an early indication of the sacrifices some of his acolytes were willing to make on his behalf. By contrast to later excesses, however, it was a comparatively mild misadventure.[330]

Naturally, Ada had her own reasons for flattering Stead. Within less than two years she managed to persuade him to set up a new journal devoted to spiritualism entitled *Borderland*, with her as co-editor on a salary of £200 and a promise that she would have full ownership rights from 1900 – once all initial risks and expenditure had been made by Stead. This unlikely enterprise probably had the cautious backing of Stout, who was perturbed that the *Review of Reviews* was being overrun with 'aberrations' such as 'Real

Ghost Stories' and palm reading, which were deterring their more serious readers. But rather than publishing his new magazine out of the same office as the *Review*, as was becoming the practice of more successful media entrepreneurs, Stead consented to rent Ada her own rooms in Pall Mall, at considerable expense to himself. Years later, Ada admitted to Edith Harper that she had insisted on this condition because of certain 'conventional austerities' which Stead 'so much deprecated'. Clearly she did not want to become a member of staff at Mowbray House because it was assumed that the couple were having an affair.[331]

The early sale of the new magazine was good, mostly because the public enjoyed the spectacle of a great journalist self-destructing before their eyes. Playing up to this morbid curiosity, Stead inserted a series of mocking 'tributes' from contemporaries. T. P. O'Connor, who had recently founded the (old) *Sun*, lamented that Stead had allowed his 'fine, beautiful mind' to be 'swept away by such nonsense'. The Bishop of Nottingham was even more direct: 'The intelligence which uses your hand,' he wrote, '...is no other than the Devil.' This was the sort of publicity Stead relished. 'I thank him for his compliment,' he told another critic, 'but if there is anything in my career which younger journalists would do well to approve, it is ... [the] gift I possess of being absolutely impervious to the ridicule and denunciation of those who imagine that anyone who sees what they do not must necessarily be a fool.' Be this as it may, within a few months Stead was publishing articles and photographs which embarrassed even Miss Freer. One of his most regrettable indulgences was a series of heavily doctored photographs of himself surrounded by the 'ghosts' of young girls. Though Ada claimed Stead to have deliberately misled their readers with such material, the sincere and typically humourless nature of the accompanying text did not give him away.

Stead's awareness of the limited nature of his powers is more clearly demonstrated by the fact that he almost never attempted to communicate 'automatically' with his male friends. '[B]low your mental telephone,' wrote Edmund Garrett from South Africa. But

Stead was willing to test his psychic powers on almost every woman that he met for the rest of his life. It was Stead's method of expressing his anxieties without directly revealing how sensitive he was to what women thought of him. It also invited greater intimacy: women were encouraged to divulge their true feelings and experiences to him, as he claimed to know them already.

One woman who was particularly receptive to Stead's mysticism was Sarah Grant; an attractive young novelist of the 'New Woman' school, who had won the admiration of George Meredith. Stead, too, had been impressed by her debut work, *The Heavenly Twins*, which explored the hypocritical social conventions that allowed bachelors to lead debauched lives while their future wives were forced to lead cloistered existences. But his staff reviewer (probably the somewhat priggish Richards) had dealt with the work censoriously. This was hardly surprising. The book was almost banned for its bold treatment of venereal disease: the heroine, Edith Beale, becomes fatally infected with syphilis by her lecherous husband, Sir Mosley Menteith, and subsequently passes the disease on to their child. On reading the negative review, the author fired off an angry letter to Stead expressing her disappointment that he had not defended her in the spirit of the 'splendid battle' and 'incessant war' which he had waged on behalf of women.[332] Within days Stead began, rather daringly, to read the book to his wife and invited Sarah for a long lunch at his favourite restaurant; an Italian bistro called Gatti's opposite Charing Cross station.

During this meal, Sarah expanded upon her thesis that 'when the sex passion is written as "objectionable or vulgar" it has been debased'. Stead was clearly sympathetic to this viewpoint for, as a sign of his appreciation, he handed her a copy of his recent booklet on Josephine Butler 'with the affectionate solicitude with which a father throws a life-belt to his daughter who is struggling in the trough of the sea'.[333] Soon he was willing to do more. Upon hearing that the new editor of the *PMG*, a flamboyant Conservative MP called Henry Cust, had written a scathing review of the book, Stead waded into the controversy on her behalf. This action was not entirely philanthropic, however, as Stead had also been mocked – with some justice – for purporting to share certain characteristics with one of the more goody-goody characters in the novel. This figure, a virtuous doctor unhappily married to a woman with more libertine inclinations than him, complains that he is unappreciated:

> She looked up, amazed at first, then, understanding, she rose. The distressing tension relaxed in that moment, her heart expanded, her eyes filled with tears and overflowed; she could not command her voice to speak, but she threw herself impetuously into her husband's arms, and kissed him passionately, and clung to him, until she was able to sob out – 'Don't let me go again, Daddy, keep me close. I am – I am grateful for the blessing of a good man's love'.

This was indeed close to Stead's idealised conception of marital – or even extra-marital – bliss, which he defended with a forthrightness that provoked almost a month of daily ridicule on the letters page of his old newspaper. His article, preposterously entitled by Cust's sub-editor 'Life from the Point of View of Tom Jones', explained that the reviewer had been wrong to suggest that Miss Grant should study the novels of Henry Fielding more closely. 'It is obvious,' intoned Stead, 'that the "Tom Jones point of view" is at its best the gratification of animal impulse and appetite whenever opportunity arises, without regard to any other consideration beyond self-indulgence...' Continuing to vent his ire, Stead explained that a modern woman would be no less disgusted by her husband's previous dalliances as the reviewer – evidently Cust – would be if he discovered that 'his bride had a family of illegitimate children somewhere down in Pimlico'. Something had snapped in Stead's brain. A facetious response from 'the shade of Mr Fielding' put it cruelly: he had given himself over to defending 'sugar-coated prurience wrapped in lily-white covers...'.[334]

The day after his article appeared, Stead informed Sarah that they were now in supernatural communication. 'You have written with my hand very curiously,' he wrote, 'and by no means so kindly as you have written with your own hand.' It is not clear what Stead believed her to have subconsciously told him, but it is obvious that he wanted more details about her private life, which he naturally supposed to be as sensational as the events outlined in her novel. He complained that her letters to him were not candid enough: 'You wear a yashmak, whereas I take my walks about without even the thinnest veils.' Even more sexually suggestive, Stead warned her that she was stoking her 'boiler' with 'hell-fire', without providing an outlet for the 'steam': 'You will burst your boiler some day if you do not change.'[335] It was advice that Stead should have heeded himself.

By the end of 1893 it was clear that Stead was close to a nervous breakdown. As Flora Shaw had predicted, he could not go on churning out such a large magazine as the *Review of Reviews* with only 'one man and a boy and a packer'. Money problems may have only been part of the reason why he could not afford to commission more external contributions: during its first few years of existence the *Review of Reviews* enjoyed an excellent circulation of about 150,000. The difficulty was that Stead liked to be in full control of his publication, and took the view that he could do the work required better than anyone else. This proved to be overly sanguine, especially when he began to dabble in fiction.

Stead's first substantial attempt in this line was his 1893 novella *From the Old World to the New*, which he printed as the Christmas annual of the *Review*. It was one of several poor decisions that undermined the sales of the magazine. Part memoir, part guidebook, part romance, it failed to succeed on all counts. But there are many signs in the book that Stead was not well. One character, a forward young woman called Irene, expresses her love for a young science professor with almost unimaginable perversity: if required, she would allow him to vivisect her. This theme was returned to later in the story when she accompanies her suitor to a Chicago slaughter-house dressed in a spotless white dress and a 'coquettish little hat'. The story comes to a bizarre climax when she slips into a pool of pig blood, only to have her soiled hand madly kissed by her companion. 'I never loved you so much,' her suitor declares, before asking her to marry him. Nothing like it exists in the whole of English literature: it cries out for psychological examination.

The truth was that Stead was approaching the borderland of insanity. Stout had become aware of this through Stead's unending flow of wayward schemes. 'Again and again,' he complained, 'when you have not (for reasons best known to yourself) thought fit to say anything to me about the incurring of liabilities there has come a time when the money has to be paid...'[336]

Some of these schemes appear to have had little or nothing to do with the magazine at all; notably the monetary gifts that Stead advanced to attractive young female novelists, almost regardless of their talent. One of these women, Annie Holdsworth, was introduced to the editor by the evangelist-cum-travel-agent Sir Henry Lunn (co-founder of Lunn Poly) who thought that she might be a welcome addition to his staff. Struck by her beauty, if not the modest novel she had recently had serialised in an obscure Dundee newspaper, Stead announced that putting her to work as a secretary would be 'like putting a race-horse to a plough'. He gifted her the princely sum of £80 to facilitate her writing. She responded by basing the hero of one of her novels on Stead: the man in question kindles a 'generous flame' in a young woman who rescues prostitutes. '[I]f the truth must be told,' Stead knowingly wrote in the guise of reviewer, the saintly woman was motivated by 'her own love for the editor in question.' After hearing this story, Stout demanded that the company cheque-book never be allowed out of his hands again.[337]

But it would be an exaggeration to claim that Stead forgot all about business. At least one of his ideas, a 'Masterpiece Library' of poetry and abridged classic literature, was a runaway success, introducing names such as Scott, Austen and Gibbon into modest homes for the first time. Yet the majority of his schemes simply took up his time and depreciated the stock of the magazine. To Stout's horror, Stead seemed willing to throw away all of their work by attempting to found his 'New Times', which he was now willing to call merely the 'Daily Paper'. A sample copy of this was tentatively offered as a supplement to the *Review* at the end of 1892. In his introductory remarks, Stead promised to begin producing the newspaper in earnest as soon as he had raised a heady 100,000 subscriptions. The sample cover advertised such unpromising features as an 'Automatic Telepathic Interview with Lady Brooke', 'Yesterdays Long Ago: The Battle of Salamis ... Xerxes in Full Flight' and a 'Calendar of Saints' beginning with St Francis of Assisi. Richards was perhaps being charitable when he later wrote that 'nobody paid it much attention'.[338]

In the hope of avoiding catastrophe, Stout called in Stead's more assiduous brother, Herbert, and his nineteen-year-old son, Willie, to help ease the editorial burden. Willie had been almost entirely educated at home by one of Stead's scholarly assistants at the *PMG*, John Underhill, who did secretarial work in the evenings for the artist Frederick Leighton. The young man was evidently keen to help his father and relished learning what a balance sheet was from Stout; but, no more than his uncle, Willie was unable to save the magazine from disintegrating if Stead broke down. Naturally curious and intelligent, it might have been better for Willie to have gone to a proper school or up to university rather than bravely attempting to keep his father under control at the office. Nevertheless, he did an admirable job and was later involved in helping to research Morley's monumental *Life of Gladstone*.

In November 1893 it was politely suggested that Stead take an extended holiday to clear his mind and free himself from the corrupting influence of London. Bernard Shaw suggested that his former editor should attend the Wagner festival at Bayreuth so as to broaden his cultural horizons. This does not appear to have captured Stead's imagination, nor was he particularly taken by Stout's sensible alternative of a Mediterranean cruise with his wife and young children. That was not Stead's style. No doubt with a slightly crazed look in his eye, Stead declared that if he was to go anywhere, he would go to Chicago: a city synonymous with vice and prostitution. Babylon was calling.[339]

CHAPTER 13

IF CHRIST CAME TO CHICAGO

I shall go and live down a slum in a room above a saloon and see whether or not I can simplify my life.
W. T. S. to Lord Esher (Christmas Day, 1893)

Stead's first transatlantic voyage did not bode well for the future. Even had Britain and America been enjoying better diplomatic relations at the time, it is hard to imagine that his reception could have been more controversial. Over the course of several frenzied months, Stead indulged his love of righteous indignation to an extent scarcely surpassed throughout his long career. By the time of his return to England the following spring, his dream of 'Anglo-Saxon reunification' appeared more ridiculous than ever. The Americans were, frankly, delighted to see the back of him.

The first alarm bell was signalled when Stead solemnly told his travelling companion, his son Willie, that he did not intend to 'attend a meeting or write a line' for the duration of their stay: he merely wished to pass his time in Chicago 'learning in silence'. Learning what? In the wake of a vastly over-blown World's Fair, the city was entering into a bitterly cold winter with half the citizens unemployed and vice and crime in the ascendancy. A less congenial environment for an ill man, particularly of Stead's disposition, to pass a meditative vacation could scarcely be imagined.[340]

Stead, of course, had personal reasons for visiting Chicago. Most notably, the amorous circle of Julia Ames was completely open to him, and he passed many happy hours discussing sex and spiritualism at the vast headquarters of the World Women's Christian Temperance Union at the intersection of LaSalle and Monroe streets. But his views were not entirely to the liking of the leader of the American branch of the organisation, Frances Willard, whose advocacy of complete prohibition of alcohol went beyond what Stead and his friend, Lady Henry Somerset, believed to be of greatest importance. Over biscuits and lemonade, Stead proposed to her, and several other prominent reformers in the Chicago area, that the churches should attempt to put the city's debauched bars out of business in a characteristically original fashion – by serving alcohol themselves.

Prostitution was a subject about which Stead and the temperance reformers could find more common ground. Through them Stead was introduced to a professor at the university who led him and his son on a tour of the city's notorious 'red-light' district, the Levee. Stead was delighted and disgusted by what he saw. Rough-looking men stood idly about, viewing the intruders with suspicion while 'painted damsels in undress' leered at them through suggestive lace curtains. On the first count Stead estimated there to be no fewer than thirty brothels on Fourth Avenue alone.

This tantalising adventure persuaded Stead to dispense with the promise that he had so recently made to his son. With a modest amount of capital grudgingly advanced to him by Stout for the purposes of his holiday, Stead proposed to rent the city's enormous (and usually excessively bawdy) Music Hall to discuss his experiences. He wanted to ask the people of Chicago, in the guise of their friend and counselor, what could be done to heal the sores of their great city. Did they know the women that worked in the Levee? And were they aware of the men and women who profited from their activities? To answer these questions, and others like them, Stead returned to the Levee to make more detailed enquiries. This time, it appears, he went alone.

Stead's first point of call was the notorious 'saloon' of Madame Hastings; probably the largest brothel in the district. To avoid any possibility that he would not see the place at its worst, Stead made his visit late on a Saturday night, just when trade was most lively. Dressed, as usual, in the clothes of a travelling salesman fallen on hard times, Stead made his way into the crowded parlour and took up a stool at the bar. Although he appears not to have actually posed as a roué, as in the case of his previous incarnation as an investigative journalist, Stead's conversation was not exactly elevating. Among other things, he wanted to hear all that could be known about 'the orgies which have given evil fame to the wine-room'. One fellow saloon-goer, presuming him to be the worst kind of lowlife, offered to make Stead the agent for his gambling house – a proposal which was apparently 'promptly accepted'.

Stead's 'hostess' was a feisty Irish 23-year-old prostitute called Maggie 'Darling'. Described by Stead as 'a brunette with long dark hair, a lively disposition ... with all the charming audacity and confidence of inexperience', Maggie completely enthralled her guest. For several hours the couple chatted – perhaps even flirted – in the only way that Stead knew: by interview. 'I don't want anything,' he told her with an indulgent smile at one stage, just a 'good talk' about the depths of human depravity.

Over the course of their conversation, Maggie regaled Stead with a variety of sensational tales, including how a police officer had arranged an assignation with her after groping her during the course of a raid. This was manna from heaven for Stead, who gleefully asked for every particular. At the end of a long discussion concerning religion, morality and spiritualism, Stead invited her to be a special guest at his meeting. Aware that this might sound dull, he promised that it would be 'quite a new kind of meeting' – one that she would truly enjoy. Through his sympathetic eyes, this enterprising and talkative prostitute became a Magdalene worthy of worship.

Stead reluctantly left Maggie's shortly before midnight and headed over to the town's central police station; presumably with the intention of confronting its officers with his 'revelations'. But the horror of what he saw in the cells provided a much-needed distraction. With the assistance of a guide, he negotiated entry to the basement where criminals, vagrants and unemployed men were held indiscriminately together. The only warmth came from a small bonfire, which choked the air with its fumes. By the time Stead returned to prepare his notes in his hotel room at 2am, he was in such a state of nervous excitement that he could hardly sleep at all.

His meeting at the Music Hall the following afternoon was a sell-out. Rarely was Stead so successful in combining his desire to reform the world with the public's insatiable appetite for entertainment. Reporters and preachers jostled for places with prostitutes, temperance reformers and the idle prurient. No one knew quite what to expect.

Stead began proceedings by reminding his audience that although some individuals had become enormously wealthy in Chicago, it remained a city of abject poverty. As ever, he saw the solution not in greater taxation or government intervention, but in a more vigorous press: those who enriched themselves by immoral means should be named and shamed. As Stead put it, the town's newspapers should act 'as a social pillory in which those who have received much and returned nothing to the community should be stigmatized…'. That was not all. In conscious plagiarism of the methods of the Salvation Army in England, Stead proposed the formation of a 'civic church' comprised of the 'hungry, naked and destitute' to agitate for moral reformation. His ideal was characteristically high: to make 'adultery and fornication … as inconceivable as incest'. The idea that Chicagoans might not appreciate such suggestions – or that they had reason to be proud that their modern Babylon was confined to one precinct alone – did not apparently register.

Stead closed his remarkable speech by giving way to a local firebrand who shocked the audience by threatening the city's wealthy with dynamite if they would not heed 'the pleadings of Editor Stead in the name of Christ'. The controversy that this provoked was outdone at the evening session when Stead incautiously allowed a 'convicted anarchist' to deliver a similar harangue, supposedly as a means of demonstrating the inclusivity of his proposed church.

With the belief that his efforts had been highly successful, Stead departed for Toronto the following morning in the hope of interviewing the British Governor General, Lord Aberdeen, for the

Review of Reviews. But before his arrival Stead lapsed into illness, complaining of a severe cold and several 'uncomfortably situated boils', the nature of which are unknown. His misery was exacerbated by the news from London that his projected *Daily Paper* had failed to secure the requisite number of subscribers. Unable to carry on with his work, Stead came to a grinding halt.

The Aberdeens, who knew Stead vaguely through their mutual friend John Morley, took pity on their visitor and invited him to stay with them until he had recovered. Stead was flattered. To Lord Esher he wrote exultantly that he was being given special treatment by his noble hostess, who apparently nursed him back to health with her own hands. So contented was Stead that he seriously considered remaining in America indefinitely to found a weekly paper in Chicago. Although he admitted that this would be 'rather bad for my ladies' in London, Stead had no reason to feel lonely. Even during his brief stay with the Aberdeens he managed to befriend a young chambermaid, who claimed, in the face of a prevailing mood of scepticism, that she could see Stead's 'astral body' in a photograph of his empty office, which the editor took with him on his travels.[341]

Stead's return to Chicago one week later was not met with universal celebration. The Chicago *Daily News* proclaimed that 'Editor Stead is again in our ... midst but he promises not to reform anything'. Such hopes proved to be groundless. Stead's first intention was to publish his sensational Music Hall speech, but when he discovered that the shorthand writers had lost their notes, he decided to produce a formidable book recounting his experiences instead. In little over eight weeks he put together one of his most accomplished and successful literary productions to date, which he gave the sensational, and typically immodest, title *If Christ Came to Chicago!* In the first three days alone the book sold over 15,000 copies, despite the powerful American Union News Company banning it from railway stations and carriages. Although Stead maintained a dove-like innocence regarding the criticism that he was catering for both ends of the market, he was not entirely

guiltless: his book contained a pullout map detailing the exact location of every brothel in the Levee.

Stead's absorption in writing this book did not prevent him
from continuing to stir up controversy on the platform. This was
particularly evident when Stead accepted an invitation to speak at a
meeting of the Women's Club (a rival organisation of the WWCTU)
two days after a subdued Christmas spent alone with his son.
Infuriated by what he took to be the well-fed and overdressed
audience, Stead commenced with the statement: 'I ... welcome this
opportunity because sitting side by side with those active workers
before me are some of the most disreputable people in Chicago.'
According to the vivid account of a reporter, 'smiles fled. Faces
blanched and reddened. Women bit their lips, [and] moved uneas-
ily in their chairs ... [while] whispering protests went up from every
row...' Stead, apparently unaware of his tactlessness, went on to ask:

> Who are the most disreputable women in Chicago? They are those
> dowered by society ... with all the gifts and ... opportunities; who
> have wealth and ... leisure; who live entirely self-indulgent lives,
> caring only for themselves, and are more disreputable than the
> worst harlot...

Stead was not done. As the women began to rise to their feet, he
continued:

> I am glad ... you are bestirring yourselves... If all those present were
> to rouse themselves ... then this great trouble ... would be a blessing
> ... which you stand in need of yourselves... For ... none are in such
> danger of losing their souls as those who are wrapped up in their
> own selfish comfort...

At this point the gathering storm burst in all its fury as Stead,
taking his hat, hurried out and slammed the door behind him. One
after the other, the women denounced his remarks and demanded
that he be 'drummed out of town for his insult to the women of

Chicago'. Not even a plea from his WWCTU friends could prevent the passage of a resolution damning Stead in the bitterest terms.

The press was even more unanimous. 'He has meddled,' thundered the *Tribune*, 'in a gratuitous, offensive, and ... insulting manner ... his methods and intemperate gabble do not commend him to Chicago...' Even his American counterpart Albert Shaw was up in arms. He could not believe that Stead had been so reckless as to damage the standing of their magazine with his 'bizarre methods of reform'.

Although Stead was delighted to have 'shaken all classes in Chicago' as never before, he made a show of penance by donning the garb of a labourer and for three hours working with a large group assigned to shovel snow in the bitter cold in return for soup and a night's shelter. This left him with an abiding image of himself as 'Christ among the citizens of Chicago', patiently toiling for the good of his fellows.

What made Stead so violently attack the comfortable women of Chicago? It may have been a desire to involve himself in a private dispute concerning the WWCTU; but, once again, it seems more likely that Stead was venting his own frustrations. In a long, though partially destroyed, correspondence with his friend, the avant-garde novelist Olive Schreiner, Stead appears to have suggested that his relationship with his wife was still not going well, and that she was jealous of his numerous female acquaintances. According to Schreiner, his and Emma's relationship had become one merely of sexual gratification, devoid of any emotional and spiritual connection. In summing up Stead's complaints, Schreiner wrote that 'the continuance of the physical relation where the highest mental relation is not possible, and where affection is given elsewhere, seems to me more terrible because a more permanent prostitution than that of the streets'.[342]

With such worries swirling around his head, Stead departed for England on 7 March.

❧

For those aware of Stead's fragile state of health on the eve of his visit to Chicago, it came as no surprise to learn that his holiday had not provided the tonic that he required. Within a few months of his return, Stead had his first serious nervous breakdown. Unable to continue editing the *Review of Reviews*, he passed the mantle to his brother Herbert, who did his best to keep the magazine alive and to quash rumours that Stead had retired. Emma, meanwhile, found the family a country house where her husband could relax and concern himself with less exciting preoccupations than broth-els and gambling dens. The property which she found, Holly Bush at Hayling Island, overlooking the sea near Portsmouth, became a favourite spot. Here Stead involved himself in family life to a greater extent than ever before. Boating, bathing and picnics were enjoyed by all, and Stead's children would never forget his improving tales of knights and princesses, which blossomed into his popular penny series 'Books for the Bairns'.

The children's governess, Alice Lawrence, recalls Stead 'reigning supreme' over a happy family circle. His ideal was to impress on his children the importance, even sacredness, of mundane household chores, which he delegated to them with the utmost solemnity. On one occasion Stead's youngest daughter Pearl, aged four, dressed in her new winter frock, was found, 'with black brooms and dust-pan', cleaning out the fireplace in his study. Other instances of Stead's parenting skills were no less comic. After family prayers, for instance, the children were called upon to select a hymn, which their father would join them in singing 'lustily though not always tunefully', regardless of its spiritual worthiness. On one occasion the choice was no more poignant than 'Three little kittens went down the lane'.[343]

Stead became happily middle-aged. Never again would he use his pen to denounce vice and immorality as savagely as he had done in Chicago. Rather, he began to accuse journalists who engaged in such muckraking of exactly what had often been charged against himself: hypocrisy. This was most spectacularly demonstrated in Stead's surprising defence of Oscar Wilde in the aftermath of his prosecution for homosexuality in the summer of 1895. Conveniently forgetting that it had been 'his' Criminal Law Amendment Act that had outlawed such practices, Stead explained that although same-sex relationships were 'unnatural for seventy-nine out of eighty persons', the majority had no right to enforce their values on others. More provocatively still, Stead announced that

> [i]f all persons guilty of Oscar Wilde's offences were to be clapped into gaol, there would be a very surprising exodus from Eton and Harrow, Rugby and Winchester, to Pentonville and Holloway.

These comments produced a long letter of thanks from Wilde's lover Lord Alfred Douglas, but Stead declined to enter into a correspondence. His defence of Wilde was as much an attack on his past critics as it was an act of genuine sympathy for his former contributor. Yet when the two men met, practically for the first time, on the streets of Paris a few years after the scandal, Stead greeted Wilde as an 'old friend'. Later he would be deeply moved by Wilde's final letter to Douglas, *De Profundis*, which he felt would 'live long after [what] all the rest of us have written will be forgotten'. In a society that had little tolerance for the outrageous, Stead and Wilde were, oddly, brothers-in-arms.[344]

SHALL I SLAY MY BROTHER BOER?

I am a voice crying in the wilderness...
W. T. S. preaching at Westminster Chapel (October 1899)

Stead's calmer approach to life was never likely to last long. Yet nothing could have prepared him for the thunderbolt of the Jameson Raid, which hurled him back into the limelight at the end of 1895. This was a feeble attempt by the supporters of Cecil Rhodes, headed by his friend, Dr Leander Starr Jameson, to incite a British-led revolution in one of the last independent territories in South Africa: the Transvaal. The debacle would have catastrophic repercussions for the 'big idea', shared by Rhodes and Stead, for a South Africa united under the aegis of the British Empire. Over the next three years, relations between the British and Dutch ('Boer') denizens of the Cape would gradually worsen until the storm of war finally broke in 1899. The conflict would be one of the great tragedies of Stead's life, for which he, with typical self-regard, believed himself to be personally responsible.

Stead's interest in South African politics can be traced to his early days at the *PMG*, when the short-lived First Anglo-Boer War (1880–81) had made the region the subject of intense media attention. This had been a struggle for independence in which the Boers had effectively succeeded in reversing the arrangement, made at a time of great national peril, whereby they received financial and military aid in return for accepting vaguely defined British 'suzerainty'. Contrary to most Liberals, including Stead's editor John Morley, who called for a policy of 'scuttle', Stead was a firm supporter of the proposed annexation. Once in control of the newspaper, he completely changed the editorial line: not only was it right for the Boers to come under imperial sway – if necessary the British should 'shoot them down'.[345]

This strange combination of philanthropy and bellicosity was typical of Stead. It was true that the Boers had little sympathy for the Liberal ideals that he cherished, such as Free Trade and protecting the rights of native Africans, but Britain's mandate to take charge in the region was extremely tenuous. Even the most fervent 'jingoes' saw little purpose in seizing the territory, principally because the country was perceived to be unworthy of the price of conquest. Only when vast goldfields were discovered on the Rand in the mid-1880s did Stead's exaggerated language come back to haunt him. Suddenly the idea of 'shooting down' the Boers became very popular indeed.

But Stead now hesitated. Rather than advocating bloodshed, he proposed that the Transvaal be absorbed by degrees. His idea, shared by what Rhodes called 'your 'boys' – Cook, Milner, Garrett and Rhodes himself – was that voting rights be given to the large number of British settlers ('Outlanders') who flocked to the mining town of Johannesburg in search of riches. But the wily Boer president, Paul Kruger, was wise to this plan: he altered the republic's constitution to deny them full citizenship. This impasse had led directly to Jameson's ill-judged expedition.

Stead was privately vexed by the Raid for at least two reasons: he viewed it as unnecessary and, more importantly, he resented not being let in on the scheme by its instigators. This was despite the fact that both Rhodes and Jameson were regular visitors to Mowbray House: 'I sit in his big armchair,' wrote 'Dr Jim', '…and in an hour I have learnt more from him than from any man in London.'[346] According to Stead, the pair had been as adamant as he that the Boer oligarchy would inevitably lose its grip on power by the simple mathematics of demographic change. Much like his unusual views about sex and adultery, Stead saw no harm in threatening the Boers with violence; but it was imperative that this was not consummated by action.

Rhodes had clearly been willing to pursue this strategy for a time. But by the mid-1890s, it had become apparent that the forces of reaction were getting stronger in the Transvaal, not weaker. The fact that most of the Outlanders cared little about their 'plight' had not helped matters. Rhodes, whose real motive was to free himself from the republic's high rates of taxation, now moved to Plan B: to engineer a revolution from the outside. For this, Stead's continual railing against the Boers was useful, but Rhodes understood that his friend would be unlikely to support an outright invasion. His willing assistant would be Flora Shaw of *The Times*.

Flora had become a highly regarded journalist specialising in South African affairs since leaving the *Review of Reviews* under a cloud in 1892. It does not appear that she kept in touch with Stead and it is highly improbable that she owed her connection with Rhodes to him. But it was his ideal of 'government by journalism' which apparently inspired her reckless attempt to help facilitate Rhodes's would-be *coup d'état*. Throughout 1895 she had acted as an informal conduit between Rhodes and the Colonial Secretary, Joseph Chamberlain; embellishing, inventing and distorting his opinions wherever it seemed to further her ends. Her deviousness is well demonstrated by a command made to her newspaper's 'correspondent' in South Africa – an army officer sent to help mobilise the rebellion – that he must '*not commence business*' on a Saturday on account of the 'Sunday papers', which might have stolen the exclusive.[347]

Chamberlain had been inclined to view Rhodes's plan with sympathy, but he told Flora that the time was not ideal for an uprising in South Africa. Crises loomed a plenty elsewhere, notably in South America where the United States was threatening war over a disputed boundary between Venezuela and British Guiana. Her interpretation of Chamberlain's judicious, but strictly 'unofficial', advice that no steps should be taken in South Africa until these problems were settled was plainly mendacious – she advised Rhodes should 'hurry up' with his invasion. When the plot fell through several months later, Rhodes proposed to use her cables, purporting to be the will of the minister, as a bargaining chip to protect and even enlarge his business interests in British South Africa.

Stead's reasons for lending a hand to this chicanery were mani-
fold, but a desire for monetary reward was almost certainly not
one of them. Although he had been made a trustee of Rhodes's last
will, and was devoted to him to an unusual degree, Stead could
not be bought – at least with cash. Like every other error of judgement that he made in his career, Stead's willingness to help Rhodes
stemmed from a sincere belief that he was doing right and that he
would be rewarded, in due course, by the 'Senior Partner'. Another
factor that cannot be ignored in this instance, however, was Stead's
obvious dislike of Chamberlain, which stemmed at least from the
time of the Dilke scandal. According to W. W. Hadley (editor of
the *Sunday Times*, 1932–50), Stead used to begin each day with
six heavy kicks forward, chanting 'That's for Joe' (afterwards he
admonished himself with the same number of reverse kicks 'on my
own behind', calling: 'William, be humble'). Whereas Stead was
willing to forgive Rhodes for all his 'sins', he proved completely
unsparing in his criticism of Chamberlain.[348]

But Stead was as dangerous as a friend as an adversary. After
resigning in disgrace as Prime Minister of Cape Colony, Rhodes
returned to England to negotiate with Chamberlain about the position of his most important possession, the 'Chartered Company'.
In return for avoiding a controversy about the government's alleged
role in the raid, Chamberlain agreed that nothing would be done to
alter the freedoms of the company, or even to alter Rhodes's controversial position as a Privy Councillor, which had been conferred
on him shortly before the raid. This made it highly embarrassing
when Stead began to speculate in the pages of the *Review of Reviews*
that Rhodes was wilfully shielding his 'co-conspirators', whom, he
hoped, would 'appreciate his reserve'.[349]

Stead does not appear to have realised the magnitude of what
was at stake. The suggestion that the British government had
inspired an act of aggression against a friendly nation threatened
war not only in South Africa but in Europe, too – Kaiser William
II had sent a congratulatory telegram to Kruger three days after the
raid, which referred contemptuously to Jameson and his troopers

as 'armed bands'. The more Stead prodded the mare's nest of the Flora Shaw cables, which he was allowed to see by Rhodes's scheming solicitor Bouchier Hawksley, the more likely it would be that Britain would have to follow Cape Colony in launching an official, and potentially humiliating, public inquiry. This led Stead to take one of his boldest steps to date: to put together a Christmas annual charging Chamberlain with conspiracy.

The History of the Mystery, as it was called, was vaunted in the *Review of Reviews* towards the end of 1896. In the guise of a quasi-Biblical novel, Stead proposed to tell the story of the Jameson Raid through the eyes of an extreme partisan of Rhodes. The most alarming feature of the book, from the government's perspective, was that he intended to reproduce extracts from Flora Shaw's cables as part of the narrative. This would have caused a huge sensation, but Stead characteristically denied any such motive. He even went so far as to inform his readers, with the utmost profession of piety, that he was doing Chamberlain a favour: the release of the 'incriminating' cables, said Stead, would provide the Colonial Secretary with a 'feather-bed' on which to land in anticipation of his demise.

Surprisingly, Chamberlain did not entirely object to Stead's plan. The minister hoped that 'these blackguards' would 'do their worst', as it would at least allow him an opportunity of refuting their charges, which had hitherto been deliberately vague. But, in the event, Stead did not allow Chamberlain even this modest luxury. Just before the pamphlet was put on general release, Stead gave in to Rhodes's demand that the text of the telegrams be omitted by asking his assistants to blacken out the offending passages. Stead also censored an entire chapter entitled 'The Serpent in Eden', allegedly, as he told his readers, because it would be 'detrimental' to the interests of the Colonial Secretary. As an experienced journalist, and lifelong master of sensation, Stead was well aware that the blackened sections would only serve to make Chamberlain appear all the more guilty.

To make matters worse, Stead sent an unexpurgated edition of his pamphlet to his friend Edmund Garrett for review in the

Cape Times. This was a cruel and cynical method of abiding by the letter of Rhodes's demands, while at the same time divulging the 'secrets' anyway. Stead knew that his former protégé was a committed supporter of Chamberlain, as Stead himself should have been, at least by the reckoning of the 'Gospel According to the *Pall Mall Gazette*'. The *History of the Mystery* threw his young friend a live grenade which he had to parry as best he could.

Garrett thought the book 'gorgeously and gloriously Steadean', but he could not understand why Stead, 'of all men on Earth', had written it. In a long review, published in the *Cape Times* of 8 December, he valiantly attempted to demolish the book's elaborate conspiracy theory. With a desire to do justice to his old friend, he even quoted extensively from one of Stead's chapters – the very one that he had been compelled by Rhodes to remove. This portrayed the sub-marine cable linking London to Cape Town as the modern tempter of Eden:

> that serpentine thing which drags its slow length along through the deep sea ooze and across the floor of the Atlantic Ocean ... it may have lied like its prototype. But Mr Cecil [Rhodes] ... trusted the serpent and did eat. He gave to Zahlbar [Jameson] and he did eat also. And the officers under him were led into Secheleland [Bechuanaland] because of the same insidious tempter's message. And all this not because of any desire on the part of anyone to deceive or to be deceived but simply and solely as the natural and inevitable result of endeavouring to condense into a coded cablegram the confidential and guarded discourse of a statesman.

Garrett was clearly devastated when he discovered what Stead had done. He had once been compelled to describe his former mentor as a 'villain'; now that word might have carried real asperity. Unwittingly, he had contributed greatly to the demand that an embarrassing official inquiry be held after all.

In the aftermath of Stead's dramatic 'revelations', the Conservative government reluctantly decided to give in to this inevitability.

Stead believed, naively, that the situation would be diffused merely if Chamberlain accepted responsibility and duly resigned. Chamberlain was willing to countenance no such recourse. And as a member of the committee formed, in part, to inquire into his involvement in the raid, he ensured that as little damage as possible was done to his reputation. This enraged Stead, but he was powerless to intervene: even the committee's most independent member, Henry Labouchere, dismissed Stead's version of events as 'fiddlesticks and nonsense'.

Although Stead would later become one of the fiercest critics of the inquiry, authoring such philippics as *The Scandal of the South African Committee* and *Joseph Chamberlain: Conspirator or Statesman?*, at the time he said relatively little. This was largely in deference to the wishes of Rhodes, who recognised the danger of attempting to place full responsibility on Chamberlain. For a time, at least, it seemed as if war in South Africa might be averted.

But Stead and his friends remained as determined as ever to annex the Transvaal, either by fair means or foul. The new method was essentially the same as the one Stead had proposed all along: to destroy Boer independence by the threat of force. For this purpose, Stead suggested that his old deputy editor, the recently ennobled Sir Alfred Milner, be dispatched to the Cape as a strong High Commissioner who could force the pace of change across the border.

Stead was quick to claim responsibility for Milner's appointment when it was announced by Lord Salisbury early in 1897, but Milner was by no means an unlikely choice for the government to have made. Since retiring from journalism at the time of the 'Maiden Tribute' campaign, Milner had become one of Britain's most distinguished civil servants, moving from department to department and amassing an impressive array of connections along the way. The idea that he owed his promotion solely to an editorial comment by Stead in the *Review of Reviews* was faintly ridiculous. But Stead was keen to assert his superiority. No matter how exalted Milner became – he became a lord in 1901 and later a viscount – Stead always viewed him, to some extent, as his underling.

Milner's appointment marked the beginning of a sharp deterioration of the situation in South Africa. In accordance with Stead's wishes he applied firm pressure to the Boer government, but to no avail. Matters came to a head at a meeting between himself and Kruger at Bloemfontein in June 1899, after which Milner informed Chamberlain that 'the case for intervention is overwhelming'. When a British ultimatum for Kruger to enfranchise the Outlanders was allowed to expire several weeks later, Lord Salisbury reluctantly advised the Queen to declare war.[350]

Stead never forgave Milner for this 'betrayal'. He later claimed that he had been willing to follow him 'blindfolded so long as he stopped short of war'. This was plainly unfair. As all of their mutual friends agreed, armed conflict had been the regrettable, though entirely foreseeable, outcome of their shared policy. The only difference between the positions of Stead and his former deputy editor was that when Milner made threats, he had to mean them.

Stead's hasty reinvention of himself as a supporter of the Boers may partly be attributed to his absorption in The Hague Peace Conference, which sat during the crucial months of the crisis. This was a meeting of diplomats from twenty-six world powers, convened at the behest of Tsar Nicholas II, to consider arms limitations and potential methods of resolving international conflicts by pacific means. With unflagging enthusiasm, Stead had made a 'Peace Pilgrimage' to Russia in anticipation of its convocation, and twice met the Tsar for confidential discussions about statecraft, bilateral arms limitation and, supposedly, the contents of the *Reviews of Reviews*. But his idea of applying the principles of The Hague to South Africa was not entirely altruistic. The delegates were scarcely more likely than Kruger and his people to accept his proposal that the nascent 'parliament of nations' be used to force the Boers to surrender their sovereignty to Britain.

Just before the outbreak of hostilities, Stead hurried back to London to compose a series of penny pamphlets on the situation. These were supposed to offer calm, judicious instruction to a generally hawkish public; but Stead's titles were anything but measured. One was called, seriously, *Shall I Slay My Brother Boer?* When these productions failed to turn the tide of public opinion against the war, Stead resorted to more vigorous language. In a lengthy sermon preached at the Nonconformist Westminster Chapel on 15 October, four days after fighting commenced, Stead assumed the position of a latter-day Elijah:

> mark my words; if I am right we shall not have long to wait before we shall find that God is not dead, neither is He asleep; and if, as I believe, He loves this England of His, and this people of His, although but a small remnant are still faithful to Him, then, as upon Israel of old when they sinned and went in opposition to the Divine will, will descend *disaster after disaster, until we turn from lying and all these evil ways into the paths of justice and truth*.[351]

It is not hard to imagine Stead's secret pleasure when this unlikely prophecy came true. During 'Black Week' in December 1899, the three most senior British generals in the field – Methuen, Gatacre and Buller – were routed by Boer commando units in a series of shock defeats. A war that was supposed to be 'over by Christmas', against a poor and ill-equipped army of peasant farmers, suddenly looked as if it might end in disaster.

Stead exulted over these reversals in a typically unusual manner: he proposed to lead a 'National Day of Humiliation' to *celebrate* the British defeats as divine 'punishment for our sins'. In language that would presumably be well understood by his curious friend Ada Goodrich-Freer, he explained that a 'national revival' could only come about if his countrymen agreed to 'kiss the rod'. The pair continued to enjoy long lunches at Gatti's throughout these years.[352]

Stead had a more reasonable, but no less unpopular, idea in founding the world's first 'Stop-the-War Committee' at the start of 1900. This attracted an impressive array of members, including two future prime ministers, David Lloyd George and Ramsay MacDonald, who admired Stead for his courage and zeal. But

Stead's intemperate language, which provoked violent mobs to infiltrate their meetings, as well as the formation of a more neutral 'South African Conciliation Committee' by the Liberal politician Leonard Courtney shortly afterwards, prevented the organisation from spearheading the 'pro-Boer' movement. Within a few months, it effectively ceased to exist beyond the personality of its founder.

Stead's isolation became more pronounced when Britain's new Commander-in-Chief, Lord Frederick Roberts, began to regain the momentum in the war later in the same year. His harsh but effective policy of destroying farms known to belong to Boer guerrilla soldiers made it impossible for them to continue moving undetected between civilian and military life. Far from recognising the desperate efficiency of this strategy, Stead was indignant: Roberts, said Stead, was waging war on 'women and children in their defenceless homes'. The reality was more nuanced. Many Boers actually welcomed the policy since it transferred the responsibility for their dependents to the enemy. Although the 'concentration camps' (as the temporary settlements for non-combatants were called) proved, for a time, to be insanitary and overcrowded, the death rate inside them was below that of the surrounding veldt by the time that Stead, and others, provoked a public outcry in mid-1901.[353]

This phase in the war marked one of the busiest periods in Stead's life. With the help of a generous cheque from the American industrialist and peace campaigner Andrew Carnegie, Stead launched a weekly newspaper entitled *War Against War in South Africa*. This publication was so extreme that it made Britain's only other 'pro-Boer' newspaper, the *Manchester Guardian,* seem (as Stead said of the fiercely anti-war Liberal leader Sir Henry Campbell-Bannerman) 'as weak as water'. This did not endear Stead to the general public, who wanted nothing more than to crush the Boers decisively. Even the make-up of his paper was considered to be gratuitously offensive. On the cover of each issue was a lurid depiction of Death the reaper with a harvest of skulls, a monocled Chamberlain viewing the hecatomb with satisfaction, and in capital type, a vehement catechism:

What do you want to do? Stop the war!
When? Immediately!
Why? Because we are in the wrong
How? By confessing our sins and doing right
What sins? Lying to cover conspiracy
Fraud in making false claims bad
Faith in going back on our word
Wholesale murder
And to do right? Expose and punish the criminals
Compensate their victims and make peace.

This was anti-war propaganda the like of which had never been seen in England before, and the paper ran at a heavy loss. After being banned from newsstands, it briefly survived as a monthly magazine until, at length, Carnegie decided that his resources would be better deployed elsewhere.

This did little to restrain Stead. In collaboration with the risqué novelist George Moore, he put together a broadsheet late in 1900 aptly entitled *Hell Let Loose: What is Now Being Done in South Africa*. This reproduced a long and sobering letter from a 'British Officer in the Field' (a relation of Moore's) which Stead 'improved upon' with a series of lurid crossheads including 'Driven to Shame by Starvation', 'Outrages by Kaffirs [i. e. Blacks]' and 'How the Women are Ruined'. As a result of such medleys, Stead became known at the War Office as 'a loathsome creature' and a 'lunatic'.[354]

Stead exulted in his rightful status as the most extreme partisan of the hated 'pro-Boer' faction. When an angry mob pelted his Wimbledon home with rocks, much as Gladstone's had been at the time of the Gordon debacle, Stead was not angry; he was grateful. '[I]n that waking moment,' he wrote, 'I was able to seize the exact sensation which the seigneurs of the Middle Ages must have had when the Jacquerie surged in tumult round their chateaux.' To the inevitable consternation of his wife, Stead refused to repair one of the windowpanes in their drawing-room as a memento of that 'historic occasion'.[355]

Such lordliness ultimately led Stead to do what he had never done before: to denounce the British public as a whole. This was most strikingly demonstrated in the aftermath of the famous Relief of Mafeking, when thousands of Londoners spontaneously poured onto the streets waving Union Jacks and chanting 'Rule Britannia'. Unlike the majority of the press, most notably the *Daily Mail* (which established the first regular circulation of over one million copies through its strong support of the war), Stead saw no reason to celebrate this 'vulgar and brutal Saturnalia'. In a stirring passage redolent of his famous leading articles on the 'Bulgarian Horrors' written some thirty years previously, Stead claims to have seen a respectable daughter

> torn shrieking from her father's arms, and kissed in succession by half a dozen ruffians who stood waiting for their prey. Any good-looking girl without an escort was seized and kissed and passed from hand to hand for similar treatment, utterly regardless of her protests ... a hundred pigs might have been stuck without a sound of their death-cries being heard above the din.[356]

In this manner Stead continued to denounce the war until it drew to an unimpressive close in May 1902. Although many viewed his actions as unbalanced, intemperate and hypocritical, Stead showed himself to be incredibly brave. His controversial views cost him not only his health, wealth and the popularity of the *Review of Reviews* (which never recovered), it also ended his decade-long partnership with Cecil Rhodes. In a codicil made months before his death in March 1902, the diamond king struck Stead's name from his will on account of his 'extraordinary eccentricity' and for being 'too masterful'. But it was more in sorrow than anger that Stead's old friends abandoned him. At a final, tearful meeting at the Burlington Hotel in Piccadilly during the last months of the war,

Rhodes took Stead's hand tenderly between his own – Hawksley actually thought that they were going to kiss – and said:

> Now, my dear Stead, I want you to understand that if, in future, you should unfortunately feel yourself compelled to attack me personally as vehemently as you have attacked my policy in this war, it will make no difference to our friendship. I am too grateful to you for all that I have learned from you to allow anything that you may write or say to make any change in our relations.

As has justly been written: 'The man who could speak thus was assuredly a great one. The man to whom it was said could not have been small.'[357]

CHAPTER 15

GRANDPA STEAD, 1902–12

Ah me! How fast they are going. Like the leaves in autumn,
the veterans fall on every side.
W. T. S., 'The Progress of the World' (May 1908)

It would be hard to exaggerate the speed with which Stead lost his fame. After being one of London's most discussed personalities for over two decades, he fell from public view with the rapidity of a lead balloon. As his former contributor George Bernard Shaw put it, cruelly though not inaccurately:

> when it turned out that he could not even see the sun crossing the heavens and the moon waxing and waning, or buy a calendar later than 1885, the younger men on Fleet Street began to wonder, not merely who Stead was, but whether he had ever been a journalist. When you told them that his leading articles had once been read by statesmen as factors in political life ... and that some of his stunts had been as successful as those of Swift and Voltaire, they simply did not believe you.[358]

It was too true. Shaggy-bearded and inclined to bore interlocutors with monologues, Stead lost touch with reality. He became, said Milner, 'a freak', more interested in the spirit world than current affairs.[359] But in his advocacy of women's suffrage, gradual constitutional reform for Russia and limiting arms proliferation, Stead continued to speak sense at a time when many of his contemporaries were hurrying the world on to catastrophe.

Perhaps the most notable feature of Stead's premature dotage was his undiminished penchant for attractive young women. Even more so than in his prime, female callers to his offices were surprised to be greeted with a kiss ('if they were pretty women'), while it was not unknown for Stead to march a particularly handsome lady to the railway station for a long weekend of enforced relaxation at Hayling Island. All this may have been perfectly innocent; but Stead's friends clearly wondered at his behaviour. To the horror of Lord Esher and Edward Cook, Stead solemnly announced, on two separate occasions, that he was not the man they knew: he was the reincarnated spirit of Charles II, returned to 'make amends for his previous life on earth'.[360]

For a man who routinely compared himself to Oliver Cromwell and publicly decried adultery as the sum of all evils, the choice of Charles II was doubly strange. But it was also apt. Month after month in the increasingly outlandish *Review of Reviews*, Stead gave pained glimpses into his tortured inner life. In February 1905 appeared a long essay entitled 'How Many Persons am I?' about the 'strange phenomena of two and even three apparently distinct personalities within one human being'. Despite ostensibly being a discussion of the findings of the famed Ukrainian psychologist Boris Sidis, Stead was effectively writing, as ever, about himself.

Stead went to the heart of the matter in a bizarre joint book review written at about the same time, critiquing the memoirs of John Wesley and Giacomo Casanova. Only Stead could have found a connection between these most unlikely of bedfellows. The paradox, said Stead, was that whereas Wesley was devoted to the 'ideals of love ... purity and self-sacrifice', it was only Casanova – 'the supreme type of the debauched libertine' – who truly experienced the ennobling influence of a woman's love. Unlike Wesley, who was 'mated with a termagant of a woman', the Italian lothario 'flitted with the rapidly and unconcern of a butterfly among the flowers'.

Did Stead, too, regard himself in the same light?

Undoubtedly he did. One young woman who came to Mowbray House expecting to meet a 'stern, rugged, elderly individual who ... would breathe hellfire upon me and rage against the wicked follies of the world ... and of my unregenerate sex in particular' was almost blown away by his extreme overfriendliness. After insisting that she conduct her interview – on the subject of women's dress – in the back of a taxi, Stead sidled up to her and, after making some suggestive remarks about her appearance, abruptly asked: 'Am I not a flirtatious person?' This was followed by a long and excited speech in which Stead explained that 'harmless flirtatiousness' added to 'the innocent gaiety of the world' – so long as one was 'absolutely faithful to one's wife'. On arriving at the railway station, where Stead was expecting to meet Emma, the editor stuck up his hand to hail his bewildered spouse and, in an aside to his companion, muttered: 'Ah, there's mother! How surprised she'll be to see you.'[361]

Although many women found this kind of behaviour to be harmless and even part of Stead's charm, others found it repugnant. The counter-feminist novelist Lynn Linton (author of such minor classics as *The Woman Who Didn't*) testily observed that it made little difference whether or not Stead was literally faithful to his wife, for he 'exudes semen through his skin'.[362]

Only privately was Stead willing to admit his strong attraction to women or, rather, theirs to him. According to one colleague, he boasted in old age that there were 'five-and-twenty women in London who would give their little finger for a kiss from me'.[363] Who these women were is not entirely clear. Madame Novikov, although the subject of a decadent biography by her former lover, was no longer of interest – she had become, said Stead, 'old and ugly ... [an] ogress'.[364] Stead's new circle was far more exciting. It included the beautiful actress Elizabeth Robins, whom Stead chastised in the *Review of Reviews* for pioneering the 'selfish' and 'immoral' role of Hedda Gabler in spite of writing of her privately (sometimes on Valentine's Day) as his 'darling Hedda'. Stead also developed a 'very warm regard' for the no less comely American adventuress Gladys Deacon, who would later boast of luring the Duke of Marlborough away from his first wife by 'witchcraft'. After Stead's death she mused that although the editor was certainly the most 'clean-living' individual she had ever known, the fact could only be believed 'after reading the "Maiden Tribute"!!!'[365]

Some of the details of Stead's extraordinary secret life were apparently recorded in a mysterious 250-page journal, which he kept securely in a small house purchased in Smith Square, Westminster, shortly before his death. Stead's official biographer, Frederic Whyte, found this book to contain innumerable instances of 'quixotry, not yet tellable': details of attractive women Stead had met; schemes to pacify his 'nervous and worried' wife; inventions; miracle cures; and much else besides. At the request of the family, however, Whyte agreed not even to refer to its existence. It has never been seen since.[366]

All of these escapades naturally took their toll on Stead's career. A man who spent his days lunching with actresses and debutantes, and brooding over a possible split personality, could hardly be expected to keep up to date with the latest happenings in the world. This was not altogether bad. For over three and a half decades Stead had placed himself at the centre of countless great national events. He had paid a heavy price for his fame. Finally, with a secure income from the *American Review of Reviews* and capable staff to whom he could delegate most of his editorial responsibilities, Stead was free to enjoy what other people would have been glad to call a 'comfortable retirement'.

Not Stead. Despite the trauma of the Boer War, he yearned to make a return to the sphere of daily journalism. He did so, however, in the most predictable and disastrous of fashions: by resurrecting his *Daily Paper*. The fact that Stead's friends and family warned him off the idea only made him more confident that it would succeed. Andrew Carnegie, who invited Stead for several long weekends at Skibo Castle to discuss the project, told him frankly that the idea was 'madness'. Edwin Stout, likewise, advised Stead against the project in the strongest terms: 'If you do this,' he warned, 'in under six weeks you will be bankrupt.'[367]

This was the sort of challenge that Stead relished. On a whim, he rented a large editorial office on Whitefriars Street, which he staffed with a considerable number of eager young journalists. They would never forget Stead's grandiose vision of 'the newspaper of the future'. He wanted the *Daily Paper* to serve not 'merely ... as a nerve centre for the collection and distribution of news ... [but also] for the inspiration, direction and organization of the moral, social, political and intellectual forces of the whole community'. As a means of furthering these objectives, Stead proposed to open special newspaper clubs all over the capital, which he planned to man, oddly, with smartly uniformed schoolgirls. 'When premises could not be got for seven years,' recalls Robertson Scott, 'they were taken for fourteen, and when they could not be got for fourteen they were taken for twenty-one.' Had Stead been a rich man, or still a brilliant editor, it may have worked. But he was neither of these things. After depriving himself of sleep for several intense weeks, Stead had a massive nervous breakdown immediately after seeing the first issue of the paper through the press. Within five weeks the *Daily Paper* had vanished from newsstands and Stead's reputation as an editor was in tatters.

Stead never recovered from this fall. But it was the death of his favourite son, Willie, in December 1907 that truly marked the end of his career. For the remaining years of his life, Stead dissipated his talents by attempting to communicate with his son's spirit in spite of Willie's professed dislike of the occult. Within a few months Stead claimed that the pair were in direct contact and offered to provide the same service to bereaved members of the general public. This was the origin of 'Julia's Bureau', a daily gathering of mediums and clairvoyants over which Stead presided in his sanctum at Mowbray House. His only condition was typical: the interested parties must never have been linked by adultery. Although many now denounced Stead as a fraud and a charlatan (he charged a nominal fee for his services), the Bureau proved expensive to maintain and actually lost Stead money. At length, with the *Review of Reviews* ailing and shunted to the empty offices of the *Daily Paper*, Stead even had to give up the lease on his beloved Mowbray House.

It was principally as the 'Director' of the Bureau that Stead became known to the politicians of the new century. This hugely undermined his credibility and ensured that even his sagest comments were exposed to ridicule. Despite being the first major commentator to recognise the potential of Winston Churchill, whom Stead predicted would become either the greatest journalist of the twentieth century 'or Prime Minister', the editor failed to make his acquaintance, let alone to become his mentor. This fairly typical letter from Stead's final years speaks for itself:

Dear Mr Churchill,

As you have been good enough to tolerate me writing once or twice when messages have come to me from the other side, I feel it is my duty to inform you that last night at the sitting of Julia's Circle, without any warning or expectation on our part, a message came purporting to come from your father [Lord Randolph Churchill (1849–95)], who professed himself to be very anxious as to the strain to which you were subjecting your nervous system. He implored us to beg you in his name to take more rest, to sleep, and not to rely upon any sedatives. With rest you would be alright. He was so urgent and so evidently anxious, I warned him that you might resent my intrusion if I sent you a message, he said he did not mind that so long as you got it.

So pray pardon me. I do not expect any acknowledgement of this letter. I have discharged my duty in sending it to you.

I am sincerely yours,

William T. Stead[368]

It would be tempting to suppose that Stead intended such advice to be taken in a jocular spirit. But he was deadly serious. In a frightening article, which appeared in the *Fortnightly Review* of January 1909, Stead explained, with chilling sangfroid, exactly 'How I Know that the Dead Return'. This told the story of a young woman on his staff whom Stead had apparently intended to dismiss but was persuaded by 'Julia' to retain since she was 'coming over to our side'. Eager to test this macabre prophecy, Stead solemnly informed two or three of his gossiping secretaries, 'under seal of secrecy', of what he had foreseen and over the following twelve months made detailed notes of the unfortunate woman's health. On one occasion she accidently swallowed a tack; another time she was stricken with a severe bout of flu. But 'Julia' told him not to worry – 'she will not come over here naturally', it was declared. Certain that the lady in question was unaware of her looming fate, Stead had several earnest conversations with her about what she was to do after death: she must return to him in 'astral' form, allow herself to be photographed and draw a special mathematical symbol with the hand of a medium. When she jumped to her death from a fourth-floor window 'in delirium' just a few days after Stead had predicted, and later 'fulfilled' her obligations to him, Stead boasted that there had never been a 'better substantiated case' of psychic aptitude. 'What more evidence, what kind of evidence, under what conditions, is wanted, before conviction is established?' he seriously asked his readers.

Thankfully for Stead, neither the police nor the press took much notice of this dark sensation. But Robert Donald, the editor of the *Daily Chronicle*, who had unhappy memories of Stead – 'that impossible fellow' – at Northumberland Street decided to follow it up with a hoax commission: he wanted him to interview the spirit of William Gladstone. After being found mumbling incoherently on the sofa at Mowbray House, Stead accepted the offer with the utmost gravity. His production secured him his first front page in years. But no one was particularly interested in what 'Gladstone' had to say. Stead had unwittingly become a figure of fun.[369]

Only abroad did Stead continue to be regarded as a serious journalist. When a revolution appeared to be looming in Russia in September 1905, for instance, Stead hurried over to St Petersburg to see what he could do to help prevent a crisis. For several busy weeks he held political meetings at the Hotel d'Europe and enjoyed brief conversations with the Tsar, his wife and his mother. Although Stead was not accorded the same level of respect that he would have liked – he complained that the Dowager Empress looked over his shoulder when he spoke to her and that her daughter-in-law, the Tsarina, regarded him as though he intended to 'bite her' – his analysis of the Russian situation was faultless, even prophetic. He foresaw 'the expropriation of the whole of the landlords' resulting in a massive reduction in yields, with all the concomitant miseries: famine, civil war and revolution. Still more presciently, Stead predicted that the well-meaning student demonstrators and their leader, Professor Pavel Milyukov, would rapidly find themselves denounced as 'renegades and traitors', and overthrown by far more dangerous radicals. Before long, Stead anticipated, a 'strong Tsar might re-establish authority and order upon the ruins of civilization'.[370] This was essentially the pattern of events which would follow the February Revolution of 1917.

Stead was no less ahead of his times in his advocacy of world peace. But, yet again, his seemingly hysterical vision of 'the shape of things to come' – so different to that of his more optimistic contemporaries – and his inability to work in collaboration with others, rendered him ineffectual. A characteristic example of his legitimate impatience with potential allies occurred at a pious meeting of the Universal Peace Congress at Glasgow, where Stead dramatically announced:

> We don't want namby-pamby resolutions affirming things... It is necessary that when nations go against the sentiment of the civilized world, there should be an explosion of pacific sentiment. I see precious little explosion here; and if a peace congress will not explode, how do you think the general public will do so?

On that occasion, like so many others, Stead was shouted down as a madman. 'While I feel as strongly as he does,' the chairman coolly intoned, 'this proposition simply makes us ridiculous – "Excommunicate of humanity"! What nonsense!' Yet, in the aftermath of two bloody world wars, many of Stead's ideas have become the bedrock of international relations.[371]

Andrew Carnegie was one of the few people who continued to have faith in Stead, despite his vagaries, until the end. But not even he could overcome the deep prejudices that Stead's name continued to arouse. When he suggested to Theodore Roosevelt that Stead be appointed to head up a 'League of Peace' for the promotion of friendly relations between Britain and Germany, the twenty-sixth President of the United States was strongly against the idea. Stead, said Roosevelt, was the kind of man who 'makes a good cause ridiculous ... [whose] proposals are rarely better than silly; and the only reason that [he is] not exceedingly mischievous is that [he is] well-nigh impotent for either good or evil'. As Stead conceded shortly before his death, he had, indeed, 'lost his influence'.[372]

～

For those who remembered Stead as the doughty crusader of Northumberland Street, his decline was pitiful to behold. No longer able to provide adequately for his family, Stead, the long-time helper of others, became the object of charity himself. When the American newspaper baron William Randolph Hearst attempted to alleviate his hardships by offering a generous salary of £5,000 in return for an insignificant fortnightly column, Stead wrote back asking if the amount could be doubled – a sum equivalent to five times what Stead had ever drawn as editor-proprietor of the *Review of Reviews*. Hearst's kindness in acquiescing was all the more touching for the fact that Stead had once described him as 'a journalist engineer to whom nothing is sacred, a man whose balance-wheel of moral principle is not dominant'.[373]

As poor Edwin Stout might have predicted, Stead squandered this lucky windfall. Besides redoubling the work of 'Julia's Bureau' and giving yet greater sums to what Frederic Whyte privately called his 'legion of darlings', Stead developed an expensive taste for touring the world in the guise of an international peacekeeper. Wherever a crisis or a peace conference loomed, Stead would descend 'bouncing with vitality, running over with human kindness towards emperors, kings, peoples, and a bevy of girls alike'. Despite his sincere abhorrence of war, Stead would often conclude a sermon on peace with a call for 'as many battleships as we could possibly build'.[374]

Nothing in Stead's career was sadder than his losing battle with obscurity. In what was to be his last 'Progress of the World', Stead announced in April 1912 that he would soon be journeying to America to speak alongside President Taft at a meeting of 'The Men and Religion Forward Movement' in New York. With something of the old fire, he explained that he and the President intended to send armies of inspectors into every American town to gather information pertaining to 'its moral, industrial, social and religious condition'. 'Every man who is got hold of,' he enthused, 'is to be indexed up and looked after.' Needless to say, Taft had heard nothing of this scheme and was not even scheduled to attend the meeting.[375]

The 'Senior Partner' had other plans for Stead, too. In what proved to be a tragically unfortunate act of generosity, his American hosts offered to send him to his destination in style: as a first-class passenger aboard the greatest ship ever to set sail – the *Titanic*.

It was a fitting climax to a life that had never been of ordinary proportions. After boarding at Southampton on 10 April, Stead delighted in rushing about its broad decks, interviewing crew members and noting as many instances of superfluous luxury as he could find. In a letter to his daughter posted en route from Ireland, he gave a wonderful glimpse of the thundering article that might have been: the ship, he wrote, was 'a splendid monstrous floating Babylon'.[376]

The grizzled editor made an unlikely complement to the ornate first-class dining-room, where he passed his four evenings on board alongside some of the richest men in the world. Even with Hearst's exuberant financial support, Stead was a desperately poor man by their standards, and few of his fellow diners showed much sign of warming to him. 'My dear fellow,' a sympathetic American lawyer was told, 'do you know he was *a pro-Boer*?'

But Stead always relished an audience, no matter how outwardly hostile. The Friday before the tragedy, he enthralled the eight men on his table with a favourite story of a cursed sarcophagus inscription. He told them that any man who recounted the events narrated by the hieroglyphs would suffer a violent death. Stead then proceeded to do exactly what the inscription had warned against. 'To prove that I am not superstitious,' he said brandishing the timepiece given to him by his first employer, 'I call your attention to the fact that it was Friday when I began this story and the day of its ending, my watch tells me, will fall upon a thirteenth.'[377]

That was Stead in his element. Late the following Sunday the ship collided with a massive iceberg and slowly began to sink. The veteran editor, who was one of the few people on deck at the time of the impact, returned to his room to read before heroically giving his lifejacket to a fellow passenger and helping women and children into the lifeboats. There were too few boats. Stead was last sighted by a survivor 'alone at the edge of the deck, in silence, and, what seemed to me, a prayerful attitude or one of profound meditation'.[378] '*One can see him!*' wrote his old ally Admiral Fisher to Lord Esher, 'and probably singing "Hallelujah"! and encouraging the band to play cheerfully… A fine death … for our Cromwellian saint.'[379]

EPILOGUE

I wish for no other epitaph upon my tomb than this: 'Here lies the man who wrote "The Maiden Tribute of Modern Babylon".'
W. T. S., 'Why I Went to Prison' (1910)

Stead's dramatic end compelled Fleet Street to pay tribute to its unacknowledged master. In the *Daily Mail* he was hailed as 'one of the most remarkable personalities of our time – a brilliant mind, an apostle of many causes, an essentially great journalist, a man of devastating sincerity and rigid principle, yet with interests as wide as the world and an inexhaustible love of adventure'. He had, said another obituary-writer, found journalism 'a thing of conventions and respectabilities' and left it 'a powerful personal force'.[380]

Critics who had lately mocked Stead for his ardent spiritualism were now willing to reassess his eccentricity. Some even accepted that Stead had predicted the tragedy in which he had perished. This was based mostly on Stead's 1893 Christmas annual, *From the Old World to the New*, in which the protagonists make a transatlantic crossing in a ship called the *Majestic*. In the course of their voyage a character with psychic powers, clearly based on Stead himself, tells the captain to divert his course because he can 'see' a group of men, whose ship has sunk, stranded on a distant iceberg. Keen, as ever, to give a factual gloss to his story, Stead used a real-life sailor, Captain Edward Smith, as the skipper in the narrative. Captain Smith would later be given the command of the *Titanic* by the White Star Line.

Stranger yet, it was said, Stead had published a story in the *PMG* of 22 March 1886 entitled 'How the Mail Steamer went down in the Mid-Atlantic – by a Survivor'. This reads like an historic account

of the famous disaster that claimed his life. After a scramble for
lifeboats, in which the captain is forced to use his pistol, 'the deck
slanted, slanted steadily, and the lift to starboard made an angle
that made it difficult to stand at all ... [a] green and white moun-
tain gleamed in the glory of the dawn, and then the ship was no
more seen.' Stead added in a haunting editorial note at the foot of
the story: 'This is exactly what *might* take place and what *will* take
place if liners are sent to sea short of boats.' He was referring to
the well-known fact that there was inadequate statutory provision
for lifeboats at the time. It was the sinking of the *Titanic* which
compelled Parliament to revisit this important area.

So even in death Stead could claim a hand in reforming the law.
But the idea that he had predicted the disaster stretches a good story
too far. Stead had planned to return to England after his American
lecture tour to write his memories and to help combat the swell
of militarism, which he correctly foresaw would result in a great
European war – a far more impressive prediction. The claim that he
had anticipated his death aboard the *Titanic* was fanciful. Dressed
in his prison garb, Stead had often told perplexed acquaintances
that 'Julia' had informed him that he would not die until he was
twice more sent to jail. And even then, it would not be by drown-
ing: he would either be 'killed on the barricades' or be 'stoned some
day in the marketplace'.[381]

Assessments of Stead's contribution to journalism tended to
be bittersweet. In the *Daily News*, a pioneer 'columnist', A. G.
Gardiner, admitted that although Stead had been the most important journalist of his era, 'his faults were many'. His methods
were 'wild, extravagant, even foolish', and his ideals – 'noble even
though besmirched'. There was an abiding note of wistfulness. In
the *Westminster Gazette* J. A. Spender lamented that 'the younger
generation cannot realise the power he was in the eighties'. The
sad, lonely figure they had come to know, careworn and decked in
tattered garments, had 'invented a new style of journalism, swayed
the decisions of Cabinets, [and] almost made himself a party in the
country'. It was hard to believe.[382]

Fittingly, it took a woman to speak the truth. In an aside to her husband at Stead's memorial service at Westminster Chapel, attended by hundreds of the most eminent personages of the day, Mrs Edward Cook observed that although everybody from Edward VII down had been 'glad enough to see Stead ... most people [were] shy of it being known'.[383] She could hardly have put it more delicately. Despite being on first-name terms with everyone from the Emperor of Russia to the crossing-sweep, Stead had few out-and-out admirers, and fewer real friends. Even the journalists to whom he had bequeathed the seeds of the future could scarcely admit the influence he had been. It was too embarrassing.

Cook was eager not to fall into the same category. In a fulsome obituary in *The Times*, he marvelled at Stead's 'ingenious and fertile mind', his 'keen sense of fun' and the 'vivacity ... [and] spontaneity' of his conversation. But Cook felt constrained to admit that this was not a portrait that many casual newspaper readers would be likely to recognise. To them, Stead was often what he was to the artist, William Rothenstein: an 'obnoxious ... man ... with no feeling for beauty, a kill-joy, a fusty-musty Puritan ... journalist, mystic, reformer, rescuer of fallen women, imperialist, and goodness knows what else'.[384]

Had Cook been able to write Stead's biography, as he had intended, he might have found a means of explaining and justifying the Stead paradox. But his attempts were thwarted by someone who knew his subject far better than he – Stead's widow. Throughout her husband's busy and varied life, Emma had assumed the role of the Virgin: silent, distantly worshipped, yet somehow unreal. Finally given the opportunity to offer an opinion, she was forthright: she 'couldn't stand' Cook's proposal.[385] Clearly, there was something fundamentally wrong in the Stead household, which even the most prying biographer could never entirely unravel. And it was not only Stead's widow who was almost shamelessly eager to escape her husband's shadow: his children, too, rebelled against him. Estelle, bucking the Nonconformist prejudice against the theatre, became an actress, and even missed her father's memorial service because it clashed with a production. As for her brother, Alfred: he abandoned his wife and children in Capri before passing the remainder of his life as an exile in Romania.[386]

If Stead had a fatal weakness, it was his unshakable belief in his own infallibility. Again and again, he staked his entire reputation on the vaguest hunches, dreams and assumptions, which often caused harm, even ruin, to innocent bystanders. The tragic story of Eliza Armstrong – who appears to have emigrated shortly after her family were forced by the controversy to leave Charles Street – is certainly the greatest example of his recklessness. Yet even after his humiliating trial, at which he lost the confidence of the majority of his contemporaries, Stead remained unrepentant. By the time of his death many of the less savoury details of that episode had been forgotten; today, as much as it is recalled at all, it is generally accepted to have been entirely to Stead's credit.[387]

Whatever Stead's failings, revisionism should have its limits. At least by the standards of his profession, he was undoubtedly a great man. He twisted facts, invented stories, lied, betrayed confidences; but always with a genuine desire to reform the world – and himself. The tabloid press that he inspired has not lived up to his ideal, but the fact remains that some of the greatest journalists can still be found among the cussed and lonely figures of the 'red-tops'.

In the history of journalism there have been more skilful writers, and sounder minds, but few have rivalled Stead for freshness, power and sincerity of style. His weaknesses were his strengths and his 'gifts' his downfall, but, taken as a whole, he remains one of the foremost exemplars of his trade. Nothing would have delighted him more than the judgement of a postmistress with whom he once lodged: 'You know, I always thought he was a wicked man – but he wasn't.'[388]

NOTES

1   *Financial Times*, 23 July 2011; *Guardian*, 15 July 2011.
2   R. Shannon, *Gladstone* (London, 1982–99), II, p. 450, n; *Review of Reviews*, XXXIX (June 1909), p. 493.
3   Whyte, *Stead*, p. 239.
4   J. A. Spender, *Life, Journalism and Politics* (London, 1927), II, p. 135.
5   *Review of Reviews*, XXX (October 1904), p. 361.
6   A. Harrison to F. Whyte, 29 June 1923. Frederic Whyte Papers (Robinson Library).
7   Scott, *Life and Death*, p. 8.
8   W. Lord, *A Night to Remember* (London, 1955), p. 16.
9   Stead, *MP for Russia*, II, p. 249.
10 Scott, *Life and Death*, p. 97; *Jarrow Guardian*, 29 February 1884.
11 *The Congregational Review*, II (1888), p. 66.
12 Scott, *Life and Death*, p. 96.
13 J. W. Robertson Scott quoted in Whyte, *Stead*, I, p. 289.
14 Whyte, *Stead*, II, pp. 341–2.
15 Ibid., p. 30.
16 Stead, *My Father*, p. 6.
17 *Jarrow Guardian*, 29 February 1884; J. Heatley, 'Recollections of the Stead Family'. Whyte Papers; K. Humby, 'The Life and Times of Rev. William Stead', *News-stead* (Spring, 2001), pp. 15–18.
18 For following, see Scott, *Life and Death*, pp. 91–3; Heatley, 'Recollections'.
19 W. T. Stead to Madame Olga Novikov, 14 November 1885. Olga Novikov Collection (Bodleian Library); *Northern Echo*, 5 July 1949.
20 Stead, *My Father*, pp. 20–21.
21 Stead, *My Father*, pp. 22–3.
22 *British Weekly*, 2 May 1912.
23 W. T. Stead, *Books Which Have Influenced Me* (London, 1887), p. 27; Stead, *My Father*, pp. 25–6; Scott, *Life and Death,* p. 242.
24 Scott, *Life and Death*, p. 242.
25 E. Mackenzie, *A Descriptive and Historical Account of the town and county of Newcastle upon Tyne* (Newcastle, 1827), I, p. 164; Whyte, *Stead*, I, p. 29.
26 *Review of Reviews*, XV (April 1897), p. 382; Stead, *Books Which Have Influenced Me*, p. 28; L. J. Dyer, 'Newcastle Mechanics Institute', *Adult Education*, XXII (December 1949), p. 125.
27 Stead, *Books Which Have Influenced Me*, p. 28; Stead, *My Father*, p. 32; *Review of Reviews*, XXIIX (October 1903), p. 411.
28 Stead, *My Father*, p. 25; *Review of Reviews*, XXIIX (October 1903), p. 411.
29 *Review of Reviews*, XXX (July 1904), p. 30; ibid., IV (September 1891), p. 237.

30 Scott, *Life and Death*, pp. 93–4.

31 Stead, *My Father*, p. 50.

32 *Review of Reviews*, XVI (October 1897), p. 387.

33 Whyte, *Stead*, I, p. 28; *Review of Reviews*, III (February 1891), p. 149.

34 *British Weekly*, 2 May, 1912. Several stories exist as to how Stead was appointed editor. This one came from a former *Northern Echo* reporter. Stead's version has Bell appearing at his office on the quayside (Stead, *My Father*, pp. 46–7).

35 For following, see S. J. Reid (ed.), *Memoirs of Sir Wemyss Reid, 1842–1885* (London, 1905), pp. 309–10.

36 J. O. Baylen, 'The "New Journalism" in Late Victorian Britain', *The Australian Journal of Politics and History*, XVIII (1972), pp. 368–9.

37 *Northern Echo*, 7 July 1949.

38 For following, see C. Lloyd, *Attacking the Devil: 130 Years of The Northern Echo* (Darlington, 1999), pp. 15–30.

39 Whyte, *Stead*, I, p. 32.

40 Stead, *My Father*, pp. 46–7; Whyte, *Stead*, p. 34.

41 Scott, *Life and Death*, p. 6

42 For following, see Stead, *My Father*, pp. 50–55.

43 Stead to Novikov, 22 October 1877.

44 Scott, *Life and Death*, pp. 92–109.

45 *Northern Echo*, 15 March 1872.

46 G. B. Shaw, quoted in Whyte, *Stead*, I, p. 304.

47 Stead to Novikov, 9 October 1879; *PMG*, 10 July 1885.

48 *Northern Echo*, 17 May; 16 March 1872.

49 S. Koss, *The Rise and Fall of the Political Press in Britain* (London, 1990), pp. 209–11; R. Shannon, *Gladstone and the Bulgarian Agitation of 1876* (London, 1963), pp. 75–8.

50 *Northern Echo*, 13 July 1876.

51 Stead, *MP for Russia*, I, pp. 242–3, 407.

52 *Northern Echo*, 18 August 1876.

53 A. J. P. Taylor, *The Trouble Makers: Dissent Over Foreign Policy 1792–1939* (London, 1969 [1957]), p. 65.

54 *Northern Echo*, 6 July 1876.

55 G. de Gaury, *Travelling Gent: The Life of Alexander Kinglake* (London, 1972), p. 137; 'Olga Novikov (1840–1925)', *ODNB*.

56 D. W. R. Bahlman (ed.), *The Diary of Sir Edward Walter Hamilton 1880–1885* (Oxford, 1972), p. 636.

57 Stead to Novikov, 15 & 19 October 1877.

58 Ibid., 28 October 1878.

59 Stead to Novikov, 30 April 1879; 25 September 1879; 15 & 24 October 1879; 19 November 1879.

60 Stead to Novikov, 30 August 1880; 11 February 1881.

61 Stead to Novikov, 30 August 1880; 7 March 1881; *The Times*, 18 April 1912.

62 Anon. [S. Morison et al.], *The History of the Times, vol. 2: The Tradition Established 1841–1884* (London, 1939), p. 304.

63 *PMG*, 3 July & 18 August 1876.

64 'Frederick Greenwood (1830–1909)', *ODNB*.

65 *Northern Echo*, 6 August 1876; *Review of Reviews*, VII (February 1893).

66 A. Watson, *A Newspaper Man's Memories* (London, 1925), p. 101; A. Milner

to Stead, 6 August 1884. Stead Papers (Churchill College); Stead to Novikov, 27 July 1880.

67 *Review of Reviews*, II (October 1890), p. 430.

68 G. B. Shaw, *Autobiography*, ed. S. Weintraub (London, 1969), p. 239. Shaw would occasionally send letters for publication in the *PMG* under pseudonyms such as 'An English Mistress', denouncing the impropriety of the English stage. The irony of these submissions was apparently lost on Stead, who published them believing them to be genuine. B. Tysan (ed.), *Bernard Shaw's Book Reviews, Originally Published in the Pall Mall Gazette from 1885 to 1888* (Pennsylvania, 1991), p. 16.

69 G. B. Shaw, quoted in Whyte, *Stead*, I, p. 305.

70 J. Morley to W. T. Stead, 14 August 1880. Stead Papers.

71 F. W. Hirst, *Early Life and Letters of John Morley* (London, 1927), II, p, 105.

72 Ibid., p. 105.

73 For following, see Watson, *Memories*, pp. 66–7.

74 Scott, '*We' and Me*, p. 16; Milner to Stead, 14 August 1884.

75 Watson, *Memories*, p. 66.

76 R. Blatchford, *God and My Neighbour* (London, 1903), p. ix.

77 Scott, *Life and Death*, p. 79.

78 *Review of Reviews*, II (November 1890), p. 429.

79 *Review of Reviews*, II (November 1890), p. 429; ibid., VII (February, 1893), p. 153; Watson, *Memories*, p. 14.

80 J. Saxon Mills, *Sir Edward Cook K.B.E.: A Biography* (London, 1921), p. 48.

81 *Review of Reviews*, VII (November 1893), pp. 424–31.

82 Watson, *Memories*, p.68; *Review of Reviews*, II (November 1890), p. 432; J. Morley to W. T. Stead, 6 April 1882. Stead Papers.

83 Scott, *Life and Death*, p. 117; *Review of Reviews*, VII (February 1893), p. 151.

84 Hirst, *Morley*, II, p. 97.

85 Whyte, *Stead*, II, pp. 321–7.

86 Scott, *Life and Death*, p. 91.

87 A. S. Wohl, *The Eternal Slum* (New Brunswick, 1977), p. 202; *PMG*, 28 June 1887.

88 J. W. R. Scott, *The Story of the Pall Mall Gazette* (Oxford, 1950), p. 185; T. Hunt, *The Frock-Coated Communist: The Revolutionary Life of Friedrich Engels* (London, 2009), pp. 223–4.

89 Wohl, *Eternal Slum*, p. 210.

90 W. S. Blunt, *Gordon at Khartoum* (London, 1911), p. 152.

91 *PMG*, 9 January 1885.

92 *Review of Reviews*, XXVI (November 1902), p. 474; Scott, *Life and Death*, p. 78; *Manchester Guardian*, 2 July 1949.

93 *Review of Reviews*, XX (July 1899), p. 21; *PMG*, 19 January 1884.

94 E. Cromer, *Modern Egypt* (London, 1908), I, pp. 389, 437.

95 *Review of Reviews*, XVII (April 1908), p. 359.

96 Cromer, *Modern Egypt*, I, pp. 435–6.

97 For following, see Blunt, *Gordon*, pp. 150–62.

98 *Review of Reviews*, XXXVII (April 1908), p. 359.

99 Marder, *Fear God*, III, p. 546.

100 Whyte, *Stead*, I, p. 147.

101 *Review of Reviews*, XVI (July 1897), p. 77.

102 A. J. Marder, *The Anatomy of British Sea Power: A History of British Naval Policy in the Pre-Dreadnought Era*, 1880–1905 (London, 1964), p. 122; *Review of Reviews*, XVI (July 1897), p. 79.

103 C. Y. Lang (ed.), *The Letters of Matthew Arnold, 1822–1888* (Charlottesville, 1996–2001), V, p. 416.

104 J. O. Baylen, 'Politics and the "New Journalism": Lord Esher's Use of the *Pall Mall Gazette*', *Victorian Periodicals Review*, XX (1987), p. 130.

105 Baylen, 'Politics and the "New Journalism"', p. 133; R. Jenkins, *Gladstone* (London, 1995), pp. 106–7; H. C. G. Matthew, *Gladstone, 1875–1898* (Oxford, 1997 [1986–95]), pp. 91–5.

106 A. N. Wilson, *The Victorians* (London, 2002), pp. 472–77; J. Walkowitz, *City of Dreadful Delight: Narratives of Sexual Danger in Late-Victorian London* (London, 1992), pp. 81–134.

107 G. Eckley, *Maiden Tribute: A Life of W. T. Stead* (Philadelphia, 2007); V. P. Jones, *Saint or Sensationalist: The Story of W. T. Stead* (Chichester, 1988); *Methodist Times*, 11 July 1885.

108 Stead to Novikov, 17 April 1885.

109 Scott, *Life and Death*, pp. 143–5.

110 Ibid., p. 111; Stead's diary, 30 January 1889. Stead Papers.

111 Scott, *'We' and Me*, pp. 123–5; Whyte, *Stead*, I, pp. 300–1; M. Belloc to W. T. Stead, 6 November 1892. Stead Papers.

112 *PMG*, 6 July 1885.

113 Hansard's Parliamentary Debates, 3rd Series, vol. 298, pp. 1181–2.

114 J. Walkowitz, 'Male Vice and Feminist Virtue: Feminism and the Politics of Prostitution in Nineteenth-Century Britain', *Historical Workshop Journal*, XIII (1982), pp. 85, 96–7.

115 B. Booth, *Echoes and Memories* (London, 1977), pp. 122–32; *PMG*, 6 July 1885.

116 *PMG*, 6 July 1885.

117 Stead to Novikov, 10 June 1885.

118 Booth, *Memories*, p. 133.

119 For following see, J. Jordan, *Josephine Butler* (London, 2007), pp. 217–35; A. Plowden, *The Case of Eliza Armstrong: A Child of 13 Bought for £5* (London, 1974), pp. 20–33; *Proceedings of the Central Criminal Court, Twelfth Session 1884–5*, pp. 894–1038; *PMG*, 6 July 1885.

120 Booth, *Memories*, p. 130.

121 Ibid., p. 150.

122 J. Morley, *Recollections* (London, 1917), I, p. 169.

123 A. Milner to F. Whyte, n.d. (copy), Whyte Papers.

124 *PMG*, 28 September 1885; H. M. Hyndman, *Further Reminiscences* (London, 1912), p. 306. A young friend of Stead's would later suggest, revealingly, that 'rescue' work should be carried out by 'better men or rather women'. E. Garrett to W. T. Stead, n.d. Stead Papers.

125 Mills, *Cook*, p. 67.

126 J. Walkowitz, 'Male Vice and Feminist Virtue', pp. 96–7; Whyte, *Stead*, I, 173.

127 *PMG*, 4 July 1885. *St. James's Gazette*, 7 July 1885.

128 Whyte, *Stead*, I, p. 169.

129 *PMG*, 9 July 1885.

130 Whyte, *Stead*, I, p. 171.
131 *PMG*, 8 July 1885.
132 H. Kingsmill, *After Puritanism* (London, 1929), p. 192.
133 *PMG*, 8 July 1885.
134 Ibid., 18 July 1885.
135 *St. James's Gazette*, 7, 8, 9, 10 July; Koss, *Political Press*, p. 262.
136 E. Charteris, *The Life and Letters of Sir Edmund Gosse* (London, 1931), p. 186.
137 Whyte, *Stead*, I, pp. 175, 304–6.
138 Milner to Stead, 8 July 1885.
139 *PMG*, 9 July 1885.
140 Ibid., 30 July 1885.
141 Whyte, *Stead*, I. p. 171.
142 *Lloyd's*, 8 November 1885.
143 *Standard*, 2 November 1885.
144 *Lloyd's*, 13 September 1885.
145 Booth, *Echoes and Memories*, p. 135.
146 *Lloyd's*, 30 August 1885.
147 Mills, *Cook*, p. 67.
148 *PMG*, 13 July 1885.
149 Scott, *Life and Death*, p. 227.
150 *PMG*, 18 July 1885; Scott, *Life and Death*, p. 133.
151 *PMG*, 17 July 1885.
152 Hansard, 3rd Series, vol. 300, col. 1408.
153 H. Yates Thompson to Stead, 19 December 1885. Stead Papers; *Lloyd's*, 8 November 1885.
154 *Lloyd's*, 12 July, 1 August & 20 September 1885.
155 E. S. Purcell, *Life of Cardinal Manning* (London, 1895), II, pp. 312, 781. Purcell considered that in his last years Manning 'lost his power of judging men aright ... the process of senile decay had set in – journalists like Stead were welcome at Archbishop's House'.
156 Bramwell Booth to Stead, 11 August 1885, Salvation Army International Heritage Centre; Stead to Novikov, 4 August 1885.
157 *PMG*, 22 July 1885.
158 Hansard, 3rd Series, vol. 300, cols 578–9.
159 Koss, *Political Press*, p. 262.
160 J. O. Baylen, 'Oscar Wilde Redivivus', *University of Mississippi Studies in English*, VI (1965), p. 77; F. Harris, *Oscar Wilde, His Life and Confessions* (New York, 1916), p. 157.
161 *PMG*, 15 August 1885.
162 *Times*, 9 November 1885.
163 W. Morris to Stead, 12 August 1885. Stead Papers.
164 *PMG*, 22 August 1885.
165 *Lloyd's*, 23 August 1885.
166 For following, see *Lloyd's*, 8 November 1885.
167 *PMG*, 20 July 1885.
168 Booth, *Echoes and Memories*, p. 139.
169 *Lloyd's*, 27 September 1885.
170 *PMG*, 25 August 1885.
171 *Lloyd's*, 27 September 1885.

172 *PMG*, 18 September 1885.

173 *Lloyd's*, 8 November 1885.

174 J. F. Archbold, *The Justice of the Peace* (London, 1840) I, p. 203; R. E. Webster, *Recollections of Bar and Bench* (London, 1914), pp. 171–3. I am grateful to Professor J. R. Spencer of the Faculty of Law at the University of Cambridge for answering a query regarding this aspect of the case.

175 *Lloyd's*, 8 November 1885

176 Stead, *My Father*, pp. 130–1.

177 W. T. Stead, *My First Imprisonment* (London, 1886), pp. 4–5.

178 Stead to Novikov, 23 November 1885.

179 G. Eckley, 'To Her Most Gracious Majesty Queen Victoria: Commuting Stead's Sentence', *News-stead* (Fall 2003), pp. 2–9.

180 Koss, *Political Press*, pp. 262–3.

181 W. T. Stead to Mrs P. Bunting, n.d. [November 1885]. Millicent Fawcett Papers (Women's Library, London).

182 Scott, *Life and Death*, p. 149.

183 H. Stead to O. Novikov, 13 November 1885. Novikov Collection.

184 Stead, *My Father*, pp. 142–3.

185 John Morley's diary, 8 December 1885. John Morley Papers (Bodleian Library); Morley, *Recollections*, I, pp. 209–10.

186 *Contemporary Review*, XXI (1886), pp. 653–74.

187 *Nineteenth Century*, XI (1887), pp. 629–43.

188 Stead to Novikov, 24 December 1885; Whyte, *Stead*, I, p. 219.

189 *Review of Reviews*, XXXVII (April 1908), p. 345.

190 Stead to Novikov, 23 November 1885.

191 Whyte, *Stead*, I, p. 219.

192 E. T. Cook's diary, 20 December 1895.

193 Scott, *Life and Death*, pp. 144–7.

194 For following, see D. Nicholls, *The Lost Prime Minister: A Life of Sir Charles Dilke* (London, 1995), pp. 177–93.

195 *PMG*, 9 June 1885.

196 C. Dilke to W. T. Stead, 18 March 1879. Stead Papers.

197 Ibid., 13 & 16 February 1886.

198 Ibid., 16 February 1886.

199 E. T. Cook's diary, 22 February 1891.

200 Stead to Novikov, 23 November 1885; 12 September 1887.

201 For following, see A. Taylor, *Annie Besant: A Biography* (Oxford, 1992), pp. 186–201.

202 N. Mackenzie and J. Mackenzie (eds), *The Diary of Beatrice Webb* (London, 1982–5), I, pp. 154, 251–2.

203 Stead to Novikov, 26 June 1880.

204 E. P. Thompson, *William Morris: Romantic to Revolutionary* (London, 1976), p. 500.

205 T. P. O'Connor, *Memoirs of an Old Parliamentarian* (London, 1929), I, p. 303.

206 Ibid., 20 & 22 April 1887; 18 December 1889.

207 F. S. L. Lyons, *Charles Stewart Parnell* (Oxford, 1977), p. 465.

208 W. T. Stead to W. Gladstone, 19, 20, 21 & 25 November 1890. Gladstone Papers (British Library).

209 *Methodist Times*, 20 November 1890.

210 Whyte, *Stead*, II, p. 20.

211 *Review of Reviews*, II (December 1890), p. 529.

212 J. L. Garvin and J. Amery, *The Life of Joseph Chamberlain* (London, 1932–69), II, p. 291.

213 Booth, *Echoes and Memories*, p. 150.

214 Scott, *'We' and Me*, p. 93; Whyte, I, p. 291.

215 Whyte, *Stead*, I, p. 290.

216 Ibid., p, 293; M. Belloc Lowndes, *Where Love and Friendship Dwelt* (London, 1943), p. 147.

217 R. Scott, *Life and Death*, p. 241; J. O. Baylen, 'W. T. Stead as Publisher and Editor of the "Review of Reviews"', *Victorian Periodicals Review*, XII (1979), p. 75, n. 73.

218 H. Belloc to W. T. Stead, 27 March 1890. Stead Papers; R. Speaight (ed.), *Letters from Hilaire Belloc*, (London, 1958), p. 20.

219 Memoir of Sir Robert Donald. Donald Papers (Parliamentary Archives); Memoir of Francis Carruthers Gould. Gould Papers (Parliamentary Archives).

220 *PMG*, 18 April 1887.

221 Ibid., 19 April 1887.

222 R. E. Lankester to W. T. Stead, 11 July 1887. Stead Papers.

223 *PMG*, 3 June 1887.

224 Ibid., 18 April 1887.

225 Ibid., 20 April 1887.

226 Ibid., 21 April 1887.

227 Ibid., 11 May 1887.

228 Ibid., 25 May 1887.

229 Ibid., 21 April 1887.

230 M. Langworthy to W. T. Stead, 5 May 1887. Stead Papers.

231 Scott, *Life and Death*, p. 221.

232 Whyte, *Stead*, I, p. 247.

233 Scott, *Life and Death*, pp. 249–50.

234 *PMG*, 21 April 1887.

235 Scott, *Life and Death*, p. 125.

236 *PMG*, 11 May 1887.

237 For following, see M. L. Friedland, *The Trials of Israel Lipski* (London, 1984), pp. 91–131.

238 Ibid., 22 August 1887.

239 Friedland, *Israel Lipski*, pp. 183–4.

240 Mills, *Cook*, p. 101.

241 B. A. Booth and E. Mehew (eds), *The Letters of Robert Louis Stevenson* (Yale, 1994–5), VI, p. 32.

242 *Star*, 27 April 1888; 26 June 1888.

243 For following, see Whyte, *Stead*, I, pp. 256–8.

244 *PMG*, 1 May 1888.

245 Ibid., 3 May 1888.

246 Baylen, ' 'Lord Esher's Use of the *PMG*', p. 135.

247 B. Roberts, *Cecil Rhodes and the Princess* (London, 1969), p. 134.

248 For following, see M. Gonne, *A Subject of the Queen* (London, 1938), pp. 80–1.
249 Stead, *MP for Russia*, II, p. 240.
250 Stead to Novikov, 25 August 1880.
251 Stead, *MP for Russia*, II, p. 251.
252 Scott, *Life and Death*, p. 146.
253 Ibid., p. 234.
254 *Review of Reviews*, XVIII (December 1898), p. 548.
255 Whyte, *Stead*, I, p. 265.
256 *PMG*, 18 June 1888.
257 Mills, *Cook*, pp. 101–2.
258 Stead's diary, 19 September 1888; E. T. Cook's diary, 13 November 1888 (Bodleian Library); *PMG*, 25 June 1888.
259 E. T. Cook's diary, 13 November 1888; Scott, *Life and Death*, pp. 149–50.
260 E. T. Cook's diary, 13 November 1888; Whyte, *Stead*, II, p. 331.
261 E. T. Cook's diary, 4 April 1889.
262 *PMG*, 28 August 1888.
263 *PMG*, 5 October 1888.
264 Scott, *Life and Death*, pp. 243–5. Some words have been corrected in accordance with the MS.
265 Whyte, *Stead*, II, pp. 341–2.
266 Scott, *Life and Death*, p. 154.
267 Scott, *Life and Death*, p. 149.
268 W. T. Stead, *The Last Will and Testament of Cecil John Rhodes* (London, 1902), pp. 81–3.
269 A. Thomas, *Rhodes* (London, 1996), p. 209; Scott, *Life and Death*, p. 151; Whyte, *Stead*, I, pp. 270–1.
270 E. T. Cook's diary, 4 April 1888.
271 W. T. Stead, *The Pope and the New Era* (London, 1889), p. 17.
272 Whyte, *Stead*, I, p. 284; W. T. Stead to Cardinal Manning, 23 & 29 October; 5 & 11 November 1889.
273 *Methodist Times*, 14 November 1889; L. Springfield, *Some Piquant People* (London, 1924), pp. 83–4.
274 For following, see R. Pound, *The Strand Magazine, 1891–1950* (London, 1966), pp. 20–9.
275 Scott, *Life and Death*, p. 154; E. T. Cook's diary, 12–14 December 1889.
276 Stead's diary, 18 September 1888.
277 E. T. Cook's diary, 9 January 1890.
278 Scott, *Life and Death*, p. 355.
279 Scott, *Life and Death*, p. 152.
280 *St. James's Gazette*, 16 January 1890.
281 G. Richards, *Memories of a Misspent Youth, 1872–1896* (London, 1932), pp. 307, 263.
282 Mills, *Cook*, p. 138.
283 Spender, *Life, Journalism and Politics*, I, p. 53.
284 G. Newnes to W. T. Stead, 28 February 1890. Stead Papers.
285 J. O. Baylen, 'The Mattei Cancer Cure: A Victorian Nostrum', *Proceedings of the American Philosophical Society*, CXIII (1949), pp. 149–76.
286 Newnes to Stead, 29 March 1890.

287 R. Sandall, *History of the Salvation Army, vol. 3, 1883–1953* (London, 1955), p. 332.

288 Whyte, *Stead*, II, p. 13.

289 T. H. Huxley, *Some Diseases and Worse Remedies: Letters to The "Times" on Mr Booth's Scheme* (London, 1891), p. 7.

290 A. Desmond, *Huxley: From Devil's Disciple to Evolution's High Priest* (London, 1997), p. 584.

291 W. T. Stead to W. Booth, 9 January 1891. Stead Papers.

292 Scott, *Life and Death*, p. 82.

293 P. Magnus, *Edward VII* (London, 1979), pp. 142–5.

294 Whyte, *Stead*, II, p. 103.

295 Scott, *Life and Death*, pp. 164–6; Whyte, *Stead*, II, p. 105.

296 Whyte, *Stead*, II, pp. 104–5.

297 W.M.S. (private secretary) to Arthur Balfour, 14 Feb, n.d. Balfour Papers (National Archives of Scotland); Lord Rosebery to W. T. Stead, 23 May 1893. Stead Papers; E. T. Cook's diary, 25 October 1892; n.d. [October 1895]; 28 March 1900.

298 M. Havers, E. Grayson and P. Shankland, *The Royal Baccarat Scandal* (London, 1977), p. 154.

299 Scott, *Life and Death*, p. 166.

300 F. E. M. Greville, *Life's Ebb and Flow* (London, 1929), p. 178.

301 For following, see G. Bennett, *Charlie B: A Biography of Admiral Lord Beresford* (London, 1968), pp. 163–5; Blunden, *Warwick*, pp. 76–89.

302 A. Leslie, *Mr Frewen of England: A Victorian Adventurer* (London, 1966), p. 123.

303 R. I. Rotberg, *The Founder: Cecil Rhodes and the Pursuit of Power* (Oxford, 1988), p. 656.

304 Whyte, *Stead*, II, p. 104.

305 F. E. M. Greville to W. T. Stead, 10 September 1893. Stead Papers.

306 Blunden, *Warwick*, p. 85.

307 For following, see Whyte, *Stead*, II, pp. 101–21.

308 Ibid., p. 28.

309 Ibid., p. 103, n.

310 Spender, *Life, Journalism and Politics*, I, p. 139.

311 Baylen, 'W. T. Stead as Publisher and Editor', p. 74.

312 O. Woods and J. Bishop, *The Story of the Times* (London, 1985), p. 158; F. Shaw to W. T. Stead, n.d. Stead Papers.

313 F. Moberly Bell, *Flora Shaw: Lady Lugard D.B.E.* (London, 1947), p. 77.

314 F. Shaw to Stead, 3 January 1890; 10 April n.d.; 13 January 1892. Stead Papers.

315 *Review of Reviews*, XXVI (October 1892), p. 373.

316 Ibid., I (June 1890), pp. 470–1.

317 E. Harper, *Stead: The Man: Personal Reminiscences* (London, 1918), pp. 28–30.

318 Whyte, *Stead*, II, p. 64.

319 For following, see S. Lowndes (ed.), *Diaries and Letters of Marie Belloc Lowndes, 1911–1947* (London, 1971), pp. 10–12.

320 Stead, *My Father*, pp. 170–6.

321 Baylen, 'Lord Esher's Use of the *PMG*', p. 132, n. 71.

322 Whyte, *Stead*, I, pp. 332; Stead, *My Father*, pp. 177–93.

323 W. T. Stead, *After Death: New and Enlarged Edition including fifteen hitherto unpublished Letters from Julia* (London, 1914 [1897]), p. 5; *Christian Commonwealth*, 9 February 1893.

324 Springfield, *Piquant People*, p. 84; Stead, *After Death*, p. 4.

325 Richards, *Misspent Youth*, pp. 126, 133.

326 Whyte, *Stead*, II, p. 56.

327 T. H. Hall, *The Strange Story of Ada Goodrich-Freer* (London, 1968), p. 15.

328 Ibid., p. 116.

329 T. Aronson, *The King in Love*, (London, 1988), p. 97.

330 *Fortnightly Review*, LV (1909), p. 56.

331 Harper, *Stead*, p. 64. Estelle Stead told Frederic Whyte that 'it would mean a great deal to my mother' if he omitted all reference to Ada in his biography of Stead. E. Stead to F. Whyte, 31 December 1924. Whyte Papers.

332 S. Grant to W. T. Stead, 15 March 1893. Stead Papers.

333 Whyte, *Stead*, II, p. 61.

334 *PMG*, 3 April, 1893 *et ante*.

335 Whyte, *Stead*, II, pp. 60–2.

336 E. H. Stout to W. T. Stead, 12 September 1895. Stead Papers.

337 Whyte, *Stead*, II, p. 59; *Review of Reviews*, X (July 1894), p. 71.

338 Richards, *Misspent Youth*, p. 306.

339 J. O. Baylen and P. G. Hogan, Jr, 'G. Bernard Shaw and W. T. Stead: An Unexplored Relationship', *Studies in English Literature, 1500–1900*, I (1961), pp. 129–33. Shaw believed that Stead would have enjoyed a trip to Bayreuth all the more for his lack of refinement: 'Your being an "utter barbarian",' he wrote, 'is a great advantage. Wagner stands or falls by the success of his appeal to "the folks" – that is, to the unsophisticated receptive natural man.'

340 For following, see J. O. Baylen, 'A Victorian's "Crusade" in Chicago, 1893–4', *The Journal of American History* (1964), LI, pp. 418–34; W. T. Stead, *If Christ Came to Chicago!* (London, 1894).

341 W. T. Stead to R. B. Brett, 25 December 1893; J. T. Saywell (ed.), *The Canadian Journal of Lady Aberdeen, 1893–1898* (Toronto, 1960), p. 34. Stead surprised his hosts by leaving 'Julia's' signature in the guestbook.

342 R. Rive (ed.), *Olive Schreiner Letters* (Oxford, 1988), I, p. 262.

343 Whyte, *Stead*, II, pp. 68–70.

344 *Review of Reviews*, XI (June 1895), p. 492; Baylen, 'Oscar Wilde Redivivus', pp. 78–86.

345 *PMG*, 6 September 1884. For following, see J. O. Baylen, 'History of the Mystery', *Journal of British Studies* (1964), pp. 104–32; Baylen, 'W. T. Stead and the Boer War: The Irony of Idealism', *Canadian Historical Review* (1959), pp. 304–14; J. van der Poel, *The Jameson Raid* (Oxford, 1951), pp. 187–99.

346 Scott, *Life and Death*, p. 242.

347 Woods and Bishop, *Story of the Times*, p. 169.

348 Scott, *Life and Death*, pp. 226–7.

349 *Review of Reviews*, XV (February 1897), p. 107.

350 J. L. Thompson, *Forgotten Patriot: A Life of Alfred, Viscount Milner of St James's and Cape Town, 1854–1925* (Madison, 2007), pp. 135–51.

351 Koss, *Pro-Boers*, p. 33.

352 *Review of Reviews*, XX (December 1899), p. 547; ibid., XXI (January 1900), p. 14; ibid., XXI (May 1900), p. 450.

353 A. Davey, *The Pro-Boers* (Tafelberg, 1978), pp. 83–7, 168–77.

354 J. O. Baylen, 'George Moore, W. T. Stead, and the Boer War', *Studies in English Literature, 1500–1900*, III (1962), pp. 49–60; Davey, *Pro-Boers*, p. 85.

355 Scott, *Life and Death*, p. 224, n.

356 *Review of Reviews*, XXII (November 1900), p. 418.

357 Stead, *Cecil John Rhodes*, p. 111–12; Whyte, *Stead*, II, p. 212; E. T. Raymond, *Portraits of the Nineties* (London, 1921), p. 182.

358 Whyte, *Stead*, p. 305.

359 Milner to Whyte, 3 June 1921.

360 H. Fyfe, *Sixty Years of Fleet Street* (London, 1949), p. 36; Whyte, *Stead*, p. 11, pp. 70–71; Brett, *Journals*, I, p. 229. Esher wrote to his son that Stead was 'wild and odd as ever': 'Pretty good loony! All his female friends he endows with the attributes of Charles' mistresses! If he wasn't so sane in other matters he would have to be shut up.'

361 Whyte, *Stead*, II, pp. 269–70.

362 Richards, *Memories*, p. 307.

363 Kingsmill, *After Puritanism*, p. 208.

364 W. T. Stead, *Blastus, The King's Chamberlain: A Political Romance* (London, 1898), pp. 73–4.

365 H. Vickers, *Gladys, Duchess of Marlborough* (London, 1971), p. 134.

366 'The Last Years. November 1910–April 1912' (suppressed chapter from Whyte, *Stead*). Whyte Papers.

367 For following, see Scott, *Life and Death*, pp. 197, 222, 246–59.

368 W. T. Stead to W. S. Churchill, 7 December 1911. Winston Churchill Papers (Churchill College).

369 *Daily Chronicle*, 1 November 1909; Harper, *Stead*, pp. 179–96. In the aftermath of the 'interview', Stead hung huge posters obtained from news vendors in the front window of his offices reading: 'Stead and Julia Exposed!'

370 *Review of Reviews*, XXXIII (June 1906), p. 562. Stead's Russian expedition is carefully examined in J. O. Baylen, 'The Tsar's "Lecturer General": W. T. Stead and the Russian Revolution of 1905', Georgia State College Research Paper No. 23 (July 1969).

371 P. Laity, *The British Peace Movement, 1870–1914* (Oxford, 2001), p. 160. Tobias Grey, reviewing the hardback edition of the present book in the *Wall Street Journal*, brings to light the fact that Stead was one of several hundred people nominated for the Nobel Peace Prize in 1901. It is, however, extremely unlikely that he was ever a 'front-runner', either at that time or in the year of his death. The peace movement never forgave Stead for his involvement in the 'Big Navy' scare of 1884.

372 D. Nasaw, *Andrew Carnegie* (New York, 2006), pp. 733–4; Scott, *Life and Death*, p. 223.

373 *Review of Reviews*, XXXIX (October 1908), p. 335.

374 H. W. Nevinson, *Fire of Life* (London, 1935), p. 219.

375 G. Eckley, *Maiden Tribute*, p. 376.

376 Stead, *My Father*, p. 342.

377 G. Marcus, *Maiden Voyage* (London, 1969), pp. 72–3.

378 Stead, *My Father*, p. 344.

379 Marder, *Fear God*, II, pp. 449–50.

380 *Daily Mail*, 18 April 1912; *The Nation*, 20 April 1912.

381 F. E. M. Greville, *Afterthoughts* (London, 1931), p. 148; E. T. Cook's diary, 25 June 1895.
382 *Daily News*, 17 April 1912; *Westminster Gazette*, 17 April 1912.
383 E. T. Cook's diary, 25 April 1912.
384 *Times*, 18 April 1912; W. Rothenstein, *Men and Memories* (London, 1978 [1931–2]), pp. 59, 64.
385 E. T. Cook's diary, 27 June 1912.
386 Scott, *Life and Death*, p. 223, n.
387 H. Evans, *My Paper Chase* (London, 2009), pp. 214–15; A. Marr, *My Trade* (London, 2004), pp. 23–4. Frederick Whyte claims to have seen a 'grateful letter' from Eliza Armstrong to Stead written years later, but this appears not to have survived (Whyte, *Stead*, I, p. 186). Census and newspaper records show that the family had left the Marylebone area by the early 1890s and had been the subject of several 'follow-up' stories in the press.
388 Scott, *Life and Death*, p. 232.

SELECT BIBLIOGRAPHY

Manuscript Collections
Bodleian Library Special Collections
British Library Manuscripts Department
Churchill College Archives Centre
London School of Economics Archives
National Archives of Scotland
National Library of Scotland Special Collections
Parliamentary Archives (London)
Robinson Library (Newcastle) Special Collections
Salvation Army International Heritage Centre
Women's Library (London) Special Collections

Newspapers and Periodicals
Borderland
Daily Mail
Financial Times
Fortnightly Review
The Guardian
Lloyd's Weekly Newspaper
The Nation
Nineteenth Century
Pall Mall Gazette
The Standard
The Star
The Times
Review of Reviews
St. James's Gazette
War Against War in South Africa

Frequently Cited Works

Brett, *Journals*:

M. V. Brett and O. S. B. Brett (Viscount Esher) (eds), *Journals and Letters of Viscount Esher*, 4 vols (London: Ivor Nicholson & Watson, 1934–8).

Marder, *Fear God*:

A. J. Marder (ed.), *Fear God and Dread Nought: The Correspondence of Admiral of the Fleet Lord Fisher of Kilverstone*, 3 vols (London: Jonathan Cape, 1952–9).

ODNB:

H. C. G. Matthew and B. Harrison (eds), *Oxford Dictionary of National Biography*, 60 vols (Oxford: Oxford University Press, 2001–4).

Stead, *MP for Russia*:

W. T. Stead (ed.), *The MP for Russia: Reminiscences and Correspondence of Madame Olga Novikoff*, 2 vols (London: Andrew Melrose, 1909).

Stead, *My Father*:

E. Stead, *My Father: personal and spiritual reminiscences* (London: William Heinemann, 1913).

Scott, *Life and Death*:

J. W. Robertson Scott, *Life and Death of a Newspaper: An Account of the Temperaments, Perturbations and Achievements of John Morley, W. T. Stead, E. T. Cook, Harry Cust, J. L Garvin and three other Editors of the Pall Mall Gazette* (London: Methuen, 1952).

Scott, '*We' and Me*:

J. W. Robertson Scott, '*We' and Me. Memories of four eminent editors I worked with, a discussion by editors of the future of editing, and a candid account of the founding and editing, for twenty-one years, of my own magazine* (London: W. H. Allen, 1956).

Whyte, *Stead*:

F. Whyte, *The Life of W. T. Stead*, 2 vols (London: Jonathan Cape, 1925).

Other Secondary Sources

Bahlman, D. W. R., (ed.), *The Diary of Sir Edward Walter Hamilton 1880–1885*, 2 vols (Oxford: Oxford University Press, 1972).

Baring, E., (Viscount Cromer), *Modern Egypt*, 2 vols (London: Macmillan, 1908).

Baylen, J. O., 'Politics and the "New Journalism": Lord Esher's Use of the *Pall Mall Gazette*', *Victorian Periodicals Review*, XX (1987), pp. 126–41.

— 'W. T. Stead as Publisher and Editor of the "Review of Reviews"', *Victorian Periodicals Review*, XII (1979), pp. 70–84.

— 'The "New Journalism" in Late Victorian Britain', *The Australian Journal of Politics and History*, XVIII (1972), pp. 367–85.

— 'Oscar Wilde Redivivus', *University of Mississippi Studies in English*, VI (1965), pp. 77–86.

— 'A Victorian's "Crusade" in Chicago, 1893–4', *The Journal of American History* (1964), LI, pp. 418–34.

— and P. G. Hogan, Jr, 'G. Bernard Shaw and W. T. Stead: An Unexplored Relationship', *Studies in English Literature, 1500–1900*, I (1961), pp. 123–47.

Bennett, G., *Charlie B: a biography of Admiral Lord Beresford* (London: Dawnay, 1968).

Blunden, M., *The Countess of Warwick: a biography* (London: Cassell, 1967).

Blunt, W. S., *Gordon at Khartoum* (London: Stephen Swift, 1911).

Booth, B., *Echoes and Memories* (London: Hodder & Stoughton, 1977 [1925]).

Booth, W. [and Stead, W. T.] *In Darkest England and the Way Out* (London: Salvation Army, 1890).

Brake, L. and Dermoor, M., (eds), *Dictionary of Nineteenth-Century Journalism* (London: British Library, 2009).

Catling, T., *My Life's Pilgrimage* (London: John Murray, 1911).

Davey, A., *The Pro-Boers* (Cape Town: Tafelberg, 1978).

Desmond, A., *Huxley: From Devil's Disciple to Evolution's High Priest* (London: Perseus Books, 1997).

Eckley, G., *Maiden Tribute: a life of W. T. Stead* (Philadelphia: Xlibris, 2007).

Friedland, M. L., *The Trials of Israel Lipski: a true story of a Victorian murder in the East End of London* (London: Macmillan, 1984).

Fyfe, H., *Sixty Years of Fleet Street* (London: W. H. Allen, 1949).

Greville, F. E. M. (Countess of Warwick), *Life's Ebb and Flow* (London: Hutchinson, 1929).

Harper, E., *Stead: the man: personal reminiscences* (London: W. Rider, 1918).

Havers, M. H., *The Royal Baccarat Scandal* (London: William Kimber, 1977).

Hunt, T., *The Frock-Coated Communist: the revolutionary life of Friedrich Engels* (London: Allen Lane, 2009).

Hyndman, H. M., *Further Reminiscences* (London: Macmillan, 1912).

Jenkins, R., *Gladstone* (London: Macmillan, 1995).

— *Sir Charles Dilke: a Victorian tragedy* (London: Collins, 1965).

Jordan, J., *Josephine Butler* (London: John Murray, 2001).

Juxon, *Lewis and Lewis* (London: Collins, 1983).

Kingsmill, H., *After Puritanism* (London: Duckworth, 1929).

Koss, S., *The Rise and Fall of the Political Press in Britain* (London: Fontana, 1990 [1981–4]).

— (ed.) *The Pro-Boers: the anatomy of an antiwar movement* (Chicago: University of Chicago Press, 1973).

Lloyd, C., *Attacking the Devil: 130 years of the Northern Echo* (Darlington: Northern Echo, 1999).

Lord, W., *A Night to Remember* (London: Longman, 1956).

Lyons, F. S. L., *Charles Stewart Parnell* (Oxford: Oxford University Press, 1977).

Magnus, P., *King Edward VII* (London: John Murray, 1979 [1964]).

Marcus, G., *The Maiden Voyage* (London: George Allen & Unwin, 1969).

Marr, A., *My Trade: a short history of British journalism* (London: Macmillan, 2004).

Moberly Bell, F., *Flora Shaw: Lady Lugard D.B.E.* (London: Constable, 1947).

Morley, J., *Recollections*, 2 vols (London: Macmillan, 1917).

Nasaw, D., *Andrew Carnegie* (New York: Penguin, 2006).

Nevinson, H. W., *Fire of Life* (London: J. Nisbet, 1935).

Nicholls, D., *The Lost Prime Minister: A Life of Sir Charles Dilke* (London: Hambledon, 1995).

Plowden, A., *The Case of Eliza Armstrong: a child of 13 bought for £5* (London: BBC Books, 1974).

van der Poel, J., *The Jameson Raid* (Oxford: Oxford University Press, 1951).

Purcell, E. S., *Life of Cardinal Manning* (London: Macmillan, 1895).

Raymond, E. T., *Portraits of the Nineties* (London: T. Fisher Unwin, 1921).

Rotberg, R. I., *The Founder: Cecil Rhodes and the pursuit of power* (Oxford: Oxford University Press, 1988).

Saxon Mills, J., *Sir Edward Cook K.B.E.: a biography* (London: Constable, 1921).

Schults, R. L., *Crusader in Babylon: W. T. Stead and the 'Pall Mall Gazette'* (Lincoln: University of Nebraska Press, 1972).

Scott, J. W. R., *The Story of the 'Pall Mall Gazette'* (Oxford: Oxford University Press, 1950).

Shannon, R., *Gladstone*, 2 vols (London: Hamilton, 1982–99).

— *Gladstone and the Bulgarian Agitation of 1876* (London: Nelson, 1963).

Spender, J. A., *Life, Journalism and Politics*, 2 vols (London: Cassell, 1927).

Stead, W. T., 'Why I Went to Prison', *Penny Illustrated Paper*, 9 November 1910.

— *The Last Will and Testament of Cecil John Rhodes* (London: 'Review of Reviews' Office, 1902).

— *The History of the Mystery* (London: 'Review of Reviews' Office, 1897).

— *If Christ Came to Chicago!* (London: 'Review of Reviews' Office, 1894).

— *From the Old World to the New* (London: 'Review of Reviews' Office, 1893).

— *The Pope and the New Era* (London: Cassell, 1890).

— *My First Imprisonment* (London: E. Marlborough, 1886).

Strachey, L., *Eminent Victorians* (London: Chatto & Windus, 1921).

Taylor, A., *Annie Besant: a biography* (Oxford: Oxford University Press, 1992).

Taylor, A. J. P., *The Trouble Makers: dissent over foreign policy 1792–1939* (London: Hamish Hamilton, 1957).

Thompson, J. L., *Forgotten Patriot: a life of Alfred, Viscount Milner of St James's and Cape Town, 1854–1925* (Madison: Fairleigh Dickinson University Press, 2007).

Walkowitz, J., *City of Dreadful Delight: narratives of sexual danger in late-Victorian London* (London: Virago, 1992).

Watson, A., *A Newspaperman's Memories* (London: Hutchinson, 1925).

Webster, R. E., (Viscount Alverstone), *Recollections of Bar and Bench* (London: Edward Arnold, 1914).

Wilson, A. N., *The Victorians* (London: Hutchinson, 2002).

Wohl, A. S., *The Eternal Slum: housing and social policy in Victorian London* (New Brunswick: E. Arnold, 1977).

Woods O. and Bishop, J., *The Story of the Times* (London: Michael Joseph, 1985).

Websites

The W. T. Stead Resource Site, created by Owen Mulpetre in 2001, contains a formidable amount of material relating to Stead. It is an excellent resource, for which I have often been grateful. (www. attackingthedevil.co.uk)

INDEX

Also available from The Robson Press

THE FIRST LADY OF FLEET STREET
Eilat Negev and Yehuda Koren

'An extraordinary story – all credit to the authors for giving the first lady of Fleet Street the byline she deserves.' Daisy Goodwin, *Sunday Times*

In the late nineteenth century, at a time when women were still denied the vote, Rachel Beer defied convention to take the helm first of *The Observer*, and then of the *Sunday Times*, becoming the first woman ever to edit a national newspaper. It was to be over eighty years before Fleet Street would see the like again. Barred from the London Clubs and the Press Gallery of the House of Commons, Rachel nevertheless managed to make her formidable voice heard on both national and international political issues – including the notorious Dreyfus Affair.

**368pp paperback, £10.99
Available from all good bookshops or order from
www.therobsonpress.com**

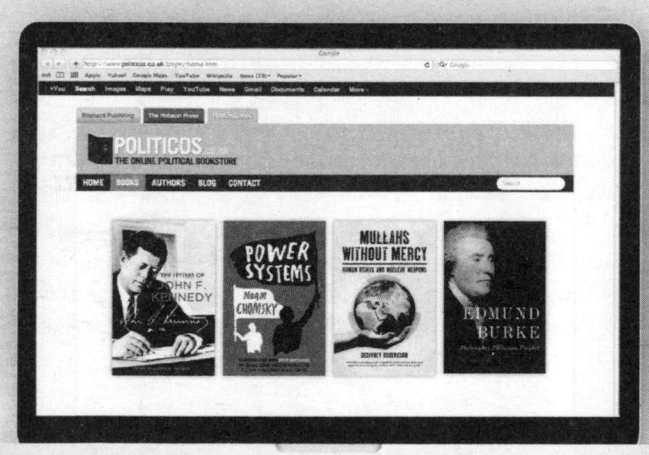